KINDRED BY CHOICE

P. 196. Men, Women
204. Second last para – the
human countenance bears
the image of divinity.
221. Where is home?

EUROPEAN CLASSICS EDITIONS:

KINDRED BY CHOICE

Die Wahlverwandtschaften

by

JOHANN WOLFGANG VON GOETHE

Translated by

H. M. WAIDSON

JOHN CALDER

LONDON

This translation from the German, first published in 1960 by John Calder (Publishers)
Ltd., 18 Brewer Street, London W1R 4AS.

Reprinted 1976.

ISBN 0 7145 0323 1 Cased
ISBN 0 7145 0324 X Paperback

Printed by Unwin Brothers Limited,
The Gresham Press, Old Woking, Surrey.

CONTENTS

v

INTRODUCTION

GOETHE contributed three major works to German literature in the novel form. *Die Leiden des jungen Werthers* (*The Sufferings of Young Werther*) made an immediate, international impact after its first publication in 1774, although the author was soon desirous of dissociating himself from many of the sentiments of his highly strung hero whose frustrations in love and social life ended in tragedy. *Wilhelm Meister* is the longest of Goethe's novels, varied in its themes and settings, with a wealth of incident and figures that makes it difficult to see it whole, though it has been of lasting influence on subsequent German prose writers and has remained of perennial fascination to students of the novel form. Like his dramatic poem *Faust,* the composition of *Wilhelm Meister* accompanied Goethe for more than fifty years of his life. The first part, *Wilhelm Meisters Lehrjahre* (*Wilhelm Meister's Apprenticeship,* 1796), gives a picture of theatre and society in eighteenth century Germany and is both optimistic and didactic in its unfolding of a young man's development to maturity. Plans for a sequel occupied Goethe from then onwards until the final version of *Wilhelm Meisters Wanderjahre* (*Wilhelm Meister's Years of Travel*) appeared in 1829. Here the author is concerned with two principal themes: the planning of a new, experimental form of society to be established in North America, and the need for self-discipline and renunciation on the part of individuals. The *Years of Travel* contain a number of inset stories which illustrate this latter theme.

Die Wahlverwandtschaften (Kindred by Choice) was first conceived by Goethe as a short tale to be inserted into the *Years of Travel.* He initially refers to it in conjunction with *Der Mann von funfzig Jahren (The Man of Fifty),* the story of a middle-aged man whose infatuation with a young girl leads him to pathetic attempts at rejuvenation. But *Kindred by Choice* took hold of its creator with unexpected tenacity, and after a quick, happy period of work in Karlsbad during the summer of 1808 Goethe made it into the full-length novel which he completed and published the following year.

It is a novel with a contemporary setting. Goethe said, on his birthday in 1808, that his intention in the work was to describe social relations and the conflicts arising from them in a symbolic manner. Edward and Charlotte belong to the country nobility of Germany in the first decade of the nineteenth century, and their life takes its course in a placid routine which is hardly troubled by money worries or by distant political disturbances; the defeat of Prussia and the dissolution of the Holy Roman Empire by Napoleon were very recent memories for Goethe at this time. This couple in early middle age practise a comfortable existence with music in the home, garden planning or any other activities they may fancy. They do not belong to the worldly, sophisticated aristocracy who habitually speak French and who are represented by the Count and Baroness, with their desiccated charm and wit; it becomes clear that Luciane has more affinities with this set than her mother Charlotte's sense of quiet responsibility. Charlotte in particular is concerned to make her and her husband's life safe and comfortable, agreeably static after the manner of enlightened eighteenth century gentry. Wild country is turned into parkland; servants and workpeople are treated kindly, but kept at a distance; the subject of death is not mentioned if it can be avoided. Goethe holds no brief for the particular activities of this domestic circle. Indeed elsewhere he refers to garden planning as 'dilettantism,' and the daily life of Edward and Charlotte, with its leisure and ease, though outwardly enviable, is liable to become tedious; Edward's restlessness is apparent already in the first chapter. The factitious liveliness introduced to the household by the tiresome Luciane and her friends is regarded by the author with overt disapproval; the *tableaux vivants,* their most serious pastime, are playthings lacking the discipline and dignity of true art.

The title of the work indicates the application of a chemical reaction to a situation involving emotional relationships between four people. If AB comes into contact with CD, A is attracted strongly to D and B to C, with the likelihood that new combinations will arise. In chemistry such elective affinities, or kinships by choice, are predestined and irresistible. When the term is transferred to human relationships, it seems as if passion may well act with no less resistible force. The novel works out the implications of this notion, fancifully outlined by Edward (Part 1, chapter 4) in terms of human character. The attraction is particularly strong in the case of Edward and Ottilie, while for Charlotte and the Captain the resistance of instinct is less difficult. There is the possibility of choice in human relations, and, whereas inanimate substances have to obey laws of nature, a civilised group of people can either submit to their passions or renounce them in the name of ethical principle. Mittler, who speaks vehemently in and out of season in support of the sanctity of marriage and will have no truck with any breach of traditional sexual morality, is something of a caricature, and his impercipience precipitates disaster more than once; but even while regarding him ironically, Goethe treats his opinions with respect, and comments on the novel made by the author at later dates, as well as the whole tenor of the *Years of Travel,* make it clear that Mittler is Goethe's mouthpiece on the subject of marriage.

Charlotte is frank, self-controlled and reasonable, at times managing and sharp. The Captain is correct and modest, responsible and intelligent, with evident affinities to Charlotte; as a character he is the least firmly outlined of the four principal protagonists. The main interest is directed to Edward and Ottilie, the middle-aged man and the adolescent girl. Edward's petulant sensitivity and egocentric imaginativeness link him with others of Goethe's men characters, for example, Weislingen, in the early play *Götz von Berlichingen,* Werther, Tasso or Faust. Eckermann reports Goethe as speaking of Edward in these words: 'I can't stand him myself, but I had to make him like that . . . There is in any case much truth in his figure, for one finds enough people in the upper classes in whom, as in him, wilfulness takes the place of character' (21 January, 1827). Goethe's work contains numerous successful portrayals of young women characters, and Ottilie is one of his most delightful creations. Innocent, clumsy, frail and not specially intelligent, her attractiveness is the more seductive because it is uncalculated. She is not only of fatal fascination to Edward, but there are few men in the novel who do not find her appealing—the architect, the assistant at the school, the old gardener, the men around Luciane, the Count. Ottilie is the only person whose character develops in the course of the narrative; she is a child when she falls in love instinctively and unrestrainedly, but it is not until after disaster has supervened that she becomes really aware of her ethical responsibility. She is by no means perfect; she shows little compunction about breaking up Charlotte's marriage, and can be suspicious, secretive and obstinate.

Her diary extracts, however, reflect Goethe's increasing fondness for aphorisms in his later years, and it is hard that Ottilie should have them saddled on her.

If some allowances are made, *Kindred by Choice* can be interpreted in terms of three-dimensional, common-sense reality with regard to its milieu and its characters. But the work is open at the edges to the supernatural; the physical resemblances of Charlotte's baby are inexplicable in terms of everyday experience, and Ottilie's posthumous miracle-working propensities are at least ambivalent; they may be of supernatural origin, or they may be due to chance and wishful thinking. Indeed, Goethe seems deliberately to have constructed his novel so that at various points we are free to interpret incidents either as reconcilable with common sense, or as representative of a scientific speculation that merges into alchemy or magic, or as indications that there is a larger spiritual world that cannot be explained away on purely rationalistic lines. Although he was on occasions severely critical of the German Romantic movement, which was in opposition to the controlling clarity of his own classicism during the 1790s, Goethe was none the less interested in this new literary school, and the Gothic-medieval elements, the hinting at the supernatural and its linking with scientific speculation are evident Romantic influences. The period of *Kindred by Choice* was also the time of the completion of *Faust I,* where fantasy and realism are inseparably and uniquely wedded.

Kindred by Choice is caught in a network of motifs and symbols, omens and portents of later events. The resemblances between Edward and Ottilie in their handwriting and their proneness to headaches, Ottilie's idiosyncratic gestures, her prefiguration as an angel in the architect's paintings in the chapel, Edward's plane-trees and his wine glass with its initials E and O; the shadowy, demonic figure of Edward's valet who suggests

the fireworks and later sets them off, who chooses
Edward's gift to Ottilie and who finally breaks his
master's precious wine glass: these and many more
motifs are exploited with highly conscious art. The
tableau of the Virgin and Child, enacted admittedly
somewhat reluctantly by Ottilie with a living baby,
is an act of *hybris* on Ottilie's part for which she has
to pay dearly later with the desperate scene in the boat
on the lake. Charlotte's irrational uneasiness when
she is in the new boat with the Captain, the bursting
of the dam which almost causes a boy's death, and
the ordeal by water of the lovers in the novella *The
Strange Young Neighbours* anticipate the catastrophic
role of this element in precipitating the final disasters.

This novel is closer to a Christian ethic than some
others of Goethe's works. In this respect it has more
in common with the *Years of Travel* than with *Faust*.
Though often hostile to institutional religion, Goethe
had a profoundly religious sense. His epic fragment
Die Geheimnisse (*The Secrets*, 1784–) makes use of the
symbol of the cross entwined with roses. In *Kindred
by Choice* irony, playfulness and worldly passion are not
condemned out of hand, but seek to wrest some kind
of acceptance from moral principle. The last words of
the novel express a confidence in a future life, just
as Faust, at the end of Part Two, is transported to
'higher spheres of pure activity.' In neither case is
Goethe necessarily thinking exclusively in terms of a
traditional Christian conception of immortality, though
there is much of the spirit of Christianity there.
Kindred by Choice is a novel by a great poet; it
contains questioning and acceptance, defiance and
resignation, sophistication and innocence, irony and
reverence.

The translation that follows has been made from the
text in volume seven of the Hamburg edition of *Goethes
Werke* (1951, E. Trunz and B. von Wiese). In addition,

other editions of *Die Wahlverwandtschaften* with a commentary are the *Gedenk-Ausgabe* (Zürich, 1949, E. Beutler and P. Stöcklein) and that of the Bibliographisches Institut (Leipzig, 1926, J. Wahle and O. Walzel).

Among English biographies of Goethe may be mentioned those of P. Hume Brown (1920), J. G. Robertson (1932) and B. Fairley (1948). See also E. L. Stahl's essay *Die Wahlverwandtschaften* (Publications of the English Goethe Society, N. S. 15, 1946).

Well-known German studies of Goethe include those of F. Gundolf (1916), E. Kühnemann (1930), G. Müller (1947), K. Vietor (1948) and E. Staiger (particularly vol. 2, 1956). Other criticism of *Die Wahlverwandtschaften* is contained in H. A. Korff, *Geist der Goethezeit* (vol. 2, 1930), W. Emrich, *Die Symbolik von Faust II* (1943), P. Hankamer, *Speil der Mächte* (1947), and H. M. Wolff, *Goethe in der Periode der Wahlverwandtschaften* (1952).

H. M. WAIDSON

Hull, 1958.

PRINCIPAL DATES OF GOETHE'S LIFE

1749 Born at Frankfort-on-the-Main

1765–8 Studied at Leipzig

1770–71 Studied law at Strassburg

1772 Spent some months in Wetzlar at the Supreme Court of the Empire

1773 *Götz von Berlichingen* (prose drama)

1774 *Clavigo* (prose drama)

1774 *Die Leiden des jungen Werthers* (novel; rev. 1783–6)

1775 *Stella* (prose drama)

1775 Invited to Weimar as companion to young duke, remained there

1776–85 *Wilhelm Meisters theatralische Sendung* (novel)

1779 *Iphigenie auf Tauris* (prose drama; changed to blank verse in 1787)

1781 *Torquato Tasso* (verse drama; completed 1789)

1786–8 Journey to Italy, sojourn in Rome

1787 *Egmont* (prose drama)

1790 *Faust* (*Fragment*) (verse drama)

1794 *Reineke Fuchs* (verse epic)

1795–6 *Wilhelm Meisters Lehrjahre* (novel, revision of the *Sendung*)

1797 *Hermann und Dorothea* (verse epic)

1797f. *Achilleis* (verse epic)

1803 *Die natürliche Tochter* (verse drama)

1808 *Faust, erster Teil* (verse drama)

1808 *Pandora* (masque in verse)

1809 *Die Wahlverwandtschaften* (novel)

1809 *Farbenlehre* (theory of optics)

1881– *Dichtung und Wahrheit* (autobiography)

1819 *Der west-östliche Divan* (poems)

1829 *Wilhelm Meisters Wanderjahre* (novel)

1831 *Faust, zweiter Teil* (verse drama, printed posthumously)

1832 Death of Goethe

KINDRED BY CHOICE

A NOVEL

PART ONE

CHAPTER I

Edward—we are referring by this name to a rich baron in his prime—had spent the best hour of an April afternoon in his orchard grafting new shoots that he had received a little earlier on to young trees. His task was finished; he replaced the implements in their case and was looking at his work with pleasure when the gardener came up and was gratified by his master's interest and industry.

'Have you seen my wife?' Edward asked, while preparing to go elsewhere.

'Over there, in the new grounds,' the gardener replied. 'The arbour which she has built by the cliff-face opposite the castle will be finished today. Everything has come on very well and is sure to please you, sir. There is an excellent view; down below is the village, a little to the right the church, beyond the top of the church-tower you can see into the distance, and opposite there is the castle and the gardens.'

'Quite right,' said Edward; 'I could see the men working a few paces from here.'

'Then,' the gardener continued, 'the valley opens up to the right, and you can see across the rich meadows with their trees into a pleasant prospect. The path up the rocks is laid out quite prettily. Her ladyship understands this sort of thing; it is a pleasure to work under her.'

1

'Go to her,' Edward said, 'and ask her to wait for me. Tell her I want to see this new creation for myself and enjoy looking at it.'

The gardener hastened away, and Edward followed soon after.

He climbed down the terraces and examined the glass-houses and hot-beds on his way past, until he came to the water, and then took a path to the place where it divided into two arms leading to the new grounds. He did not take the one which went by the graveyard fairly directly to the cliff, but went by the other path which wound its way up gently on the left through pleasant shrubs; at the spot where the two paths met again he sat down for a moment on a convenient seat, then stepped up the slope itself which led him by means of all kinds of steps and terraces along the path, which sometimes narrowed until it finally reached the arbour.

Charlotte received her husband at the door and made him sit down in such a position that he could see at one glance through door and windows the various views which showed the landscape as through a frame. He was pleased at this, hoping that spring would soon enliven the whole scene more richly. 'There's just one thing,' he added, 'the arbour seems to me rather too cramped.'

'But spacious enough for us two,' Charlotte replied.

'Yes, that's true,' Edward said, 'and there's room for a third person as well.'

'Why not?' Charlotte replied, 'and for a fourth. We should really want to prepare other places for larger groups of people.'

'Since we are sitting here undisturbed and alone,' Edward said, 'and in a quiet, serene mood, I must confess to you that I've had something on my mind for quite a time which I would like, in fact must, confide to you, but which I can't bring myself to do.'

2

'I've noticed something of the sort,' Charlotte answered.

'And I can but confess,' Edward continued, 'that I might have kept silent even longer if the postal messenger had not pressed me and if we had not to make up our minds today.'

'What is it then?' Charlotte asked in a friendly and accommodating manner.

'It concerns our friend the Captain,' Edward answered. 'You know what a sad position he has been placed in, like so many others, through no fault of his own. How painful it must be to a man of his knowledge, talents and accomplishments to see himself inactive, and—I will no longer delay telling you what it is that I wish for him—I should like us to have him with us here for a time.'

'That must be thought over and needs looking at from more than one angle,' Charlotte said.

'I'm ready to let you have my views,' Edward replied to her. 'There is a subdued expression of deepest discontent in his last letter; not that he is lacking anything in particular, for he knows how to keep within bounds, and I have looked after what is necessary; nor does he feel awkward at taking something from me, for in the course of our lives we have come to be so mutually indebted that we can't reckon out how our credit and debit stand toward each other—what really torments him is that he is without occupation. His pleasure, indeed his passion, consists of making available for the use of others the many abilities that he has developed in his own personality. And now to fold his hands in his lap or to go on studying further, acquiring further skills, because he can't make use of what he possesses in full measure—in short, my dear, it is a painful situation; the unpleasantness of which he feels doubly, indeed three times as strongly in his solitude.'

'But I thought he had offers from various sources,'

said Charlotte. 'I myself have written on his behalf to many active friends, and as far as I know, this was not without effect.'

'Quite so,' Edward replied; 'but it is just those various affairs, those offers which cause him fresh pain and disturbance. None of the posts is suited to him. It is not a question of his having to have activity, but he would have to sacrifice himself, his time, his opinions, and his whole personality, and that is impossible for him. The more I think of it, and feel it, the more intensely I desire to see him here with us.'

'It is very good and kind of you to think of a friend's position with such sympathy,' Charlotte answered; 'but let me ask you also to think of your own, our own in fact.'

'I have done this,' Edward said to her. 'We can only promise ourselves advantage and pleasure from having him near. I won't talk about the expense, which in any case will only be a slight one for me if he comes here, especially when I consider at the same time that his presence won't cause us the least discomfort. He can live in the right wing of the castle, and everything else will work out. Think how much this will help him, and of the pleasure and advantage we shall have from his company! For a long time now I should have liked the property and the district to be surveyed; he will be able to look after and direct this. Your intention is to administer the property yourself in future, as soon as the lease of the present tenants has elapsed. What a precarious undertaking this is! Think what a help his knowledge and experience would be to us! I feel only too clearly how I miss a man of this type. The country people have the right knowledge; but the information they give is confused and dishonest. Men who have studied academically in the town are certainly clear thinking and orderly, but they haven't the direct insight into the business. I can expect both these qualities

4

from our friend; and then a hundred other matters will result from the situation which I like to anticipate and which will concern you, and from these I can foresee much that is good. Now it is good of you to have listened to me in this friendly way; but do speak freely and in detail at this point, and tell me everything that you have to say; I won't interrupt you.'

'Very well then,' Charlotte replied, 'I will begin at once with a general observation. Men think more of what is specific and immediate, and rightly so, for it is their duty to be active, whereas women think more of what relates to life as a whole; they are equally right to do so, because their lot and the lot of their families is linked with this continuity, and it is precisely this sense of continuity that is required from them. Let us therefore cast a glance at our present and our past life, and you will admit that this invitation to the Captain doesn't coincide so exactly with our intentions, plans and arrangements.

'I like so much to think of our earliest links! When we were young we loved each other so dearly; we were separated; you from me, because your father, with his insatiable craving for property, married you to an older, rich woman; I from you, because, being a person with no special prospects, I had to bind myself to a well-off man whom I did not love, though I did respect him. We two became free again; you earlier than myself, as your older wife died leaving you in possession of a large fortune; I became free later, just at the time when you came back from your travels. And so we found each other again. We were happy in our memories, lived in them, and there was nothing to stop us living together undisturbed. You urged our marriage; I didn't consent at once, for as we are about the same age, I being a woman have become older, but you as a man have not. Finally, I didn't want to refuse you what you seemed to regard as your only happiness. You wanted to rest

5

at my side and recover from all the disturbances that you had experienced at court, in the army, on your travels, to be restored in spirit and to enjoy life; but again, with me alone. I sent my only daughter to a boarding-school, where indeed she can develop in a less limited manner than if she remained in the country; and I sent not only her, but also Ottilie, my dear niece, who might have developed into a domestic companion more suitably under my direction. All this took place with your agreement, simply so that we could enjoy undisturbed the happiness we had earlier longed for so intensely and had now at last attained. In this way we took up our life in the country. I was to be responsible for internal matters, you for outside things and anything of a general character. I have arranged my life to be accommodating to you in all things, and to live only for you; let us at least make the effort for a time to see how we may suffice each other in this manner.'

'Since what is continuous, as you put it, is really your element as a woman,' Edward said 'we shouldn't listen to you talking in a sequence of ideas nor decide that you women are right; though you may well have been right before today. The way of life that we have planned for ourselves up to now is good as far as it goes; but are we to build nothing further on it, and is nothing further to develop from it? What I have achieved in the garden, and you in the park, has this been done only for hermits?'

'That is all very well,' added Charlotte. 'So long as we don't introduce anything that hinders us and is alien! Remember that our plans concerning our entertainment too were dependent only on our both being together. You wanted first of all to disclose to me in orderly sequence your travel-diaries, and thereby to put into order much that belongs here among your papers, and with my support and help to create out of

6

these invaluable, but confused notebooks and papers a whole which would be enjoyable for ourselves and for others. I promised to help you with copying, and we thought how comfortable, pleasurable and charming it would be to travel in memory through the world, which we were not destined to see together. Indeed, the start has already been made. Then you have taken up your flute again in the evenings, accompanying me at the piano; and there are plenty of visitors, people living in the neighbourhood as well as those who visit us. I at least have made for myself out of all this the first truly happy summer of my life, as happy as any I ever thought to enjoy.'

'The only thing is,' Edward replied, rubbing his forehead, 'with all that you repeat to me so lovingly and sensibly, there might always be the thought that the Captain's presence will destroy nothing, rather it will hasten and give fresh life to everything. He too has shared in a part of my travels; he too has noticed much, and in various ways; if we were to use this together, it would then become a beautiful whole.'

'But let me confess to you in all sincerity,' Charlotte replied somewhat impatiently, 'that this goes against my feelings and that I have a premonition which holds no good in store.'

'With this type of argument you women would certainly be invincible,' Edward replied, 'in the first place sensible, so that we can't contradict; affectionate, so that we are glad to give way; sensitive, so that we would not care to hurt you; full of intuitive premonitions, so that we are terrified.'

'But I'm not superstitious,' Charlotte said, 'and I have no interest in these dark impulses, if this is what they are; but they are mostly the unconscious memories of the happy and unhappy consequences which we have experienced as a result of our own or other people's actions. There is nothing more important in any circumstance than the intervention of a third person. I have seen friends, brothers and sisters, lovers, married couples, whose relationship has been absolutely changed and their position completely reversed by the chance or intentional advent of another person.'

'That might perhaps happen,' Edward replied, 'in the case of people who live blindly on, not in the case of those who have been enlightened by experience and are more aware.'

'Awareness, my dear, is no adequate weapon, in fact it is often a dangerous one, for the man who makes use of it,' Charlotte countered; 'and at least one thing emerges from all this—that we shouldn't be in too much of a hurry. Just give me a few more days, don't make a decision!'

'As things are now,' Edward answered, 'we shall still be in too much of a hurry even after several days. Between us we have expressed the reasons for and against; it's a matter for decision, and really it would be best to decide it by lot.'

'I know you like to gamble or throw dice in cases of doubt; but in such a serious matter as this I should regard anything of the sort as criminal.'

'But what am I to write to the Captain?' Edward exclaimed; 'for I must sit down to it right away.'

'A calm, sensible and comforting letter,' Charlotte said.

'That's as good as none at all.'

'And yet in many cases it is necessary and a more friendly act to write about nothing than not to write at all.'

CHAPTER II

ALONE in his room, Edward found that Charlotte's recapitulation of the fateful events of his life and the recollection of the position and intentions of the two of them had excited his lively spirit in a pleasant way. In her presence and with her companionship he had felt so happy that he began thinking out a letter to the Captain which should be friendly and sympathetic, but soothing and without any specific suggestions. But when he went to the writing-desk and took up his friend's letter to read it through once more, he immediately envisaged the good man's sad position again: all the emotions which had tormented him in the last few days re-awakened, and it seemed to him impossible to leave his friend to such an anxious situation.

Edward was not accustomed to denying himself anything. From his early years onward the only, spoilt child of rich parents, who were able to persuade him into a strange, but most advantageous marriage with a much older woman, pampered by her again in all kinds of ways, since she tried to respond to his good behaviour towards her by great generosity, his own master after her death within a short time, independent in his travels, free to move about and change his way of life as he pleased, without excessive desires, though desirous of much and many kinds of things, frank, beneficent, open, indeed courageous if need be—what in the world could oppose his wishes!

Up to now everything had gone according to his desires, he had even obtained the hand of Charlotte, whom he had acquired after all by his obstinate, indeed romantic fidelity; and now he felt himself for the first time contradicted and crossed, just as he was about to attract the friend of his youth to him and so to speak to round off his whole existence. He was annoyed and impatient, and picked up the pen and laid it down again more than once, because he could not make up his mind what he wanted to write. He did not want to go against his wife's wishes, nor indeed was he capable of resisting a requirement of hers; restless as he was, he was unable to write a quiet letter; it would have been quite impossible for him. The most natural thing was to seek delay. In a few words he asked his friend's forgiveness because he had not written lately and because he was not writing at length today, and promised to send a satisfying and more substantial letter in the near future.

The next day, while they were strolling toward the same spot, Charlotte seized the opportunity of taking up the subject again, perhaps with the belief that there is no surer way of blunting an intention than to discuss it frequently.

This renewal of the conversation suited Edward well. As usual he showed himself to be friendly and engaging; for though he easily flared up, being easily susceptible to impressions, even though his lively desires became importunate and his obstinacy made him impatient, all his words were rendered so gentle by his complete consideration of the other person that it was impossible not to go on thinking him amiable even when he was clearly being troublesome.

In such a way he first of all this morning brought Charlotte into the gayest of moods, and then completely discomposed her by the pleasant turns of his conversation, until she finally exclaimed: 'I'm sure you want me to concede to my lover what I refused to my husband. At least, my dear,' she went on, 'you should

10

realise that your wishes and the friendly spiritedness with which you express them, don't leave me untouched and unmoved. They force me to a confession. Up to now I too have hidden something from you. I find myself in a similar position to yours and have often restrained myself in the same way that I am expecting restraint of you.'

'I'm glad to hear that,' Edward said; 'I see that you have to have a quarrel from time to time in married life, in order to get to know things about each other.'

'Well then, you are to hear from me,' Charlotte said, 'that I feel the same way about Ottilie as you do about the Captain. I'm not at all happy to think of the poor child in a boarding-school where conditions for her are very oppressive. My daughter Luciane, who is born for life in society, is being trained there for social life; she is acquiring languages, history and anything else they may teach her, like sight-reading notes and their variations at the piano; with her lively nature and happy sense of memory she is able, so to speak, to forget everything and then in a moment to remember everything; she can distinguish herself before all the others through her easy behaviour, her graceful dancing, and her suitable freeness in conversation, and through her innate commanding personality she can make herself queen of her little circle; the headmistress of this place regards her as if she were a little goddess who is getting on well now that she is in her care, doing her credit and awakening general confidence and causing other young people to come to the school too; the first pages of her letters and monthly reports are constant rhapsodies on the excellence of such a child, which I of course know how to translate into my own prose; but when she finally comes to mention Ottilie there follows excuse on excuse that a girl who is growing up so well in one way, does not wish to come on and display any talents or accomplishments. The little that she adds to this is similarly no puzzle to me, since I can recognise in this dear child the whole character of her mother, my closest friend, for she grew up beside me; if I were a teacher or tutor, I am sure I could have brought up this daughter of hers to become a magnificent person.

'But since it doesn't fit into our plan and we shouldn't always be chopping and changing our plans for living and bringing in something new, I prefer to put up with it, and in fact I repress the unpleasant feeling I have when my own daughter, who knows full well how completely dependent Ottilie is on us, explains her advantages over her in an insolent manner and in this way to some extent makes null and void our own good action toward Ottilie.

'Yet who is not so well educated that he would not on occasion assert his superiority over others in a cruel way! Who is so highly placed that he might not have to suffer from pressure from time to time! Ottilie's worthiness is increased by these trials; but ever since I have come to see clearly the disagreeable position she is in, I have been trying to find some other place for her. At any moment I am expecting a reply, and when the time comes I shan't hesitate. That's the way things are, as far as I am concerned, my dear. You see, both of us have similar cares hidden within a loyal, friendly heart. Let us bear them together, since they cannot be mutually cancelled out.'

'What strange creatures we are,' Edward said with a smile. 'As soon as we banish something that worries us from our presence, we believe that's the end of it. In large matters we can sacrifice much, but as for giving way on a small point, that is a requirement which we are seldom big enough to fulfil. My mother was like that. When I lived with her as a boy or a youth, she could not rid herself of the cares of the moment. If I was late when I'd gone riding, she thought I'd had an accident; if I got wet in a shower of rain, she thought

12

I would get a temperature. When I went away from her on my travels, it was as if I scarcely belonged to her any more.

'If we look at the matter more closely,' he continued, 'we are both behaving in a pettish and irresponsible manner, by allowing two of the noblest souls who are so close to our hearts to remain in worried and oppressive circumstances, just so that we shan't be exposed to any danger. If this doesn't deserve to be called selfish, I don't know what does! You take Ottilie, and let me have the Captain, and let us make a trial of it, in God's name!'

'We might consider it,' Charlotte said with some misgiving, 'if the danger were only for ourselves alone. But do you really think that it is advisable to have the Captain and Ottilie together under the same roof—he a man of roughly your own age, just at the age when a man first becomes capable of love and worthy of it (this flattering remark I can say to you only as we are on our own), together with a girl of Ottilie's attractiveness?'

'I really don't know how you can make so much of Ottilie!' Edward replied. 'I can only explain it by saying that she must have inherited the affection you had for her mother. She's pretty, there's no denying it, and I remember the Captain pointed her out to me when we came back a year ago and met her with you at your aunt's. She's pretty, and in particular she has lovely eyes; but I can't say that she made the least impression on me.'

'That's very praiseworthy,' Charlotte said, 'for I was there too; and although she is much younger than I am, still the presence of the older friend had so many attractions for you that you passed over her budding, promising beauty. This too is part of your nature and is why I am so happy to share my life with you.'

Although she seemed to be speaking frankly, Charlotte was hiding something. In fact, she had introduced Ottilie

13

and Edward just as he was back from his travels, in order to give her beloved foster-daughter the chance of such a good match; for she no longer thought of Edward in connection with herself. The Captain too had been asked to draw Edward's attention to her; but Edward, obstinately mindful of his love for Charlotte, looked neither to right nor to left and was happy only in the feeling that it might be possible to be the possessor of a good fortune that a sequence of events had put beyond his reach apparently for ever.

The couple were just on the point of going down the new gardens to the castle when a servant came up hastily toward them and with laughter on his lips made himself heard from below: 'Do come along quickly, my lord and lady! Mr. Mittler has come galloping into the courtyard. He shouted and brought us all together, telling us to go in search of you and to ask if there is need of him. ''If there is need,'' he called after us, ''do you hear? But hasten, quickly!'' '

'The funny man!' Edward exclaimed; 'hasn't he come just at the right time, Charlotte?—Return quickly!' he ordered the servant; 'tell him there is need, great need! Tell him to dismount. Look after his horse; take him into the castle and give him some breakfast! We are just coming.

'Let's take the nearest way back!' he said to his wife and set off along the path by the graveyard, which he usually avoided. But how surprised he was to find Charlotte here too had spared people's feelings. While taking the greatest possible care of the old monuments, she had managed to arrange and to order everything in such a way that it appeared as a pleasant place where the eye and the imagination could gladly dwell.

She had given suitable honour to the oldest stone of all. The stones had been erected, fitted in or otherwise arranged against the wall according to age; the tall base to the church itself had been repeated and ornamented by this. Edward felt strangely surprised as he came in through the little door; he pressed Charlotte's hand, and there was a tear in his eye.

But the eccentric visitor banished this tear at once. For he had had no peace in the castle and had ridden without delay through the village up to the cemetery-gate, where he halted and called over to his friends: 'I hope you're not having me on. If it's really necessary, I'll stay for lunch. Don't keep me! I've still got a lot to do today.'

'As you've come such a way,' Edward called out to him, 'you might as well ride in properly; we meet at a serious spot: and see how beautifully decked out this sad place is.'

'I'm not coming in here, either by horse, by carriage or on foot. Those who are lying peacefully here are no concern of mine. I shall have to put up with it when the time comes for me to be carried in, feet first. It's something serious, then?'

'Yes,' Charlotte called. 'Really serious! This is the first time we newly-weds are in trouble and confusion which we cannot settle on our own.'

'It doesn't look like it,' he answered, 'but I am willing to believe it. If you are having me on, I shall leave you in the lurch another time. You just follow me quickly! My horse can do with the rest and refreshment.'

Soon the three were together in the hall of the castle; breakfast was served, and Mittler recounted his deeds and plans for the day. This strange man had earlier been a minister of religion and with his restless activity he had succeeded during the course of his duties in settling the differences, both domestic and neighbourly, firstly of individuals, and then of whole parishes and of a number of landowners. While he was in office, no married couple had had a divorce, and the local judiciary had been spared all contentions and law-suits of that nature. He soon realised how essential legal knowledge was to him. He devoted all his studies to this subject and

15

soon felt himself a match for the cleverest lawyers. His sphere of activity expanded miraculously; and there was a move to transfer him to the governmental headquarters where he might complete from the top what he had begun at the bottom, when he won a considerable sum in a lottery, bought himself a moderate-sized estate which he rented to a farmer and which he made the centre of his activity, with the firm intention, or rather according to his old custom and inclination, not to stay in any house unless he could act as a reconciler and helper there. Those who are superstitious about the significance of names believe that the name of Mittler (mediator) was the reason for his following this strangest of vocations.

The sweet was served when the guest admonished his hosts in all seriousness that they should not hold back any longer with their disclosures, because he would have to go immediately after coffee. Husband and wife made their confessions at some length; but he had scarcely comprehended what the point of the business was when he got up from the table in some annoyance, moved to the window and ordered his horse to be saddled.

'Either you don't know me,' he exclaimed, 'you don't understand me, or else you are very spiteful. Is there any quarrel here? Is any help necessary here? Do you think that I'm here to give advice? That is the silliest job anyone can take up. Each one should advise himself and do what he can't help doing. If it goes well, let him rejoice in his wisdom and good luck; it it goes badly, then he can turn to me. The man who wants to be rid of an evil always knows what he wants; the man who wants something better than he has already is completely blind —Yes, yes, you can laugh—he is playing blind-man's-buff, perhaps he will make a catch; but what? Do what you like: it's all the same! Invite your friends, or keep them away; it's all the same! I have seen the most sensible arrangements break down, and the silliest ones succeed. Don't worry your heads about it, and if it does go badly one way or the other, still don't worry your heads about it! Just send for me, and you shall receive help. Until that time, goodbye!'

And with that he leapt on to his horse without waiting for his coffee.

'Here you can see what little use it is bringing in a third person, when things are not in complete harmony between two people who are tied closely to one another,' Charlotte said. 'At the moment we are surely even more confused and uncertain than before, if that is possible.'

The couple would probably have been hesitant even longer, if a letter from the Captain had not come in reply to Edward's. He had decided to take one of the posts that had been offered to him, although it was in no way suited to him. He was to share the tedium of living with elegant and rich people who would entrust him with the task of dispelling their boredom.

Edward saw this whole situation quite clearly and could describe it in sharp terms. 'Do we want to leave our friend in such circumstances?' he exclaimed. 'You can't be so heartless, Charlotte?'

'That strange man, our good Mittler, is right after all,' Charlotte added. 'All such undertakings are a leap in the dark. What can come of them, no man can foresee. Such new arrangements can be pregnant with happiness and unhappiness, without our needing to ascribe to ourselves any particular merit or guilt. I don't feel strong enough to oppose you any longer. Let's make the experiment! There's only one thing I ask of you: it should only be for a short while. Allow me to act on his behalf more actively than up to now and to make full use of my influence and connections in order to secure him a post which can guarantee him a certain amount of contentment in his own way.'

Edward assured his wife of his liveliest appreciation in the pleasantest manner possible. He hastened, free and

17

happy in mind, to tell his friend in writing of the proposals. Charlotte had to add her approval in her own writing in a postscript and to join her friendly requests to his. She wrote with a skilled hand pleasingly and politely, but yet with a kind of haste that was unusual for her; and, unexpectedly for her, she spoiled the sheet of paper at the end with a blot of ink which annoyed her and became bigger, the more she tried to remove it.

Edward made a joke of it and, as there was still room, he added a second postscript to say that his friend should see from this sign with what impatience he was awaited and should arrange for his journey to be made in accordance with the speed with which the letter had been written.

The messenger went off, and Edward thought that he could not express his gratitude more convincingly than by insisting once and again that Charlotte should at the same time send for Ottilie from school.

She asked for delay here and was able to arouse Edward's interest that evening in musical entertainment. Charlotte played the piano very well, while Edward played the flute not so proficiently, for although he had made considerable efforts from time to time, he lacked the patience and persistence that are necessary for the development of such a talent. Consequently he executed his part very unevenly, some sections well, though perhaps too quickly, whereas with others he would stop because he was not familiar with them, and as a result it would have been difficult for anybody else to have got through a duet with him. But Charlotte could adapt herself to this; she would pause and then let herself be rushed along by him again, and thus fulfilled the double duty of a good conductor and of a wise wife, who are always able to hold the right measure on the whole, even though individual passages may not always remain in tempo.

18

CHAPTER III

THE Captain came. He had first sent a very sensible letter which reassured Charlotte completely. Such insight into himself and such clarity about his own position and that of his friends made a bright and cheerful prospect.

As usually happens among friends who have not seen each other for some time, the conversations during their first hours together were lively, indeed almost exhausting. Toward evening Charlotte arranged for a walk in the new gardens. The Captain liked this part very much and noticed every beauty spot which had been made visible and enjoyable for the first time by the new paths. His eye was practical and at the same time easily pleased; although he recognised very clearly what was desirable, he did not cause those who were showing him round their property ill-humour by expecting more than circumstances permitted, or by recalling something more satisfying that he had seen elsewhere.

When they reached the arbour they found that it had been decked out in the happiest way, only with artificial flowers and evergreen branches, it is true, but to these there were added such fine sheaves of natural wheat and other fruits of the field and forest, that they were a credit to the artistic sense of those who had made the arrangement. 'Although my husband doesn't like having his birthday or name-day remembered, I'm sure he won't be annoyed with me today for offering these few wreaths to a triple celebration.'

'A triple one?' Edward cried.—'Yes, certainly!' Charlotte replied: 'We may quite fairly treat our friend's

19

arrival as a festive occasion; and then, hasn't it occurred to you that today is your name-day? Aren't you both called Otto?'

The two friends shook hands across the little table. 'You remind me of that youthful gesture of friendship.— When we were children we were both known by that name; but when we lived together at school and considerable confusion came of it, I voluntarily resigned to him this pleasing and concise name.'

'And you weren't being all that generous about the matter,' the Captain said. 'For I remember well enough that you liked the name Edward better, as indeed this name has a specially pleasant sound when spoken by charming lips.'

Thus all three were now sitting round the same little table at which Charlotte had spoken so keenly against the guest's coming. In his contentment Edward did not wish to remind his wife of those hours, but he could not refrain from saying: 'There would still be room enough for a fourth person too.'

At that moment bugles could be heard from the castle, as if to affirm and reassure the good opinions and intentions of the friends who were now together. They listened in silence, while each looked into himself and felt doubly his own happiness in so pleasant a union.

It was Edward who broke the silence by getting up and stepping out to the front of the arbour. 'Let's take our friend straightway to the hill-top,' he said to Charlotte, 'so that he won't believe that this limited valley is all our inheritance and estate; up above the view becomes more open, and we feel we can breathe more freely.'

'In that case we shall still have to climb up the old and rather difficult footpath,' Charlotte added; 'but I hope that my steps and paths will lead more comfortably right to the top.'

And in this way they made their way over rocks and

through bushes and undergrowth to the topmost level, which in fact was not a plateau but a continuous and fertile ridge. The village and castle at the rear were no longer in sight. Down below could be seen lakes spread out, on the other side hills with vegetation which were skirted by the lakes, and finally steep rocks which by their perpendicular drop in no uncertain way limited the last of the pools, and reflected their emphatic shapes upon the water's surface. Half hidden in the ravine where a rushing stream poured into the lakes lay a mill which appeared to be a friendly resting-place in such a setting. In the whole semi-circle which was in view there was a manifold variety of depths and heights, and thickets and forests whose first green leaves were a promise of a most luxuriant prospect later. Individual groups of trees also occasionally held the eye. In particular, a mass of poplars and plane-trees at the edge of the middle pool could be distinguished with particular advantage below the feet of the watching friends. This group of trees stood in its best growth, fresh, healthy and striving outward with its branches.

Edward drew his friend's notice to these trees in particular. 'I planted these trees myself in my youth,' he cried out. 'They were young shoots which I saved when my father had them uprooted in the middle of summer when he was laying out a new part of the large castle-garden. Without any doubt they will excel themselves again this year in a gratifying manner with new shoots.'

They turned back contented and cheerful. The guest was allocated friendly and spacious accommodation in the right wing of the castle, and here he had very soon set up and arranged his books, papers and instruments so that he could continue in his accustomed activities. But Edward would not leave him in peace for the first few days; he showed him around everywhere, now on horseback and now on foot, and made him familiar with the neighbourhood and the estate; at the same time he confided to him the desires which he had been cherishing for a long time for the better knowledge and more advantageous use of the property.

'The first thing that we ought to do would be for me to plot the district with the compass,' the Captain said. 'This is an easy and pleasant job, and even if it doesn't give absolutely accurate results, it is nevertheless always useful and, in the first place at least, gratifying; what is more it can be carried out without requiring much assistance and one knows that one can finish the work. If you should think at a later date of a more exact survey, it would always be possible to take advice on that.'

The Captain was very experienced at this kind of surveying. He had brought the necessary apparatus with him and started at once. He instructed Edward and some huntsmen and peasants who were to assist him in the work. The days were favourable; he spent the evening and the early mornings at map-drawing. In a short time it was all shaded and coloured, and Edward could see his possessions growing in the clearest manner from the paper like a new creation. He thought that he was getting to know them and that they seemed to belong to him now for the first time.

The occasion for talking about the district and the gardens could be offered much more suitably after such a survey had been made than when one was making sporadic attempts to control the natural situation according to chance impressions.

'We must make this clear to my wife,' Edward said.

'Don't do that!' the Captain replied, for he did not like to see other people's convictions crossing his own, and he had learnt by experience that people's views are much too varied for them to be united at one point, even when the most sensible ideas are put forward. 'Don't do that!' he cried, 'she could easily go wrong. She is like all who only concern themselves with such things as a hobby—she is more concerned that she should do some-thing than that something should be done. Such a person makes tentative approaches to nature, and has prefer-ences for this little spot or that one; he wouldn't venture to remove this or that obstacle, or be bold enough to sacrifice some specific thing; he can't imagine in advance what may arise, he experiments, it works or it doesn't work; he makes changes, perhaps changing what should have been left alone, leaving what should have been changed and the result is that it remains a hotch-potch that may be pleasing and stimulating, but doesn't satisfy.'

'Confess to me honestly,' Edward said, 'you are not pleased with her garden planning.'

'If the conception, which is very good, had been realised in the execution, there would be nothing to criticise. She has picked her way wearisomely through the rocks and now makes everyone whom she takes up pick his way equally wearisomely, if I may say so. One cannot walk with any freedom either side by side or in succession. At every moment the pace is inter-rupted; and what other objections could not be raised besides!'

'Then would it have been easy to do it any other way?' Edward asked.

'Quite easy,' the Captain went on; 'all she had to do was to break off the one corner of cliff, which in any case is insignificant because it consists of small pieces, and she would have made a finely swung curve up the ascent and would have at the same time superfluous stone for building up those parts where the path would have been narrow and crippled. But let this be said between us in strictest confidence; otherwise she will be confused and annoyed. Furthermore, what has been done must be left as it is. If you want to spend more money and give more trouble, there would still be a number of things to be done and much that is pleasant to be achieved from the arbour upwards and over the peak.'

While the two friends in this way had plenty of occupation with what was before them, there was no lack of vivid and pleasant reminiscence about past days, and here Charlotte usually took part. They also made up their minds to take up the accounts of their travels and to conjure the past again in this way, as soon as the most urgent tasks had been disposed of.

What is more, Edward had less to talk about to Charlotte alone, especially since he took to heart the criticism of her park-planning, which seemed to him to be such justifiable criticism. For a long time he said nothing about what the Captain had confided to him; but when he finally saw his wife occupied with working herself up once more with little steps and paths from the arbour up to the top, he restrained himself no longer, but after some preamble acquainted her with his new views.

Charlotte stood dumbfounded. She was intelligent enough to see quickly that the men were right; but what had already been done contradicted this; after all, it had been constructed in that way; she had found it right and desirable, and even what was criticised was dear to her in each particular part; she resisted the conviction, she defended her little creation, and she scolded the men who straightaway thought in large-scale, grandiose terms, who wanted to turn a pastime into a labour, and who did not think of the expenses which are inevitably entailed by an extension of the plan. She was upset, hurt and irritable; she could not let the old idea go, nor could she wholly reject the new one; but decided person as she was, she immediately stopped the work and gave herself time to think the matter over and let it mature within her.

Now that she also missed this active pastime, and since the men were busied about their own affairs ever

more companionably and in particular were looking after
the decorative beds and the glass-houses with zeal, and
in between also continuing the usual riding pursuits such
as hunting, and the buying, exchanging, tending and
breaking in of horses, Charlotte felt daily more lonely.
She continued her correspondence the more energetically,
also on the Captain's account, and yet she had many a
lonely hour. The reports which she received from the
boarding-school were all the more agreeable and pleasant
in consequence.

An extensive letter from the headmistress, which as
usual dwelt with satisfaction on her daughter's progress,
had appended to it a short postscript as well as a note
contributed in the handwriting of one of the male
assistants at the school, both of which we are repro-
ducing.

Postscript of the Headmistress

All I could say about Ottilie, Madam, would be to
repeat what is contained in my previous reports. I
could have no reason to blame her, and yet I cannot
be pleased with her. She is modest and agreeable to
others, now as always; but I cannot be content with
this self-effacement and humbleness. Madam recently
sent her money and various materials. She has not
taken up the former and the latter are still lying there
untouched. It is true she keeps her things very cleanly
and well and seems to change her clothes, not in order
to look well, but for reasons of cleanliness. I cannot
praise her great temperance in food and drink either.
There is no superfluity at our table; however, there
is nothing I would rather see than children eating their
fill of tasty and healthy food. What has been prepared
and served with care and thought, should be eaten up
as well. I can never persuade Ottilie to this. Indeed
she invents some task in order to fill out an interval
when the serving-women are delayed, only in order to
miss a course or the dessert. We must take into
consideration, however, with all this, that she often

25

has a headache on the left side of her head, as I have only recently found out, and that this affliction can be painful and not insignificant, even if it is only transient. So much for this otherwise so attractive and dear child.

Note by the Assistant

Our good Headmistress usually lets me read letters in which she makes observations about her pupils to their parents and guardians. I always read those letters which are addressed to you, Madam, with double pleasure; for while we have to congratulate you on a daughter who combines all those brilliant qualities which enable one to rise in the world, I at least must consider you no less fortunate in having in your adopted daughter a child who was born to serve the well-being and contentment of others and surely also to serve her own happiness. Ottilie is almost our only pupil about whom I cannot agree with our esteemed Headmistress. I by no means take exception to this active lady because she demands an outward and visible token of the fruits of her care; but there are concealed fruits which are the true, healthy ones and will sooner or later develop to fine life. Your foster-daughter is certainly of this type. As long as I have been teaching her, I have seen her go slowly, very slowly, forward, always at the same pace, but never back. If it is ever necessary to begin at the beginning with a child, it certainly is with her. She cannot understand anything that does not follow from what has gone before. She stands incapable, even obstinate, when confronted with an easily understandable matter if it has no connection with anything else for her. But if one can find the relationships and make them clear to her, she will comprehend the most difficult things.

With this slow rate of progress she remains behind her fellow-pupils who, with their quick, different, abilities, are always rushing ahead and can easily grasp, remember and apply everything, even the most unconnected facts. Consequently she learns nothing at all and has no benefit from a rapid teaching-method;

this is the case in some classes which are taken by teachers who are excellent, but quick and impatient. Complaints have been made about her handwriting and her inability to grasp the rules of grammar. I have gone into these complaints; it is true, she does write slowly and stiffly, if the point is pressed, but not hesitantly and clumsily. What I taught her step by step about French, which is admittedly not my subject, she easily understood. Indeed it is strange: there is much that she knows, and knows well; only when she is questioned, she seems to know nothing.

If I am to close with a general observation, I would like to say this: she does not learn like someone who is being educated, but like someone who wishes to be an educator; not as a pupil, but as a future teacher. Perhaps, Madam, you will think it strange that I myself, as educationist and teacher, do not believe that I am any longer praising anyone except when I declare such a person to be one of my own sort. Madam's better insight and deeper knowledge of people and the world will deduce the best from my limited, well-meaning phrases. You will be convinced that much joy may be expected of this child. I take my leave of you, Madam, and ask your permission to write again as soon as I believe that my letter will have something significant and pleasant to report.

Charlotte was pleased at this note. Its contents coincided quite closely with her own conception of Ottilie; at the same time she could not restrain a smile since the teacher's feelings seemed to be warmer than those usually aroused by insight into the virtues of a pupil. With her calm and unprejudiced way of thought she let such a situation, like so many others, take its course; she appreciated this sensible man's interest in Ottilie; for she had had sufficient opportunity in the course of her life to realise how highly any true affection is to be esteemed in a world where indifference and dislike are actually only too much at home.

CHAPTER IV

THE topographical map was now ready; on it the estate with its environs had been depicted in a fairly large scale, and shown in its characteristics and made comprehensible through pen-and-ink work and colours, while the Captain had been able to base the map firmly on some trigonometrical calculations; for hardly anyone managed with less sleep than this active man, as his day was always devoted to the purpose of the moment, and consequently something had always been achieved by the evening.

'Let us turn now to what is left,' he said to his friend, 'to the description of the estate, for which there must already be sufficient preparatory work which will lead afterwards to deeds of tenancy and other things of the sort. Let us establish and arrange one thing only: separate everything that is actual business from living. Business demands seriousness and severity, life requires caprice; business is a matter of strictest necessity, while life often needs inconsequentiality, in fact it is pleasant and exhilarating. If you are safe with the one, you can be all the freer in the other; whereas if there is a confusion of the two, security is torn away and destroyed by freeness.'

Edward perceived a gentle reproach in these suggestions. Although admittedly not disorderly by nature, he could never bring himself to separate his papers according to subjects. What he had to negotiate together with other people was not separated from what depended on himself alone; similarly he did not keep business and occupations, conversation and distractions, adequately apart. He was relieved now that a friend was assuming this troublesome task, and that a second self was effecting the separation into which the one self may not always like to split.

They set up in the Captain's wing of the house a basket for current papers and a repository for matters that had already been dealt with; they collected together all documents, papers and reports from various containers, rooms, cupboards and boxes, and in a short time the confused mass was brought into pleasing order and lay sorted in properly marked pigeon-holes. What was required was found in a more complete state than they had hoped. In this connection an old copy-clerk was very useful who stayed at his desk the whole day through and even part of the night, a person with whom until now Edward had always been dissatisfied.

'I don't know him any more,' Edward said to his friend, 'how busy and useful the fellow is!'

'The reason for that,' the Captain replied, 'is that we don't give him anything new to do until he has finished the previous task in his own time; and consequently he accomplishes a great deal, as you see; as soon as anyone interrupts him, he can't do anything.'

After spending their days in this way together, the friends did not fail to visit Charlotte regularly in the evening. If there were no company from neighbouring places and estates, which often was the case, their conversation and reading were chiefly devoted to such subjects as are conducive to the well-being, the advantages and entertainment of middle-class society.

Charlotte, accustomed in any case to make use of the present moment, felt herself personally helped when she saw her husband contented. A number of domestic arrangements which she had wanted for a long time but had not been able to introduce properly, were made effective by the Captain's actions. The household medicine store, which up to now had only consisted of a few items, was expanded, and Charlotte was placed, through comprehensible text-books and also through conversations, in a position where she could exercise her active and philanthropic nature more frequently and more effectively.

Since thought was given also to emergencies, which although usually only too often came as a surprise, everything that might be necessary for rescuing the drowning was acquired all the more extensively, because with the proximity of so many lakes, streams and water-constructions some accident of this kind frequently happened. The Captain looked very conscientiously after this aspect of first-aid, and Edward let fall the remark that a case of this type had been in the strangest way of epoch-making significance in his friend's life. But when the latter was silent and seemed to be avoiding a sad memory, Edward stopped likewise, and Charlotte also went on to discuss some other subject, for she was in general no less informed about it.

'We may well praise all these precautionary measures,' the Captain said one evening; 'but we still lack what is most essential, a good man who knows how to deal with all this. I can suggest for this purpose a field-surgeon who is well known to me and is to be had for a reasonable offer, a first-rate man in his line who has often given me more satisfaction even in the treatment of serious internal troubles than a famous doctor would have done; and first-aid is after all always what is most missed in the country.'

A letter was at once written to this man too, and the married couple were happy that they had found reason to spend on the most essential purposes many a sum of money which would have been available for superfluous expenditure.

In this way Charlotte used the Captain's knowledge and energy for her own purposes too, and began to be fully contented with his being there and at ease about any possible consequences of this. She made a habit of preparing a number of questions, and as she had a love of life, she attempted to remove anything that might be harmful or death-bringing. The lead-glaze on pottery ware, the rust on copper vessels had before now caused her considerable anxiety. She was glad to receive instruction on these matters, and naturally it was necessary to go back to the basic laws of physics and chemistry.

Edward's pleasure at reading aloud to company gave a chance, but ever welcome impetus to such conversations. He had a very melodious, deep voice and in earlier days had been popular and well known for his lively and sensitive recitation of works of poetic and rhetorical nature. Now it was other things that occupied him, other types of writing which he read from, in particular for some time now predominantly works of a physical, chemical and technical content.

One of his special traits, which however, he perhaps shared with a number of people, was that he found it unbearable if anyone should be looking into the book while he was reading. Formerly, when he read poems, plays and stories, it was the natural consequence of the keen desire to surprise, to make pauses and to arouse expectations, which someone who is reading aloud has just as much as the poet, the actor and the storyteller, and it clearly goes very much against the desired effect if a third person is knowingly looking ahead with his eyes. It was therefore also his custom in such a case always to sit so that he had no one behind him. Now that there were the three of them this precaution was unnecessary; and since there was no intention this time of arousing feeling or surprising the imagination, he himself did not think of being particularly careful.

Only one evening, after he had sat down without thought, he did notice that Charlotte was looking over his shoulder. His old impatience awakened, and he

31

reprimanded her, in a rather brusque manner; they should once and for all get out of the habit, like so many other habits which were of an unsociable kind. 'If I am reading to someone, isn't it as if I were telling him something orally? What is written, the printed word, comes in place of my own thought and my own heart; and would I take the trouble to talk at all, if a little window were fixed in front of my forehead or my breast so that the person to whom I wish to relate my thoughts and to offer my emotions in turn could already know a long time in advance what I was aiming at? When somebody looks over into my book, I always feel as if I were being torn into two pieces.'

Charlotte's skill in larger or smaller social groups showed itself particularly in her ability to put on one side any unpleasant, passionate or even simply lively remark, to interrupt a conversation that was becoming too lengthy and to stimulate one that was slowing down; this time too she was not deserted by her happy gift. 'I am sure you will pardon my mistake when I confess what happened to me at that moment. I heard something being read about kinship, and then I thought at once about my kindred, about some cousins who are on my mind at this very moment. My attention returns to your reading; I hear that the talk is about quite inanimate things, and look into your book in order to find where I am again.'

'What has been misleading and confusing you is a figure of speech,' Edward said. 'Here it is a matter only of soils and minerals, but man is a true Narcissus; he likes to see his own reflection in everything; he makes himself a foil to the whole world.'

'How true!' the Captain went on. 'This is the way he deals with everything that he finds outside himself; he lends to animals, plants, the elements and the gods his own wisdom and folly, his own will and caprices.'

'As I don't want to divert you too far from your interest of the moment,' Charlotte added, 'would you teach me quite briefly what is actually meant here by kinships?'

'I'll be glad to do that,' the Captain replied, Charlotte having turned to him; 'indeed, only as well as I am able to from what I learned and read about ten years ago. Whether people still think the same way about it in the scientific world, and whether it agrees with the new teaching, I couldn't say.'

'It's bad enough that we can't now learn any one thing for our whole life-time,' cried Edward. 'Our ancestors adhered to the information that they'd been given in their youth; but now we have to learn everything afresh every five years, if we're not going to be out of fashion completely.'

'We women are not so particular,' Charlotte said: 'and to be frank, I'm only concerned with understanding the word: for nothing makes you look sillier in company than if you use an unfamiliar, artificial word in the wrong way. Therefore I should only like to know in what sense this term is used in this context. What the scientific connotation may be, we can leave to the men of learning who in any case, as I have observed, are hardly ever in agreement.'

'But where shall we begin now, in order to get to the point most quickly?' Edward asked the Captain after a pause, and the latter, having thought it over, replied a little later:

'If I may be allowed to appear to go back a long way, we shall soon arrive at the spot.'

'Be assured that I am all attention,' said Charlotte, putting down her work.

And the Captain began like this: 'The first thing that we notice about all living creatures is that they have connections with one another. It certainly sounds curious when one says something which is taken for granted any way: but it's only when we are fully clear about what is known that we can step forward together to the unknown.'

'I should have thought,' Edward interrupted, 'we could make the matter easy for her and us by some examples. If you think of water, oil or quicksilver, you will find a unity and coherence of their parts. They do not leave this unified state except as a result of force or some other intervention. Then if this is removed, they immediately come together again.'

'There's no question about that,' Charlotte said in agreement. 'Drops of rain tend to unite into streams. And even when we are children, we play wonderingly with quicksilver, separating it into little balls and letting it come together again.'

'And therefore I may perhaps mention in passing an important point,' the Captain added, 'that is, that this completely clear connection, made possible by the liquid state, is always distinguished in a definite manner by the spherical shape. The drop of water, as it falls, is round; you have talked mostly about little balls of quicksilver; even a lump of running, molten lead comes out in the shape of a sphere, if it has time to solidify completely.'

'Let me go on,' Charlotte said, 'to see whether I can grasp what you are aiming at. Just as each thing has a connection to itself, so it must equally have a relationship to others.'

'And that will vary according to the variations in the different species,' Edward continued hastily. 'Soon they will meet each other as friends and old acquaintances who come quickly together, become united without changing anything about each other, just like wine mixing with water. On the other hand other things will linger near to each other as strangers, and will refuse to bind themselves even after mechanical mixing and fricture; just as oil and water, when shaken together, separate themselves again a moment later.'

'It doesn't require much effort of imagination to see in these simple forms people whom we have known,' Charlotte said; 'in particular we remember here the

34

social groups in which we have lived. But most similarity with these inanimate beings is found in the masses who stand opposed to one another in the world, and the social classes, the professions, the nobility and the third estate, the soldier and the civilian.'

'And what is more, just as these classes may be unified through customs and laws, so there are mediating factors too in our world of chemistry which can unite those things which otherwise repel one another,' Edward added.

'In this way we combine oil and water by means of alkaline salt,' the Captain interposed.

'Only not too quickly with your lecture!' Charlotte said, 'so that I can show that I am keeping in step. Haven't we already arrived at this point at the affinities?'

'Quite right,' the Captain replied; 'and we are going to get to know them right away in their full power and purpose. Those natures which, on meeting, grasp each other quickly and affect each other mutually, are known as related. This relationship is striking enough in the case of the alkalis and acids which, although they are in opposition to one another and perhaps just for that reason, seek and seize each other, modify each other and form a new body together in the most decisive manner. Let us just consider lime, which expresses its great attraction, its definite desire for unity, towards all acids! As soon as our chemical apparatus arrives, we will let you see various experiments which are very entertaining and give a better insight than words, names and technical terms.'

'Let me confess,' Charlotte said, 'that when you call these curious creatures related, they appear to me less as blood relations than as kindred of mind and soul. It is in just this way that truly significant friendships arise among human beings; for contrasting qualities make a more intimate union possible. And so I will wait and see how much of these secret activities you will be bringing before my eyes. Now I won't interrupt you any further

35

in your reading aloud,' she said, turning to Edward, 'and, being so much better informed, I shall listen to your reading with attention.'

'But since you've called upon us, you won't get away so easily,' Edward answered; 'for it's the complicated cases which are in fact the most interesting. It is only with these that one gets to know the degrees of kinship, the nearer and stronger, the more distant and slighter connections; the relationships are only interesting when they effect divorces.'

'Does this sad word, which unfortunately we hear so often in society now, also occur in the natural sciences?'

'To be sure!' Edward replied. 'It used in fact to be a characteristic honorary title for chemists to call them past masters in separation.'

'So people don't do it any longer, and a good thing too,' Charlotte added. 'Combining is a greater art and service. An artist in unification would be welcome for every occasion in the whole world. Now then, let me know of a few such cases, since you are in full swing for once in a way!'

'Well, let's link up right away with what we were just defining and discussing,' the Captain said. 'For example, what we call limestone is a more or less pure lime-earth which is intimately connected with a delicate acid which is known to us in the form of air. If we put a piece of such stone into diluted sulphuric acid, this latter will seize hold of the lime and appears with it as sulphate of lime; but that delicate acid from the air disappears. Thus a separation and a new combination have taken place, and one now believes that it is justifiable to apply the word elective affinity, because it really does look as if one kinship was preferred to the other and chosen before it.'

'Excuse me, just as I excuse the scientist,' Charlotte said; 'but I would never see a choice here, but rather a necessity of nature, and possibly not even this; for after all it may be perhaps only a matter of opportunity.

36

'Opportunity occasions relationships, just as it makes thieves; and if we're talking about your natural materials, it seems to me that choice lies merely in the hands of the chemist who brings these things together. Once they are together, then God help them! In the present case I just feel sorry for the poor acid contained in the air which must move around in the infinite once more.'

'All it's got to do is to combine with water and in the shape of a mineral spring to be of refreshment to the healthy as well as the sick,' the Captain added.

'It's all very well for the sulphate of lime to talk,' Charlotte said; 'it is now complete, it is a body, it's provided for, whereas the substance that has been expelled can have a difficult time before it finds a home once more.'

'I may be mistaken, but I think there's some slight cunning hidden behind your words,' Edward said with a smile. 'Just own up to your guile! I am after all in your eyes the lime which is seized by the Captain, as the sulphuric acid, and withdrawn from your pleasant company and transformed into refractory gypsum.'

'If your conscience compels you to such observations,' Charlotte replied, 'I needn't worry. These allegorical speeches are pretty and entertaining, and who wouldn't be glad to play with such resemblances! But man is after all raised by so many stages above these elements, and if he has been rather free and easy in his use of the lovely words choice and kinship by choice, he does well to retreat once more into himself and to make a proper consideration on this occasion of the value of such expressions. Unfortunately I know cases enough, where an intimate, and apparently indissoluble union of two persons has been broken up by the chance arrival of a third person, and one of the previously so happily united couple has been driven out into the unknown distance.'

'The chemists are much more gallant in this connection,' Edward said; 'they bring up a fourth substance, so that no one goes empty away.'

'Yes, indeed!' the Captain added; 'these cases are in fact the most important and peculiar ones, where it is possible to describe attraction and relationship, this parting and uniting, so to speak in a really crosswise fashion, where four substances, up to now linked together in two pairs, are brought in contact with each other, abandon their previous union and bind themselves together afresh. In this process of letting go and seizing, of fleeing and seeking, you really do believe you're seeing a higher destiny; you ascribe to such substances a kind of wishing and choosing and take the invented words "kinship by choice" as wholly justified.'

'Give me a description of such a case!' Charlotte said.

'One shouldn't attempt this sort of thing in words,' the Captain replied. 'As already said, as soon as I can show you the experiments themselves, everything will become more tangible and more agreeable. Just now I would have to fob you off with awful technical terms which even so wouldn't give you any picture. These creatures, that seem to be dead and yet are always inwardly prepared for activity, must be seen active before one's eyes and observed sympathetically in the way they seek each other out, attract, seize, destroy, swallow and consume one another, and after that emerge again from this most intimate union in renewed, novel and unexpected shape: it's then that one believes them capable of eternal life, even mind and reason, because we feel that our senses are hardly adequate to observe them aright and that our reason scarcely suffices to comprehend them.'

'I don't deny that the strange jargon must seem burdensome, in fact ridiculous, to someone who has not become reconciled to it through direct observation and comprehension,' Edward said. 'But we could easily express the relationship we were talking about, by letters for the time being.'

'If you won't think it pedantic,' the Captain went on, 'I'm sure I can sum up briefly in the language of signs. Think of an A that is intimately bound to a B and inseparable from it, even though many means and much force are used; now think of a C which is related in a similar way to a D; bring the two pairs into contact: A throws itself at D, C at B, without our being able to say who first felt the other or who first united itself with the other again.'

'Well now!' Edward interposed; 'until we do see all this with our eyes, let us look at this formula as a figure of speech from which we may deduce a lesson of immediate use. You represent the A, Charlotte, and I your B; for really I do depend completely on you and follow you as A follows B. The C is obviously the Captain, who just at the moment is withdrawing me from you to some extent. Now it is only fair that you should be provided with a D if you are not going to disappear into thin air, and this is absolutely without question the dear little lady Ottilie, whose approach towards you, you may not resist any longer.'

'Very well!' Charlotte replied. 'Even if the example doesn't really fit our situation, as it seems to me, I do think it is fortunate that today we fully agree for once, and that these relationships through science and through choice should hasten a confidential communication between us. I will therefore only admit that I have been determined since this afternoon to summon Ottilie here; for my confidante and housekeeper, so loyal up to now, is going to leave in order to get married. This would come from my initiative and for my sake; what determines me from Ottilie's point of view, you can read aloud to us. I won't look at the page over your shoulder, but in fact its contents are already known to me. Still, you just read it!' With these words she took out a letter and handed it to Edward.

39

CHAPTER V

The Headmistress's Letter

MADAM will excuse me if I express myself very briefly today; for I have to report to all the parents and guardians the progress we have achieved during the past year with our pupils; what is more, I may be brief, because I can say much in a few words. Your daughter has shown herself as the first girl in every sense. The enclosed certificates and her own letter, which contains a description of the prizes she has won and at the same time expresses the pleasure that she feels about such a successful achievement, will reassure you and indeed be gratifying to you. My pleasure is to some extent qualified by my foreseeing that we shall no longer have cause to retain in our midst a young lady who has made such good progress. I send you my best respects and will take the liberty in the near future of expressing my thoughts about what I consider may be most advantageous for her. My friendly assistant is writing about Ottilie.

The Assistant's Letter

Our respected headmistress allows me to write about Ottilie, partly because, from her way of thinking, it would be disagreeable for her to disclose what has to be disclosed, and partly too because she herself owes an apology which she prefers to let me make.

As I know only too well how little our good Ottilie is in a position to express what is in her and what she can do, I had a certain anxiety at the prospect of the public examination, all the more so as no preparation at all is possible for it, and also, if it were to be

40

conducted in the usual way, Ottilie could not apparently be prepared. The results have justified my anxiety only too clearly: she did not win any prize, and furthermore she is one of those who have not been awarded any certificate. What am I to say? In handwriting others had scarcely such well formed letters, but a much freer manner; in arithmetic everybody else was quicker, and difficult problems, which she can solve better, were not included in the examination. In French many could talk more fluently and coherently; in history she did not have names and dates at her fingertips; her geography showed a lack of attention to political divisions. There was neither time nor leisure for the performance of her few, modest tunes. She would certainly have won a prize for drawing; her outlines were clear and her execution was both careful and intelligent. Unfortunately she attempted something on too large a scale and did not complete it.

When the girls had withdrawn and the examiners took counsel together and allowed us teachers to have some small say in the matter, I soon noticed that Ottilie was not mentioned at all, or if she was discussed, it was with indifference if not disapproval. I hoped that I might win some support for her by a frank description of her character and behaviour, and ventured to do this with double zeal, firstly because I could speak according to my own convictions and secondly because I had found myself in exactly the same sad position when I was younger. I was listened to with attention; but when I had finished, the chairman of the examiners said to me, in a friendly but nevertheless laconic voice: 'We assume that ability is there, but it must be converted to accomplishment. This is the aim of all education, this is the clear, express purpose of parents and guardians and the quiet, only half-realised purpose of the children themselves. This too is the subject of the examination, by which teachers and pupils are judged at the same time. From what we have heard from you we may hope well for the child, and it is certainly to your credit that you take exact account of the ability of the girls. If you transform such ability into accomplishment in the course of a year, there will be no lack of applause for you and your favoured pupil.'

I was already resigned to what followed from this, but had not been apprehensive about something still worse that took place soon afterwards. Our good headmistress, who like a good shepherd did not like to see a single one of her lambs lost or, as in this case, undecorated, was unable to hide her disappointment after the examiners had gone, and said to Ottilie, who was standing very quietly by the window while the others were rejoicing over their prizes: 'But tell me, for heaven's sake, how is it possible to look so stupid when in fact one is not?' Ottilie replied quite calmly: 'Forgive me, dear Mother, I've got one of my headaches again, just today as it happens, and rather a bad one.'—'Nobody can know that!' replied the lady who is usually so sympathetic, and she turned away in irritation.

Now it is true: nobody can know it; for Ottilie does not change her facial expression, and I have not even seen that she has once put her hand to her forehead. But that was not yet all. Your daughter, Madam, who is usually lively and open, was unrestrained and presumptuous in the feeling of her triumph today. She was jumping around the rooms with her prizes and certificates and waved them in front of Ottilie too. 'You've come off badly today,' she cried. Ottilie answered quite calmly: 'The final test hasn't come yet.' 'And even so you'll always be last,' the young woman exclaimed, making off again.

Ottilie appeared composed to everybody else, only not to me. An inner emotion of an unpleasant and intense quality, which she is resisting, shows itself through an uneven colouring on her face. Her left cheek becomes red for a moment, the right one becoming pale. I took our headmistress to one side and talked seriously with her about the matter. The good lady recognised her mistake. We took counsel and discussed the matter at length, and, without

making that a pretext for my being any more long-
winded, I will put our decision and suggestion to you,
Madam—that you should have Ottilie with you for a
time. You will see the reasons for this best yourself. If
you do decide on this, I will say more about how the
good child should be managed. If your daughter does
leave us in due course, as may be presumed, we shall
be glad to see Ottilie come back to us.

One more thing, which I might perhaps forget later;
I have never seen Ottilie demand anything or even
make an urgent plea for anything. On the other hand
it does happen, though only seldom, that she tries to
refuse something that is asked of her. She does this
with a gesture which is impossible for anyone who has
understood its meaning to refuse. She presses together
the palms of her hands, lifts them into the air and
moves them against her breast, bending just slightly
forwards as she does it and looking at whoever makes
this urgent request with such a glance that he is glad
to withdraw whatever it might be that he has been
demanding or wishing for. If you ever see this gesture,
Madam, though it is unlikely with your manner of
treatment that you will, do think of me and spare
Ottilie.

Edward had read these letters aloud, not without
smiling and shaking his head. There were bound to be
also remarks about the people and the situation.

'Enough!' Edward finally exclaimed; 'it's decided,
she's coming! You will be looked after, my love, and
we may now press on with our suggestion. It is most
necessary for me to move over to the Captain in the
right wing of the house. Really the best time for working
together is last thing at night and early in the morning.
You for your part will receive the finest room on your
side of the building for yourself and Ottilie.'

Charlotte did not object, and Edward described her
future way of life. Among other things he exclaimed:
'It really is quite obliging of our niece to have slight

headaches on the left side of her face; I often have one on the right. If they coincide and we sit facing each other, I myself leaning on my right elbow and she on her left, holding our heads in our hand according to different sides, it will make a pair of nice counter-pictures.'

The Captain thought that might be dangerous. Edward on the other hand cried: 'You just be careful of the D, my dear friend! What should B do if C were snatched from him?'

'Oh, I should have thought that could be taken for granted,' Charlotte replied.

'Certainly,' Edward exclaimed; 'it would return to its A, its Alpha and Omega!' he cried, jumping to his feet and pressing Charlotte close to his breast.

CHAPTER VI

A CARRIAGE bringing Ottilie had arrived. Charlotte went out to meet her; the dear child hurried towards her, threw herself down at her feet and embraced her knees.

'Why the self-abasement?' said Charlotte who was somewhat embarrassed and wanted to lift her up. 'It isn't intended to be so humble,' added Ottilie, remaining in her previous position. 'I like so much to remember the time when I didn't reach any higher than your knees and when I was already so sure of your love.'

She got up, and Charlotte embraced her warmly. She was introduced to the men and at once treated with special respect as a guest. Beauty is everywhere a very welcome guest. She seemed attentive to the conversation though she did not take part in it.

The next morning Edward said to Charlotte: 'She's a pleasant, entertaining girl.'

'Entertaining?' Charlotte put in with a smile: 'but she hasn't opened her mouth yet.'

'Really?' Edward replied, and seemed to be thinking the matter over, 'that would certainly be strange.'

Charlotte gave the new arrival only a few hints about fitting in with the household. Ottilie had quickly seen the whole ordering of things, and, what is more, had sensed it intuitively. She easily understood what it was she had to see to for all, and for each one separately. Everything took place punctually. She knew how to arrange matters without appearing to be giving orders, and if anyone neglected a task, she at once carried it out herself.

45

As soon as she realised how much spare time she had, she asked Charlotte if she might arrange her times regularly, and these times were now observed precisely. She performed her duties in the way which Charlotte was familiar with from the Assistant. She was allowed to do things in her own way. Sometimes she would give her used quills, in order to suggest a freer type of handwriting to her; but soon these too would again be cut sharp.

The ladies had agreed amongst themselves to talk French when they were alone; and Charlotte insisted on this all the more, since Ottilie was more talkative in the foreign language, by making practice in French a duty for her. Here she often said more than she seemed to want to. Charlotte was particularly entertained by her casual, though exact and at the same time affectionate description of the whole school institution. Ottilie became a pleasant companion to her, and she hoped that she would later find in her a trusty friend.

Meanwhile Charlotte took out again the old papers referring to Ottilie in order to recall how the headmistress and the assistant had judged the dear child, so that she could compare these comments with her personality. For Charlotte believed that one could not get to know quickly enough the character of people with whom one has to live, in order to know what can be expected of them, how far they are capable of development, or what it will be necessary once and for all to concede to them and pardon them for.

It is true that she did not find anything new as a result of this investigation, but much that was known became more significant and striking to her. Thus, for example, Ottilie's moderation in eating and drinking might indeed cause her anxiety.

The next thing that concerned the women was the matter of dress. Charlotte required of Ottilie that she should wear clothes that were richer and more distin-

guished. At once the good, busy child cut out the
materials that had previously been given to her and, with
only a little help from others, was able to adapt them
quickly and most becomingly. The new, fashionable
dresses enhanced her figure; for although the pleasant
characteristics of a person do make themselves noticeable
beyond the external covering, we always believe that we
can see them anew and in more charming form if the
person discloses her qualities to a new background.

As at first, now even more, she certainly caught the
eye of the men in this way, to put the matter bluntly. For
if the emerald through its magnificent colouring pleases
the sight, in fact even has some healing power on this
noble sense, human beauty works with much greater
power on the outward and the inner senses. Whoever
perceives beauty cannot be approached by anything
evil; he feels in harmony with himself and the world.

Thus the company had profited in several ways by
Ottilie's arrival. The two friends kept more regularly to
the hours, even the minutes, of the meetings. They did
not keep the ladies waiting longer than was reasonable
either for meals, or for tea, or for walks. They did not
hurry so soon from the table, especially in the evening.
Charlotte certainly noticed this and did not fail to
observe the two men. She tried to find out whether one
man rather than the other might be the reason for this;
but she could not notice any difference. Both showed
themselves altogether more sociable. In their conversations they seemed to be considering what might be suitable to arouse Ottilie's interest, and what would be
suitable to her views and the rest of her knowledge.
When reading aloud and giving an account they paused
until she came back. They became gentler and altogether
more communicative.

In response to this Ottilie's willingness to make herself
useful grew every day. The more she became acquainted
with the house, the people and the conditions, the livelier

was her intervention and the more quickly did she understand every glance, every movement, a half word, a sound. Her quiet attention remained consistently the same, as did her calm alertness. And in this way her sitting and standing, going and coming, fetching and carrying and sitting down once again were without appearance of disquiet, a constant change, a constant pleasant moving about. Added to this was the fact that one did not hear her walk, she moved so quietly.

This discreet serviceability of Ottilie's gave Charlotte much pleasure. There was one thing that did not seem to her to be quite in order, which she did not conceal from Ottilie. 'It is one of the praiseworthy services for us to bend down quickly if someone drops anything from his hand and to try and pick it speedily up,' she said to her one day. 'Through this we so to speak admit ourselves to be owing of service to him; only one ought to consider in wider society to whom one shows such devotedness. I don't wish to prescribe to you any rules about it with regard to women. You are young. It is a respect to those who are higher in station and age, a politeness toward your own sort, and to those who are younger and more lowly you are thereby showing humane feeling and goodness; but it isn't really proper for a woman to show herself devoted and submissive to men in this way.'

'I will try to get out of the habit,' Ottilie replied. 'However, you will forgive me this awkwardness when I tell you how I came upon it. We were taught history; I haven't remembered as much of it as I suppose I should; for I didn't know what I could use it for. Only a few isolated incidents did make a great impression on me, such as the following one: When Charles the First of England was standing before his so-called judges, the gold knob of the small stick which he carried fell off. Accustomed to everyone putting themselves out for him on such occasions, he seemed to be looking round and expecting that someone would render him the small service this time too. Nobody moved; he bent down himself to pick up the knob. That seemed to me so distressing, I don't know whether rightly so, that from that moment on I haven't been able to watch anybody drop anything without bending down for it myself. But as it certainly may not always be proper and as I can't tell my story every time,' she added, smiling, 'I will restrain myself more in future.'

Meanwhile the useful activities to which the two friends felt themselves called continued without interruption. Indeed they found every day new reasons for considering and undertaking something or other.

When they were walking together one day through the village, they noted with displeasure how inferior it was as regards order and cleanliness in comparison with those villages where the inhabitants had to be careful of both because space was short.

'You remember,' the Captain said, 'how we expressed the wish while we were travelling through Switzerland that we would really improve a country estate by setting up a village placed in such a park, not in the Swiss style of building, but with Swiss order and tidiness, those qualities which are so encouraging to all who frequent the village.'

'That would be suitable here for example,' Edward replied. 'The castle hill runs down towards a jutting edge; the village is built in a fairly regular manner in a semi-circle opposite; the stream flows in between, and one man protects himself against its flooding with stones, another with stakes, another with beams, and his neighbour again with planks, but nobody helps anyone else; on the other hand each one brings disaster and loss to himself and to the rest. In the same way the road goes clumsily, now up, now down, at one time through the water, at another over stones. If the people would give a hand, it wouldn't need a large additional sum of money in order to set up a wall in a semi-circle, to raise the level of the road behind to that of the houses, to provide a fine open space, to encourage cleanliness and by means of an operation conceived on a large scale to banish all petty, niggling care once and for all.'

'Let's try!' the Captain said as he cast his eyes over the situation and made a quick judgment.

'I don't like to have anything to do with tradespeople and peasants unless I am in a position to give them orders,' Edward added.

'You're not far wrong there,' the Captain replied, 'for I have also had a lot of trouble in my life from jobs of that sort. How difficult it is for man to weigh rightly in the balance what he must sacrifice against what is to be gained, how hard it is to desire the end and not to despise the means! Many people even confuse ends and means, taking pleasure in the means without keeping the end in view. Every evil, they say, should be remedied at the spot where it becomes visible, and they are unconcerned about that point where it does in fact take its origin and derive its force. That is why it is so difficult to have consultations, especially with the ordinary people who are quite sensible in everyday life, but seldom see further ahead than from one day to another. Then you've got to take into account that one man will gain, another lose in a communal project, so that nothing at all can be achieved in the way of compromise. All real contributions to the common good must be achieved by means of unrestricted authoritarianism.'

As they stood talking, a beggar who looked insolent rather than needy accosted them. Edward disliked being interrupted and disturbed and reprimanded him after he had several times beckoned him in a more patient manner to go away without effect. The fellow went off with short steps, grumbling and answering back, and insisted on the rights of the beggar who may well be refused alms but who may not be insulted because he is just as much under the protection of God and the authorities as anybody else; at this Edward completely lost his self-control.

The Captain said afterwards, in order to calm him down: 'Let us see this incident as an invitation to give our country police authority here as well! Alms have to be given; but it is better not to give them personally, especially at home. There one should be moderate and uniform in all things, including philanthropy. Too generous a gift only attracts beggars, instead of getting rid of them, whereas if you are on your travels, flying past, you appear to the poor man at the street corner as a figure of chance good fortune and you may well throw him a surprisingly generous gift. Such an arrangement is made easy for us here by the situation of the village and the castle; I've already thought about it before.

'At the one end of the village lies the inn, at the other live an old couple, good people; what you want to do is to deposit a small sum of money at both these places. The person who is leaving the village, not the one entering, should receive something; and as the two houses at the same time are situated on the roads which lead up to the castle, everybody who might wish to go up to the castle will have to pass the two places.'

'Come,' said Edward, 'let's arrange it straightaway; we can always see to the details later.'

They went to the innkeeper and to the old couple, and the matter was decided.

'I know well enough,' Edward said, as they were making their way up to the castle hill again, 'that everything in life depends on a clever idea and a firm decision. Thus you judged my wife's plans for the garden very accurately and gave me too a hint for improving things, and I won't deny that I passed it on to her right away.'

'I could guess that, but I couldn't approve,' the Captain replied. 'You have confused her; she has let

things lie and is at odds with us about this one matter;
for she avoids speaking about it and hasn't invited us
up to the arbour again, although she goes up there now
and again with Ottilie.'

'We mustn't let ourselves be put off by that,' said
Edward. 'If I have a conviction about something good
that might and ought to be put into effect, I don't have
any peace until I see it realised. After all we are sensible
enough about making other innovations! Let us take
out the English descriptions of parks with their copper-
plate illustrations for our evening entertainment, and
then afterwards your plan of the estate! At first we can
tackle it just as a joke and a possibility; a serious discussion will develop from it pretty soon.'

After this was agreed upon, the books were consulted
in which in every case one could see the outline of the
district and its physical features in their first, rough
natural conditions, and then on other pages one found a
sketch of the alterations that had been consciously
undertaken in order to make use of and enhance the
good that was already present. From this discussion it
was easy to proceed to talking about their own possessions and their own district and about what they might
be able to make of them.

It was now a pleasant occupation to take as a basis
the map that had been drawn up by the Captain; only
it was not possible to tear oneself away completely from
that first idea which Charlotte had taken up at the
beginning. However, they did work out an easier ascent
to the heights; they decided upon a summer-house on
the upper slopes in front of a pleasant little wood; this
building was to stand in relation to the castle; it should
be visible from the castle windows, and from the
summer-house the eye should sweep over castle and
gardens.

After thinking it over carefully and surveying the
land, the Captain brought up for discussion the path

down to the village, the wall by the stream and the question of filling it in. 'If I construct a comfortable path to the heights, I shall gain just as many stones as I need for that wall,' he said. 'As soon as one project is dovetailed into another, both can be accomplished more cheaply and more quickly.'

'But now there's my worry,' Charlotte said. 'Of necessity a definite sum must be set aside; and if you know how much you need for such a plan, you can divide it out, if not over weeks, at least over months. The cash is in my hands; I look after the papers and I do the accounts myself.'

'You don't seem to trust us much,' Edward said.

'No, not in matters of discretion,' Charlotte replied. 'We are better at restraining caprice than you men.'

The arrangement was made, the work quickly begun; the Captain was always present, and Charlotte was now almost daily a witness to his serious and exact mentality. He too got to know her more intimately, and they both found it easy to work together and to achieve something.

Working together is like dancing together: people who keep step together become indispensable to one another; a mutual esteem must necessarily result from this; and there was a sure proof that Charlotte was well disposed to the Captain since she had become better acquainted with him—quite calmly she let him destroy a fine resting-place which she has chosen and adorned with special care in her first gardening plans, without having even the slightest unpleasant feeling about it.

CHAPTER VII

As Charlotte and the Captain were now occupied together. Edward consequently spent more time in Ottilie's company. In any case his heart had for some time been filled with a quiet, friendly feeling towards her. She was obliging and accommodating to everybody; his vanity made it appear that she was most obliging towards himself. Now there was no doubt about it: she had already noted exactly what foods he liked and how he liked them prepared; she did not fail to observe how much sugar he took in his tea and similar details. She was especially careful to shield him from all draughts, for he showed an exaggerated sensibility toward these and as a result frequently came into conflict with his wife, who could not have enough fresh air. In the same way Ottilie was knowledgeable about the orchard and the flower-garden. She tried to further his wishes and to avoid anything that made him impatient, in such a manner that she soon became indispensable to him, a friendly protective spirit, and he began to feel distressed if she were not present. In addition to this was the fact that she seemed more talkative and frank when they were alone together.

As he grew older Edward still retained a child-like quality which was particularly congenial to Ottilie's youthfulness. They were happy in their memories of earlier days when they had seen one another; these memories went back to the first period of Edward's affection for Charlotte. Ottilie liked to recall them as being the most attractive couple at the court; and when

54

Edward denied that she would have such a recollection of what had happened in her early childhood, she insisted that she still remembered very clearly one episode when she had her head in Charlotte's lap at Edward's entry, not from fear, but from childish astonishment. She might have added that it was because he had made such a vivid impression on her and she had liked him so much.

Under these circumstances much of the business which the two men had earlier undertaken together now came to something of a standstill, so that they found it essential to draft some essays and write letters in order to obtain a clear view of the situation again. They therefore arranged to meet at their office, where they found the old clerk without occupation. They went to work and soon found him things to do, without noticing that they were burdening him with much that they otherwise used to do themselves. The very first essay of the Captain and Edward's very first letter both would not come right. They took up a certain time with drafting and writing out, until at last Edward, who was having least success, asked what time it was.

It then transpired that the Captain had forgotten to wind up his watch, for the first time for many years; and they seemed to sense, if not to realise clearly, that time was beginning to be of little account to them.

While the men were becoming slacker in their activities, the activity of the women appeared to increase. In general the normal way of life of a family, which is composed of given people and necessary circumstances, has an extraordinary tendency to absorb a nascent passion like a vat, and a fair time can elapse before this new ingredient causes a noticeable fermentation and spills foaming over the edge of the vessel.

For our two friends the decisive mutual affections were of the pleasantest effect. There was a sharing of confidences, and a general feeling of good will was developed from the will of each individual. Every section of the community felt happy, and no one begrudged the other his good fortune.

Circumstances like these lift up mind and heart, and everything that we do or undertake turns in the direction of the immeasurable. For instance, the friends too were no longer confined to their house. Their walks were spread farther, and if Edward went on ahead with Ottilie to choose the path and to prepare the ways, the Captain, talking seriously with Charlotte, and showing interest in many a newly discovered little place and many an unexpected view, quietly followed the track of those who had gone hastily on ahead.

One day their walk took them through the castle-gate of the right wing down to the inn, over the bridge towards the pool. They walked beside it for as far as one usually followed the water, the bank of which then ceased to be fit for walking as it became enclosed by a bushy hill and then precipitous rocks.

But Edward, who was familiar with the district from his hunting expeditions, pressed on with Ottilie along a path that was overgrown, knowing full well that the old mill that was hidden between the rocks could not be far off. However, the little-used path soon disappeared, and they found that they were lost among thick undergrowth between moss-covered rocks; though not for long, for the sound of the mill wheel soon made known to them the proximity of the place they were looking for.

Advancing forwards on to a steep rockface, they saw the curious old black wooden building in the valley below, overshadowed by steep cliffs and tall trees. They made up their minds without delay to make their way down over moss and boulders, Edward going first; and as he now looked up and saw Ottilie following him fearlessly and unhesitatingly from rock to rock with easy steps and most beautiful poise, he believed it was some angelic figure that he saw hovering over him. And when she occasionally took his outstretched hand at a doubtful spot, or leaned on his shoulder, he could not deny that he was feeling the touch of the most delicately charming feminine creature. He almost wished she might lose her balance and slip so that he could take her in his arms and clasp her to his heart. But he would not have done this under any circumstances, for more than one reason; he was afraid of offending or hurting her.

What is meant by this, we may discover at once. For as soon as he had come down and was sitting opposite her under the tall trees by the rustic table, and the friendly miller's wife had gone off to fetch milk while her welcoming husband went to meet Charlotte and the Captain, Edward after some hesitation began to speak:

'I have a request, dear Ottilie; excuse my asking, even if you refuse it! You make no secret of the fact, and there's no reason why you should, that you wear a miniature on your breast below your dress. It is the picture of your father, that good man whom you hardly knew and who in every sense deserves a place near to your heart. But forgive me: the miniature is clumsy and large, and this metal and glass cause me a thousand fears when you lift a child into the air or carry something in front of you, when the coach sways, or when we make our way through undergrowth, as happened just now as we were coming down from the rocks. It is terrible for me to think that any unexpected push or fall or touch might possibly be harmful and dangerous to you. For my sake do remove the miniature, not from your mind or your room; indeed, give it the most beautiful and most sacred place where you live; only do remove from your breast something the closeness of which seems to me so dangerous, possibly from exaggerated anxiety!'

Ottilie was silent and had looked straight ahead, as he spoke; then without undue haste or hesitation, with a glance directed up above rather than to Edward, she unfastened the chain, took out the miniature, pressed it against her forehead and handed it to her friend, saying: 'Keep it for me until we come home! I can think of no better way of showing you how much I appreciate your friendly care.'

Edward did not dare to press the miniature to his lips, but he took her hand and pressed it against his eyes. Perhaps they were the two most beautiful hands that had ever been clasped together. He felt as if a stone had fallen from his heart, as if a barrier between himself and Ottilie had been removed.

Guided by the miller, Charlotte and the Captain came down by an easier path. They greeted one another gladly, and took refreshment. They did not want to return the same way, and Edward suggested a cliff path on the other side of the stream, by which the pools would again come into view, though the path necessitated a certain amount of effort. They now made their way through scattered groups of trees and saw in the distance various villages, groups of houses and dairy-farms with their green and fertile surroundings; the first that they encountered was a farm lying pleasantly on the heights in the midst of the trees. The prosperity of the district could be seen at its best, in front and behind, on the gently rising hill, and from here they proceeded to a delightful little wood; when they emerged from here, they found themselves on the heights facing the castle.

How happy they were to arrive there, so to speak, in this unpremeditated manner! They had made a circle round a little world; they were standing on the site of the new building and were looking once more into the windows of their own home.

They went down to the arbour and for the first time the four of them were there together. Nothing was more natural than that they should all express the wish that the path they had taken today, slowly and not without difficulty, should be made possible to follow in a sociable, easy and comfortable manner. Each made suggestions, and they calculated that the route which had taken them several hours would bring them back to the castle in one hour, if it were properly made up. Their thoughts were already devising a bridge which would shorten the distance and beautify the scenery, to be placed below the mill where the stream flowed into the pools, when Charlotte put a check on their inventive imagination by reminding them of the expense of such an undertaking.

'We can do something about that,' Edward put in. 'We have only got to sell that farm in the woods which seems to be so pleasantly situated and yet brings in so little, and use the money for these plans and we shall have the pleasure of using the interest from well-invested capital on a delightful walk, whereas all we get from it now, with some trouble and after the final accounts at the end of the year, is a miserably small income.'

Charlotte herself as a good housekeeper could not find much to say against this. The matter had already been discussed earlier. Now the Captain brought forward a plan for dividing up the land among the forest peasants; Edward, however, suggested a procedure which he thought would be quicker and easier. The present tenant, who had already come forward with suggestions, might have the property, paying for it by instalments, while they themselves could undertake the planned alterations piece by piece, also on the instalment system.

Such a sensible and cautious arrangement could not but meet with general approval, and the whole company was already seeing in their minds' eye the new paths winding in and out as well as hoping to discover the pleasantest resting places and vantage points on or near these paths.

In order to be able to picture it all in more detail, they took out the new map immediately in the evening at home. They saw the path they had taken and realised how it might perhaps be directed even more effectively at some places. All the previous suggestions were reconsidered and linked with the latest ideas; the siting of the new summer-house opposite the castle was approved again and the circle of paths leading to it was finally decided upon.

Ottilie had kept silent during all this, when Edward finally moved the plan, which up to now had lain in front of Charlotte, over to her, at the same time inviting her to give her opinion; when she hesitated a moment he affectionately encouraged her not to remain silent; after all, it didn't matter yet, for nothing had been settled, he said.

Putting her finger on the highest level part of the hill, she said: 'I would build the house here. You wouldn't see the castle, it's true, for it would be concealed by the little wood; but to make up for that, you would find yourself in a different, new world, while at the same time the village and all the houses would be hidden. The view toward the pools, the mill, the hills, mountains and countryside is extraordinarily fine; I noticed it while passing by.'

'She's right!' Edward cried. 'How is it we didn't think of it! That's what you mean, isn't it, Ottilie?' He took a pencil and drew in a rather long rectangle on the hill in a really emphatic and rough way.

The Captain was very hurt at this, for he did not like to see a careful and neatly drawn up plan spoiled in this way; however, he controlled himself after a slight expression of disapproval and took up the idea. 'Ottilie is right,' he said; 'we do enjoy a long walk in order to have coffee or eat fish which wouldn't have tasted so well if we had had it at home, don't we? We require a change and fresh things around us. An earlier generation sensibly built the castle here, for it is protected from the winds and has all our daily requirements close at hand; but it would really be quite suitable to have a building over there, more for short pleasure visits than for living in, and it would provide most pleasant hours during the fine weather.'

The more they discussed the matter, the more favourable it appeared, and Edward could not conceal his elation that it was Ottilie who had had the idea. He was as proud as if it had been his own discovery.

CHAPTER VIII

First thing in the morning the Captain inspected the situation and drew up a plan, first of all a rough plan and then, when the others had once more expressed their agreement on the spot itself, an exact plan together with an estimate and all that was necessary. There was no lack of adequate preparation. The business about the sale of the farm was also taken up at once again. Together the men found a new cause for activity.

The Captain drew Edward's attention to the thought that it would be gracious, in fact it would be an obligation, to celebrate Charlotte's birthday by the laying of the foundation-stone. It did not require much effort to overcome Edward's old dislike of such festivals; for it quickly occurred to him that Ottilie's birthday, which came later, could similarly be celebrated in a really festive way.

The new gardening plans and what was to be undertaken in connection with them seemed important and serious to Charlotte, indeed almost suspicious, so that she spent a lot of time going through on her own the estimates and the plans for the distribution of time and money. The company saw less of each other in the daytime, and came together all the more eagerly in the evenings.

Meanwhile Ottilie was already completely at home with the housekeeping, and how could it be otherwise with her quiet and confident behaviour. Furthermore, her whole mentality was directed toward the house and domestic matters rather than to the world at large and outdoor life. Edward soon noticed that in fact she only came along with them on walks as a matter of courtesy, and that she only stayed for any length of time outside in the evening as a matter of social duty, often indeed seeking an excuse in domestic activity in order to go indoors again. He was therefore soon able to arrange their communal walks in such a way that they were back home again before sunset, and he began to read poetry aloud, which was something he had not done for a long time, choosing especially such poems the recitation of which allowed for the expression of a pure, but passionate love.

In the evenings they usually sat round a small table in seats that had been drawn up to it: Charlotte on the sofa, Ottilie on a chair facing her, and the men taking the other sides. Ottilie sat on Edward's right, and it was in this direction also that he placed the light when he was reading. Then Ottilie would edge up closer in order to look into the book, for she too trusted her own eyes more than strange lips; and Edward similarly edged along in order to make it comfortable for her in every way, indeed, he often made lengthier pauses than was necessary, so that he need not turn over the page before she had finished reading it.

Charlotte and the Captain certainly noticed it and often looked at each other with a smile; but they were both surprised by another indication in which Ottilie's quiet inclination towards Edward was occasionally revealed.

On one evening, which had been partly lost for the little group by the presence of tedious callers, Edward suggested that they should stay together a little longer. He felt in the mood for taking out his flute, an instrument which had not been on the agenda for a long time. Charlotte looked around for the sonatas which they usually played together, and as they could not be found,

Ottilie confessed after some hesitation that she had taken some up to her room.

'And you can, you will accompany me on the piano?' Edward cried, his eyes sparkling his happiness. 'I think I could manage it,' Ottilie replied. She brought along the notes and sat down at the piano. The listeners were attentive, and were surprised how completely Ottilie had learnt the music, but even more surprised to realise how she succeeded in adapting the music to Edward's manner of playing. 'Adapting' is not the right word; for if Charlotte's skill and free will allowed her to wait at one point and to hurry at another for the sake of her husband who was now hesitant, now impetuous, it seemed that Ottilie, who had heard Charlotte and Edward play the sonata a few times, had only learnt the piece in the manner in which Edward played his part. She had made his shortcomings so much her own that once more a kind of living whole grew out of it that certainly did not keep in time, but still sounded very pleasant and agreeable. The composer himself would have had pleasure at seeing his work distorted in so charming a manner.

The Captain and Charlotte looked silently upon this strange, unexpected event with the sort of feeling with which one often regards childish actions, which because of their worrying consequences one cannot exactly approve of and yet one cannot reprove them, perhaps one must only enjoy them. For as a matter of fact the inclination of Charlotte and the Captain towards one another was growing just as much as that of the other two, and was perhaps only the more dangerous since they were both more serious, more assured and more capable of self-restraint.

The Captain was already beginning to feel that custom was threatening to link him irresistibly with Charlotte. He brought himself to the point of avoiding the hours when Charlotte usually came to the gardens, by getting up very early in the mornings to put his things in order and then retiring to work in his own wing of the castle. For the first few days Charlotte thought that this was by chance; she looked for him in all the probable places; then she believed she understood his reasons and respected him all the more on that account.

If the Captain now avoided being alone with Charlotte, he was all the busier preparing and hastening the garden plans for an impressive celebration of the approaching birthday; for while constructing the easy path from below upward, from behind the village toward the castle, he arranged for work to be done starting from the top as well, ostensibly in order to break up stones, and he had so ordered and calculated everything that the two sections of the path should not be joined until the last night. The cellar of the new house at the top also was more broken into than properly excavated, and a handsome foundation-stone was shaped with compartments and covering-sheets.

The outside activity and these little friendly secret intentions, combined with more or less suppressed inward feelings, prevented social activity becoming lively when the company came together; consequently Edward, who felt that something was missing, called upon the Captain to bring out his violin and to play together with Charlotte at the piano. The Captain could not refuse the general requests, and so the two performed together one of the most difficult compositions with such feeling, ease and lack of restraint that it gave them and the two listeners the greatest pleasure. They promised to repeat the occasion frequently and to practise together more.

'They can do it better than we can, Ottilie!' Edward said. 'We will admire them, but still enjoy playing together ourselves.'

CHAPTER IX

THE birthday had come, and everything was ready:
the whole wall, which raised the village road and protected it from the water, and also the way past the
church which then continued for a time as the path laid
out by Charlotte, wound its way up the rocks with
the arbour above on the left after making a complete turn and in this way gradually reached the top of
the hill.

A lot of visitors had come on this day. They all went
to church where they found the parishioners assembled
in festive dress. After the service the boys, youths and
men left first, as was arranged; then came the gentry
with their visitors and retinue; girls, young women and
women came at the end.

At the bend of the road an elevated space in the rocks
had been set up; here the Captain arranged for Charlotte
and the guests to be seated. From this point they had a
view of the whole path, the column of men walking up
in front and the women coming after who were now
passing by. It was a lovely sight in the splendid weather.
Charlotte felt surprised and moved, and warmly pressed
the Captain's hand.

They followed the quietly proceeding crowd which
had now already formed a circle round the site of the
new building. The proprietor of the house that was to
be erected, those belonging to him and the most distinguished guests were invited to step down below to where
the foundation-stone, propped up on one side, lay just
ready for putting into place. A stonemason in his best

clothes, bearing a trowel in one hand and a hammer in the other, made a graceful speech in rhyme, which we can only reproduce in incomplete form in prose.

'Three things are to be observed when erecting a building,' he began: 'it should stand on the right spot, have good foundations and then be well executed. The first matter is actually the proprietor's business; for although in a town only the Prince and the municipality can decide where the building is to be, in the country the landowner has the privilege of saying, "My house is to stand here, and nowhere else." '

Edward and Ottilie did not dare to look at each other during these words, although they were standing near to one another.

'The third matter, the execution of the building, is the care of many guilds; indeed there are few that would not be active here. But the second matter, the foundation, is the stonemason's business and, to put it boldly, the most important part of the whole undertaking. It is a serious concern, and our invitation to you is serious; for this solemn occasion is a matter of depths. Here inside this narrow, hollowed out space you do us the honour of appearing as witnesses to our secret work. We are about to lower this well hewn stone, and soon these earthen walls, now adorned by the presence of fine and worthy personages, will no longer be accessible, and will be filled in.

'We could put into place without further ado this foundation-stone, which represents with its corner the true corner of the building, with its rectangular shape the regularity of the building, with its horizontal and vertical position the trueness of the walls, inside and out; for the stone would lie firm with its own weight. But here too there must be no lack of mortar, the binding medium; just as people who turn towards each other by nature are held together even better when they are cemented by law, so stones also, which fit together already by their shape, are combined even better by this unifying force; and since it is not fitting to be idle when others work, you will not be above collaborating on this occasion.'

At this he handed his trowel to Charlotte, who used it to throw mortar underneath the stone. Several people were asked to do likewise, and the stone was then lowered; after that the hammer was handed to Charlotte and the others, so that the union between the stone and the ground might be expressly blessed by a threefold knocking with the hammer.

The speaker continued: 'The stonemason's work, although now in the open air, takes place, if not invariably in concealment, at least for a hidden purpose. The regularly planned foundations are filled in, and even in the case of walls which we erect above the ground, we are hardly ever thought of. The labours of the stone-cutter and sculptor attract more attention, and we even have to give our blessing when the painter covers over the trace of our handiwork with whitewash and annexes our work by covering it over and smoothing it down and colouring it.

'Who is more concerned than the stonemason in doing what he does in a way that will be right for himself? Who more than he has reason to cherish the awareness of his worth? When the house is finished, the floor smoothed and plastered, the exterior covered with ornamentation, he sees through all the coverings into the inside and can still recognise those regular and careful joints to which the whole owes its existence and support.

'But just as anyone who has done wrong must fear that the wrong will be brought into the light, in spite of all efforts to conceal it, the man who has done good in secret must expect that this too will come into the open against his will. Here in these holes of different size varying objects are to be placed as a testimony to a distant posterity. These sealed metal quivers contain

68

written messages; all sorts of curious information is inscribed on these metal sheets; in these fine glass bottles we are burying the best old wine, with an indication of its vintage; there are some coins bearing this year's date; all these things have been presented through the generosity of our proprietor. Here too there is room enough if any guest or spectator would care to bequeath something to posterity.'

The workman looked round after a short pause; but as often occurs in these cases, nobody was ready and everyone was surprised, until finally a young and cheerful officer gave the lead and said: 'If I may make a contribution of a kind that has not yet been deposited in this treasury, I must cut off a few buttons from my uniform, for these too surely deserve to be passed down to posterity.' No sooner said than done, and now a number of people had similar ideas. The ladies did not hesitate to include some of their little hair-combs; bottles of smelling-salts and other dainty objects were not begrudged. Ottilie alone was hesitant until a friendly word from Edward drew her attention from the contributions that had been put down. She then unfastened from her neck the golden chain on which her father's picture had hung, and placed it with gentle hand on top of the other treasures; at this point Edward in some haste arranged that the well constructed cover should be lowered and affixed at once.

The young workman who had shown himself the most active up to now put on his oratorical mien again and went on: 'We are laying this stone for ever, as a security for the longest possible enjoyment for the present and future owners of this house. But while we are so to speak burying treasures here, we are thinking at the same time, during this most thorough of all occupations, of the transience of the human condition; we are thinking of the possibility that this firmly sealed lid may be lifted again, an eventuality that could only happen if all this

69

that we have not even constructed yet, were to be destroyed once more.

'But precisely so that this building may go forward, away with thoughts of the future and back to the present! Let us at once press on with our work after today's ceremony is over, so that none of the guilds that are working on our site need be idle, so that the building may rise speedily to completion and so that the proprietor and his family and guests may happily enjoy the view of the district; and now let us drink the health of these people and of all who are now present!'

And with this he drank the contents of a finely shaped goblet and threw it into the air; for to destroy a glass that has been used on an occasion of gaiety is a token of an overflowing joy. But this time it happened differently; the glass did not fall to the ground, and, furthermore, there was no miracle about this.

In order to get on with the building, the foundations had already been fully dug at the opposite corner, and a start had even been made to construct the walls, and for this purpose scaffolding had been erected, to as high a point as it would be necessary.

The scaffolding had been provided with a platform of planks specially for the occasion, and a crowd of spectators had been allowed up; this had happened for the benefit of the workpeople. The glass flew up in that direction and was caught by one of them, who saw this chance as a happy omen for himself. He showed it to those around him without letting it out of his hand, and the letter E and O could be seen cut into it in very graceful interlacing: it was one of the glasses which had been made for Edward in his youth.

The scaffolding stood empty again, and the more active of the guests climbed up to have a look round and could not find praise enough for the beautiful view on all sides; for many are the additional marvels to be discovered by someone standing only one storey higher

than a high vantage-point. Looking over the countryside
one could perceive several new villages, the silver thread
of the river was clearly visible, indeed one person
claimed he could see the towers of the capital city. To
the rear, behind the wooded hills, rose the blue peaks
of a distant mountain range, and the immediate neighbourhood could be viewed as a whole. 'The only thing
that is needed now,' somebody cried, 'is for the three
pools to be joined together into one lake; then the view
would possess everything that is magnificent and
desirable.'

'That could indeed be done,' the Captain said; 'for
in some distant age they did form a mountain lake.'

'Only I should like to ask you to spare my group of
plane-trees which stand so well by the middle pool,'
Edward said. 'Look,'—he turned to Ottilie and led her a
few paces forward, pointing down—'I planted those
trees myself.'

'How long have they been there?' Ottilie asked.

'About as long as you have been alive,' Edward
replied. 'Yes, dear child, I was planting trees already
while you were still in your cradle.'

The company returned to the castle. After having a
meal, they were invited to take a walk through the
village in order to inspect the new developments here
too. Here the inhabitants had assembled in front of their
houses at the Captain's request; they did not stand in
rows, but were grouped naturally together in families,
and some were busy with their evening tasks while
others were resting on the new seats. It was laid upon
them as a pleasant duty to renew this cleanliness and
tidiness at least every Sunday and holiday.

Intimate companionship based on affection, as it had
developed among our friends, cannot but be unplea-
santly disturbed by the presence of a considerable
company. The four of them were all relieved to be alone
once more in the large drawing-room; but this domestic

feeling was somewhat upset by a letter brought to
Edward which announced the arrival of new guests the
next day.

'It's just as we imagined,' Edward said to Charlotte;
'the Count won't fail, he's coming tomorrow.'

'Then the Baroness won't be far away,' Charlotte
added.

'Certainly not!' Edward replied; 'she too will be
arriving tomorrow from another direction. They ask if
they can stay the night and want to continue their
journey together the day after tomorrow.'

'Then we shall have to make our arrangements in
good time, Ottilie!' Charlotte said.

'What are your orders in this respect?' Ottilie asked.

Charlotte outlined her wishes to her, and Ottilie left.

The Captain enquired about the relationship of these
two people, which he only knew of in a most general
way. At a time when they were already both married,
they had fallen passionately in love. Two marriages
could not be broken without causing some stir; they did
think of divorce. In the Baroness's case it was possible,
but not in the Count's. They had to give the appearance
of being separated, but their liaison continued; and if
they could not be together during the winter in the city,
they made up for this during the summer in holiday
travel and visits to spas. They were both rather older
than Edward and Charlotte and had all been good
friends during earlier days at Court. They had always
remained on good terms with one another, although one
could not approve of everything about one's friends.
Only this time their arrival was not particularly welcome
to Charlotte, and if she had gone into the reason precisely, her misgivings were in fact on Ottilie's account.
It would be better if the good, pure child were not made
aware of such an example so early in her life.

'They might have left it a few days longer,' Edward
was saying, when Ottilie reappeared, 'until we have

settled the sale of the farm. The draft is ready, and I
have the one copy here; but we haven't got a second
copy, and our old clerk is really ill.' The Captain offered
his services, and Charlotte too; but there were some
objections here. 'Just give it to me!' Ottilie cried in
some haste.

'You won't finish it,' Charlotte said.

'It's true, I ought to have it the day after tomorrow,
and that's asking a lot,' Edward said. 'It shall be
ready,' Ottilie cried and already had the paper in her
hands.

The next morning, when they were looking out for the
guests from the upper storey, for they did not want to
miss going out to meet them, Edward said: 'Who's that
riding so slowly along the street?' The Captain described
the figure of the rider more exactly. 'Oh, it is him, then,'
Edward said; 'for the details, which you can see better
than I can, fit very well into the whole, that I can see
quite well. It's Mittler. But what's he doing, riding
slowly, so slowly?'

The figure came nearer, and it really was Mittler.
They gave him a friendly reception as he came slowly
up the steps. 'Why didn't you come yesterday?' Edward
called out to him.

'I don't like noisy celebrations,' the owner replied.
'But I'm coming today to celebrate my friend's birthday
with you quietly and after the event.'

'But how can you spare the time?' Edward asked
jokingly.

'You owe my visit, for what it's worth to you, to an
observation that I made yesterday. I spent half the day
in a truly happy manner in a house where I had brought
peace, and then I heard that a birthday was being celebrated here. "After all, people might consider it selfish
of you if you only share happiness with those whom you
have reconciled," I thought to myself. "Why don't you
for once in a way join in the happiness of friends who

keep and cherish peaceful relationships?'' No sooner said than done! Here I am, just as I planned.'

'You would have found a large company here yesterday, today you only find a small one,' Charlotte said. 'You will find the Count and the Baroness, who have already given you something to do in the past.'

With irritable haste the strange, though welcome man moved away from the middle of the four friends who had surrounded him, and he at once looked for his hat and riding-whip: 'There is always an unlucky star hovering over me, as soon as I make up my mind to relax for once and to do good to myself! But why do I leave my own character? I shouldn't have come, and now I am being driven away. For I won't stay under the same roof with that couple; and you look out, they bring nothing but disaster! Their nature is like yeast, which reproduces its own contagion.'

They tried to smooth him down, but to no effect.

'Anyone who attacks marriage,' he cried, 'anyone who undermines, through word or deed, this foundation of all moral society, will have to reckon with me; or if I can't get the better of such a one, I have nothing more to do with him. Marriage is the beginning and the culmination of all civilisation. It makes the brutal man gentle, and the most educated man can have no better opportunity of demonstrating his humane spirit. It must be indissoluble; for it brings so much happiness that the individual instances of unhappiness cannot be taken into account. And what is this talk about unhappiness? When someone is overcome from time to time by impatience he is pleased to consider himself unhappy. Once one allows the moment to pass, one will consider oneself fortunate that what has endured so long still endures. There are really no sufficient grounds for separating. The human condition is granted so much, both in pain and joy, that it is quite impossible to work out what the partners in a marriage owe to each other. It is an infinite debt, which can only be paid off in eternity. Marriage can be uncomfortable at times, I can well believe, and that's as it should be. Are we not also wedded to our consciences, which we should often like to get rid of because they are more disturbing than any husband or wife could ever be?'

Thus he talked in lively fashion and would probably have gone on talking a long time, had not the sound of coachmen's horns announced the arrival of the visitors, who drove into the courtyard of the castle, as if by prearrangement, from either side at the same time. When those who were living in the house hurried out toward them, Mittler hid himself and, after arranging for his horse to be brought to him, rode away in annoyance.

CHAPTER X

THE guests were welcomed and ushered in; they were
happy to be once more in the house and in the rooms
where they had spent so many a happy day in the past
and which they had not seen for a long time. Their
presence too was very pleasing to the friends. The Count
and the Baroness could be counted among those up-
standing, attractive personalities whom one almost prefers to see in middle age rather than in youth; for even
if such people have lost something of their first freshness
of youth, they do now elicit a distinctive confidence and
affection. This couple too showed themselves most
accommodating now. The easy manner in which they
dealt with circumstances, their gaiety and apparent
openness were immediately infectious, and their
behaviour as a whole was controlled by a high degree of
propriety, without any feeling of constraint being
noticeable.

This effect was felt at once by the others. The visitors
came straight from the world of society, as could be
seen even from their clothes, appurtenances and all that
surrounded them; they consequently formed something
of a contrast to our friends and their circumstances of
country living and secret passion, though this contrast
was very soon lost as old memories were mingled with
sympathy for present interests and quick, lively conversation soon linked them together.

All the same, it was not long before there was a split
in the company. The ladies withdrew to their own wing
and found plenty of entertainment there, having various

confidences to exchange and at the same time beginning to examine the latest shape and cut of spring dresses, hats and the like, while the men concerned themselves with the new coaches and the horses, at once beginning to talk about prices and to make exchanges of horses.

They did not reassemble until the meal-time. Clothes had been changed, and here too the newly arrived couple showed themselves to advantage. Everything that they wore was new and, so to speak, unseen, and yet already tried out and therefore familiar and comfortable.

The conversation was lively and varied, and, as happens when such people are present, everything and nothing seemed to be of interest. They spoke French so that the servants should not follow what they were saying, and the conversation strayed with playful zest to affairs of society, both in high and in less elevated circles. There was one point where the conversation remained fixed longer than was reasonable; this was when Charlotte enquired about a friend of her youth and heard with some surprise that she had just had a divorce.

'It is disagreeable when you believe that your absent friends are safe and sound, and that a beloved friend is well cared for,' Charlotte said; 'before you know where you are, you have to hear that her fate is in the balance and that she is about to step on to a new and probably once more uncertain path in her life.'

'Actually, my dear,' the Count replied, 'it is our own fault if we are surprised in this way. We do so like to think that earthly things, and in particular marital ties, are really permanent, and, as far as this latter is concerned, we are misled by the comedies, which we see always being repeated, to illusions such as do not fit in with the way of the world. In comedy we see a marriage as the final fulfilment of a desire that has been put off by the hindrances of several acts, and at the moment when it is attained the curtain falls and the temporary satisfaction it occasions lingers in our minds.

77

In life it's a different matter; the play goes on behind the scenes, and when the curtain rises again, we would be glad not to see or hear any more about it.'

'It can't be as bad as all that,' Charlotte said, smiling, 'as one can see that even people who have stepped off this stage are quite glad to play a part on it at a later date.'

'There's nothing to be said against that,' the Count said. 'One is glad to take over a new role again, and when you know the world, you can see that in marriage too it is only this definite eternal duration amid so much that is transient in the world, that has something awkward about it. One of my friends whose good humour displayed itself in making suggestions for new laws maintained that every marriage should be undertaken only for a five-year period. This, he said, was a lovely odd and holy number, and such a length of time was just sufficient for getting to know each other, having a few children, separating and, what is best of all, being reconciled once more. He used to say: "How happily the first period would pass! Two or three years at least would go by in a pleasurable manner. Then surely one of the parties would be interested in seeing the relationship last, and mutual considerateness would increase the closer one approached the end of the period. The partner who was indifferent, perhaps even discontented, would be placated and persuaded by such behaviour. One would forget that time was passing, just as one forgets the time when in good company, and one would be most pleasantly surprised to notice after the set time had passed that it had in fact already been prolonged." '

Although this sounded pleasant and gay, and, as Charlotte felt, although it would be possible to give this joke a deep moral meaning, she did not find such remarks pleasant, particularly on Ottilie's account. She knew full well that there is nothing more dangerous than an over-free conversation which treats a culpable or semi-culpable situation as if it were usual, general, and even praiseworthy; and surely anything that attacks the marriage union comes into this category. She therefore attempted in her clever way to direct the conversation; as she was not able to do this, she was sorry that Ottilie had seen to everything so well that there was no reason for asking her to get up. The quietly observant girl made herself understood to the house-steward by glances and gestures, so that all was excellently arranged, although a few new and clumsy servants were in attendance in livery.

And so the Count, not sensing Charlotte's attempt to change the subject, continued to express himself on this theme. He was not otherwise in the habit of being in any way a burden in conversation, but this concern lay too near to his heart, and the difficulties of living apart from his wife made him bitter against anything to do with marriage, although he himself eagerly desired to marry the Baroness.

'That friend of mine made another suggestion for a law,' he continued. 'A marriage should only be regarded as indissoluble when either both parties or at least the one party get married for a third time. For as far as such persons are concerned, they are undeniably confessing that they consider marriage as something indispensable. Now it will already be known how they have behaved in their previous marriages, whether for instance they have those peculiarities which often give more cause for separation than do bad qualities. Thus one would have to make investigations on both sides, and to keep a watch on the married just as much as on the single, because one doesn't know how cases may turn out.'

'There's no doubt that would increase curiosity in society,' Edward said; 'for in fact, now that we're married, nobody takes any further interest either in our virtues or our faults.'

'According to such an arrangement our host and hostess would have already gone happily through two stages and might be preparing for the third,' the Baroness interposed with a smile.

'They've managed things well,' the Count said; 'in this instance death has willingly accomplished what the divorce-courts are usually reluctant to carry out.'

'Let's leave the dead in peace,' Charlotte added with a glance that was in part serious.

'Why?' the Count replied, 'we can, after all, think of them with due honour. They were modest enough to limit themselves to a few years in return for the many good things that they left behind.'

'So long as the sacrifice of one's best years is not necessary in such cases!' the Baroness said with a suppressed sigh.

'True enough,' the Count replied, 'it's enough to make you despair, if it weren't for the fact that so little in this world comes up to expectations. Children don't fulfil their promise, and young people do only seldom, and if they keep their word, the world doesn't keep its word to them.'

Charlotte, glad that the conversation was taking another turn, put in cheerfully: 'Oh well, we must in any case accustom ourselves soon enough to enjoying what is good in life in an incomplete and fragmentary manner.'

'Certainly,' the Count answered, 'both of you have had very good times. When I look back at the years when you and Edward were the most handsome couple at Court, there's no talk now either of such brilliant times or of such outstanding personalities. When you danced together, all eyes were fixed upon you, and how sought after you both were, while at the same time you both were only interested in each other!'

'As so much has changed,' Charlotte said, 'we can perhaps listen with modesty to such compliments.'

'I have often blamed Edward for not being more persistent,' the Count said; 'for his odd parents would have given way in the end; and it's no small thing to gain ten years of one's youth.'

'I must put in a word for him,' the Baroness interposed. 'Charlotte wasn't wholly free from blame and not entirely innocent of casting her eyes around, and although she loved Edward sincerely and secretly intended him as her husband, I was myself a witness of how much she tormented him so that it didn't take much to persuade him to the unfortunate decision of travelling and going away and becoming used to being without her.'

Edward nodded to the Baroness and seemed grateful for her support.

'And then I must add one thing to excuse Charlotte,' she continued; 'the man who was courting her at that time had already been showing his affection towards her for a long time, and was certainly a pleasanter person, when one got to know him more closely, than you others are willing to admit.'

'My dear,' the Count said in a rather lively tone, 'we might as well admit that he wasn't completely indifferent to you, and that Charlotte had more to fear from you than from anybody else. I find that a very attractive feature about the ladies, that they still continue their attachment to a man and don't let this feeling be distorted or stopped by any kind of separation.'

'Perhaps men possess this quality even more,' the Baroness put in; 'at least as far as you are concerned, dear Count, I've noticed that nobody has more power over you than a woman who once had a hold on your affections. Thus I have seen that you would take more trouble to arrange something at the request of such a woman than you would do for the woman friend of the moment.'

'One can perhaps tolerate that sort of reproach,' the

Count replied; 'but as far as Charlotte's first husband is concerned, the reason why I couldn't put up with him was that he seemed to force apart a grand couple, who were really made for one another, and who, once they had been united, needed to have no fear of a five-year period nor to look forward to a second, let alone a third marriage.'

'We shall try to make up for what we have missed so far,' Charlotte said.

'You'll have to keep to that,' the Count said. 'Your marriages were after all really marriages of the unpleasant kind,' he went on with some vehemence, 'and unfortunately marriages in general—excuse the rather outspoken expression—have something clumsy about them; they spoil the most tender relationships, and the fault does in fact lie only in the crude sense of security which at least one of the partners takes advantage of. Everything is taken for granted, and the couple seem to have come together only so that one or the other of them may now go his own way as he pleases.'

At this moment Charlotte, desirous of breaking off this discussion once and for all, made use of a bold turning of the conversation, and succeeded in this. The conversation became more general, and both couples and the Captain could take part in it; even Ottilie was induced to express her opinion, and the dessert was enjoyed in the happiest atmosphere, to which the wealth of fruit, set out in elegant baskets, and the gayest mass of flowers, beautifully displayed in fine vessels, contributed the principal share.

The new arrangements in the park were also discussed, and a visit was paid there immediately after the meal. Ottilie withdrew under the pretext of domestic duties; but in fact she went to do some copying out. The Count was entertained by the Captain; Charlotte joined him later. When they reached the top of the hill and the Captain had obligingly hurried back to fetch the plan, the Count said to Charlotte: 'I like this man very much. He is very well informed and sees the whole perspective. What is more, his activity seems to be very serious and logically thought out. What he is accomplishing here would be considered of great importance in higher circles.'

Charlotte heard this praise of the Captain with warm pleasure. However, she restrained herself and confirmed what was said with calm and clarity. But how surprised she was when the Count continued: 'This new acquaintance comes at a very convenient time for me. I know a position which would be most suitable for the man, and by recommending him I can make him happy and at the same time be of good service to a friend in a high position.'

It was as if a thunder-clap had descended upon Charlotte. The Count did not notice anything; for ladies, used to restraining themselves at all times, still retain a kind of apparent self-control even in the most unusual eventualities. But she was already no longer listening to what the Count said, as he went on: 'When I have made up my mind about something, I get on with it quickly. I've already drafted my letter in my mind, and I am eager to write it down. Do procure me an express messenger whom I can make use of this very evening.'

Charlotte was torn in two inwardly. Surprised by these suggestions, as also by her own reaction to them, she was unable to utter a word. Fortunately the Count went on speaking about his plans for the Captain, and the advantages of these plans became only too obvious for Charlotte. It was time for the Captain to appear and to expound his qualifications to the Count. But how differently she looked at her friend, now that she was to lose him! She turned away with a perfunctory bow and hurried down to the summer-house. She had not gone more than half-way down when tears started from her eyes, and now she rushed into the small space of the little hermitage and yielded unreservedly to a pain, a passion and a despair the possibility of which she had not in the least suspected a few moments earlier.

On the other side of the hill Edward had gone down to the pools with the Baroness. This clever woman, who liked to be in the know about everything, soon noticed in the course of an exploratory conversation that Edward became expansive in his praise of Ottilie, and in a most natural manner she gradually induced him to talk so that she finally had no doubt that in this case it was not a question of incipient passion, but of one that was fully developed.

Even when there may be no love lost between them, married women nevertheless give tacit support to each other, especially against young girls. The consequences of an attachment such as Edward's became all too quickly obvious to the world wise mind of the Baroness. In addition, she had already spoken to Charlotte about Ottilie earlier in the day and had disapproved of this child's staying in the country, particularly with Ottilie's quiet character, and had suggested that she should take Ottilie to a friend of hers who was devoting great care to the education of her daughter and was now only looking for a suitable companion to enter the family as a second child and to share in all the advantages of such a life. Charlotte had undertaken to think the matter over.

Now, however, her insight into Edward's feelings turned the Baroness's suggestion to Charlotte into a firm resolve, and the more rapidly this change took place within her, the more she complied outwardly with Edward's wishes. For nobody was more self-possessed than this woman, and this self-possession in unusual circumstances habituates us to use deception even in an ordinary case and makes us inclined, since we exercise so much control over ourselves, to extend our power over other people too, so that we can, as it were, compensate ourselves through our outward gains for our inner losses.

Linked to this attitude of mind there is often a kind of secret malicious pleasure at the blindness of others and at the unconscious manner in which they walk into traps. We are pleased not only at an achievement in the present, but at the same time we also look forward to the surprise of a humiliation to come. And thus the Baroness was malicious enough to invite Edward to come with Charlotte to the vintage harvest on her estate and, when he asked whether Ottilie could come as well, to answer in terms which he could interpret in his own favour if he liked.

Already Edward was talking enthusiastically about the wonderful country, the large river, the hills, rocks and vineyards, the old castles, trips on the water, the joyful celebration of the harvesting and of pressing the juice from the grapes, and so forth, and in the innocence of his heart saying how he was looking forward to the impression which such scenes would make on Ottilie's unspoiled heart. At this moment they saw Ottilie approaching, and the Baroness quickly asked Edward not to say anything to Ottilie about this planned autumn journey; for so often what one looked forward to a long time in advance did not come about. Edward gave his word, but encouraged her to move more quickly to meet Ottilie and in the end hurried several paces ahead, towards the dear child. His whole being was expressive of heartfelt pleasure. He kissed her hand, pressing into it a bunch of wild flowers which he had picked on the way. The Baroness felt almost embittered in her heart at this sight. For although she might not condone what might be culpable about this affection, she could not help envying this insignificant greenhorn of a girl what was lovable and pleasant about it.

When they sat down together for dinner, a completely different mood had come upon the company. The Count, who had already written and sent off the messenger before the mealtime, was conversing with the Captain, whom he was sounding more and more in an understanding and unassuming manner. The Baroness, who was sitting to the Count's right, found little entertainment from that side, and just as little from Edward who, being firstly thirsty and then excited, drank a lot of wine and conversed in a lively manner with Ottilie whom he had drawn to his side; Charlotte, who was sitting on the other side by the Captain, found it difficult, indeed almost impossible, to conceal her inward feelings.

The Baroness had time enough to make her observations. She noticed Charlotte's displeasure, and as she was thinking only of Edward's relations with Ottilie, she could convince herself without difficulty that Charlotte was uneasy and irritated at her husband's behaviour, and she considered how she could now best fulfil her aims.

There was a split in the party after dinner as well. The Count, who wanted to get to know the Captain thoroughly, had to use a number of approaches to find out what he wanted in the case of such a quiet and by no means vain and generally laconic man. They walked together up and down one side of the room, while Edward, excited by wine and hope, was talking playfully with Ottilie by a window; but Charlotte and the Baroness walked silently together up and down the other side of the room. Their silence and idle waiting about eventually brought the rest of the company to a standstill. The women withdrew to their wing, the men to the other, and thus it seemed that the day was ended.

CHAPTER XI

E DWARD accompanied the Count to his room and was quite willing to be induced to stay chatting to him for a time. The Count became lost in memories of earlier times, conjured up in a lively manner Charlotte's beauty, which as a connoisseur of such things he expiated upon with much fieriness: 'A pretty foot is one of nature's great gifts. Such grace is indestructible. I watched her walking today; it would still be a pleasure to kiss her shoe and to repeat the somewhat barbaric but nevertheless deeply felt honour of the Sarmatae, who know of nothing better than to drink the health of a beloved and respected person out of one of his shoes.'

The tip of the foot was not the only object of praise among a couple of men on intimate terms. They went from her personality on to old stories and adventures, and mentioned the obstacles which had once been put in the way of the two lovers' meetings, the trouble they had taken, the tricks they had devised, just to be able to tell one another that they loved each other.

'Do you remember,' the Count continued, 'in what a friendly and unselfish way I helped you in an adventure, when our highest masters visited their uncle and met in the rambling castle? The day had been spent in solemnities and formal clothes; part of the night at least should go by in free, affectionate conversation.'

'You'd certainly made a note of the way to the quarters of the ladies-in-waiting,' Edward said. 'We found the way all right to my beloved.'

'And she thought more of the proprieties than of my

87

comfort and had kept a very ugly chaperone by her,' the Count added; 'so that while you two were very happily exchanging looks and words together, a most unpleasant lot befell me.'

'It was only yesterday, just when you were arriving, that I reminded my wife of the story, especially of our retreat,' Edward went on. 'We lost the way and came to the ante-room of the guards. Believing that we could now find our way quite well, we thought we could get through here too without any difficulties and go past the sentry, as past the others. But how astonished we were on opening the door! The path was strewn with mattresses on which these giants lay sleeping stretched out in several rows. The one waking man on duty looked at us with amazement; but we in our youthful courage and mischief strode quite calmly over the stretched out boots without even one of these snoring children of Enoch being woken up.'

'I had an urge to stumble,' the Count said, 'so that there should be a noise; and what a curious resurrection we should have seen!'

At this moment the castle clock struck twelve.

'It is full midnight,' the Count said with a smile, 'and just the right time. I must ask you a favour, dear Baron: lead me today, as I led you then; I have promised the Baroness to visit her again. We haven't talked alone together all day, we haven't seen each other for so long, and there is nothing more natural than to be desirous of an intimate hour together. Show me the way there. I'll find the way back, and in any case there won't be any boots for me to stumble over.'

'I shall be glad to do this favour for a guest,' Edward replied; 'the only thing is, the three women are over there together in that wing. Who knows whether we may not find them still together, or whether we may not start some other troubles which will come to look rather odd.'

'Don't worry!' the Count said; 'the Baroness is expecting me. She is bound to be alone in her room at this time.'

'It's an easy matter in other respects,' Edward added, and he took a light which he held up before the Count as they went down a secret staircase which led to a long corridor. At the end of this corridor Edward opened a little door. They climbed a spiral staircase; up above at a narrow resting-place Edward pointed out to the Count, handing him the light, a hidden door on the right which opened at once at the first attempt, admitted the Count and left Edward behind in the dark space.

Another door to the left went into Charlotte's bedroom. He could hear talking and listened. Charlotte was speaking to her maid. 'Has Ottilie already gone to bed?' —'No,' was the reply, 'she is still sitting downstairs writing.' 'Light the night-light then,' Charlotte said, 'and go off now: it's late. I'll put out the candle myself and go to bed on my own.'

Edward was delighted to hear that Ottilie was still at her writing. 'She is being busy on my account!' he thought exultantly. Enclosed in upon himself through the darkness, he saw her sitting and writing in his mind's eye; he imagined himself approaching her, seeing her as she would turn round towards him; he felt an insurmountable desire to be close to her once more. But there was no way from here to the entresol room where she lived. Now as he found himself directly by his wife's door, a strange confusion took place in his soul; he tried to turn the handle, the door was locked, he knocked softly, Charlotte did not hear.

She was walking up and down in the fairly large dressing-room. She repeated to herself time and time again what she had been turning over and over in her mind since that unexpected suggestion of the Count. The Captain seemed to be standing in front of her. He it was who filled the house with his presence and still gave life to the walks outside, and he was to go away, and all was to become empty! She said everything to herself that can be said, she even anticipated, as one usually does, the wretched consolation that even pains such as these are healed by time. She cursed the time that it would take to heal them; she cursed the deadly time when they would have been healed.

Finally then the resort to tears was all the more welcome, and she seldom indulged in it. She threw herself on to the sofa and gave herself up completely to her pain.

Edward for his part could not leave the door; he again knocked, and a third time rather more loudly, so that Charlotte heard it quite clearly through the quiet of the night and started up in fright. Her first thought was that it might, it must be the Captain; her second thought, that this was impossible. She thought she might be deceived, but she had heard it, she wanted and was afraid to have heard it. She went into the bedroom, stepped quietly to the bolted door. She was impatient with herself because of her fear. 'It might easily be that the Baroness needs something!' she said to herself, and called out in a controlled and sedate voice: 'Is anyone there?' A soft voice answered: 'It's I.' — 'Who?' Charlotte replied, unable to distinguish the tone of the voice. In her imagination the Captain's figure stood before the door. Rather more loudly she heard 'Edward!' She opened the door, and her husband stood before her. He greeted her in a joking manner. She could take up the conversation in a similar tone. He wrapped up the mysterious visit in mysterious explanations. 'But I must confess to you the real reason why I've come,' he said finally. 'I have taken a vow to kiss your shoe this very evening.'

'You haven't thought of that for a long time,' Charlotte said. 'All the worse,' Edward replied, 'and all the better!'

She had sat down in a chair in order to hide her scanty night attire from his glance. He threw himself down at her feet, and she could not stop him kissing her shoe nor, when the shoe was left in his hand, seizing her foot and pressing it tenderly to his breast.

Charlotte was one of those women who are temperate by nature and who without intention and effort continue in their married life the manner of young lovers. She never deliberately stimulated her husband, indeed she scarcely responded to his desire; yet without coldness or repelling severity she continued to be like a loving bride who still feels a sensitive shyness even from what is permissible. And this, in a double sense, was how Edward found her this evening. How intensely she would have liked her husband not to be there; for the imagined figure of her friend seemed to be reproaching her. But what should have alienated Edward only attracted him more. A certain agitation was visible in her. She had been crying, and if gentle people mostly lose attractiveness because of this, those whom we usually know as strong and controlled personalities gain infinitely thereby. Edward was so loving, so affectionate, so pressing; he begged her to let him remain with her, he did not demand, he endeavoured to persuade her, now seriously, now playfully, he did not think that he had rights, and finally he roguishly put out the candles.

In the obscurity of the remaining lamp, inner attraction and imagination at once asserted their rights over reality: Edward held only Ottilie in his arms, it was the Captain who, more closely or more distantly, hovered at the threshold of Charlotte's mind, and in this way the absent and the present, strangely enough, were entwined in attractive and radiant confusion.

And yet the present will not be deprived of its monstrous rights. They spent part of the night in all kinds of talk and levity which were all the freer since the heart unfortunately had no part in them. But when Edward woke the next morning in his wife's arms, the day seemed to him to be looking in upon him with foreboding, the sun seemed to him to be lighting upon a crime; he stole quietly away from her side, and when she awoke she found herself, strangely enough, alone.

CHAPTER XII

W H E N the company reassembled for breakfast, an attentive observer could have deduced from the behaviour of the individual members the varied state of their inner thoughts and feelings. The Count and the Baroness came together with the cheerful happiness which a pair of lovers feel when they consider themselves secure in their mutual affection after enduring a period of separation; on the other hand Charlotte and Edward met the Captain and Ottilie as it were with shame and remorse. For that is love's way, that it alone believes it can be right, and all other rights disappear in face of love. Ottilie was happy in a childlike way, she could be called open, for her. The Captain appeared first; in the course of his conversation with the Count, who had aroused in him all those considerations which for some time had been quiescent and dormant, it had become only too obvious to him that he really could not fulfil his vocation here and that fundamentally he was only wasting his time in semi-active idleness. The two guests had scarcely withdrawn when once again fresh visitors arrived; these were welcome to Charlotte who wanted to get out of herself and to be distracted, but unwelcome to Edward who felt doubly attracted to being with Ottilie; similarly Ottilie found the visitors burdensome, as she had not yet finished making the copy that was so necessary for the next morning. And so she too hurried at once to her room when the visitors at last departed.

It was now evening. Edward, Charlotte and the Captain, who had accompanied the visitors on foot for a stretch before they got into their coach, agreed to go for a further walk round the pools. A boat had arrived which Edward had ordered from far away at considerable expense. They wanted to try if it could be easily moved and steered.

It was tied up at the edge of the middle pool not far from a few old oak-trees which had already been considered as part of the future plans for the estate. A landing-stage was to be set up here, and an architecturally designed resting-place was to be erected under the trees towards which those who might be traversing the lake would have to steer.

'Now where will be the best place to arrange for landing on the other side?' Edward asked. 'I should think, by my plane-trees.'

'They're a bit too far to the right,' the Captain said. 'If we landed farther down, we should be nearer the castle; but it needs thinking over.'

The Captain was already standing in the rear part of the boat and had grasped an oar. Charlotte stepped in, as did Edward, and he took the other oar; but just as he was about to push off, he thought of Ottilie and thought that this trip by water would delay him so that he would not know when on earth he would be back. He made up his mind there and then, jumped back on land, handed the Captain the other oar and hurried home, excusing himself casually.

There he learned that Ottilie had retired to her room to write. Although it was pleasant to know that she was doing something for him, he felt an intense frustration at not seeing her present. His impatience increased every moment. He went up and down in the large drawing-room, took up various things, but nothing was able to hold his attention. It was she whom he wanted to see, and to see her alone, before Charlotte should come back with the Captain. Night fell, and the candles were lit.

Finally she came in, radiant with good feeling. The

feeling that she had done something for her friend had raised up her whole personality beyond its usual level. She placed the original and the copy on the table in front of Edward. 'Shall we check them?' she said with a smile. Edward did not know how to reply. He looked at her and examined the copy. The first pages were written with extreme care in a delicate, female handwriting, and then the characters seemed to change and become easier and freer; but how surprised he was when he cast his eyes over the last few pages! 'Good heavens!' he cried, 'what's this? That's my handwriting!' He looked at Ottilie and then again at the papers, and the conclusion in particular was just as if he had written it himself. Ottilie was silent, but she looked at him with the greatest satisfaction. Edward raised his arms: 'You love me!' he cried, 'Ottilie, you love me!' and they held each other embraced. It would not have been possible to say who first clasped the other.

From this moment on the world was turned upside down for Edward, he was no longer what he had been, nor the world what it had been. They stood facing each other, he held her hands, and they looked into each other's eyes, about to embrace again.

Charlotte and the Captain came in. Edward smiled covertly when they made apologies for staying out a long time. 'Oh, how much too early you have come!' he said to himself.

They sat down to the evening meal. The personalities of the visitors of that day were criticised. Edward, pleasantly excited, spoke well of each of them, always considerately and often approvingly. Charlotte, who was not entirely in agreement with him, noticed this mood of his and joked with him for being so gentle and indulgent today, whereas he usually sat in strictest judgment with his words over departing visitors.

Edward spoke up with fire and warm conviction: 'If you really love one person from the bottom of your

heart, then everybody else appears to be lovable!'
Ottilie cast her eyes down, and Charlotte looked straight
in front.

The Captain took up the theme and said: 'After all,
there's something similar too about feelings of reverence
and respect. You only come to recognise what is estimable in the world when you find an opportunity of
exercising such an attitude on one object.'

Charlotte soon made towards her bedroom, in order
to give herself to the memory of what had happened
that evening between herself and the Captain.

When Edward, by jumping ashore, had pushed the
boat from the bank and had entrusted his wife and his
friend to the uncertainly swaying element, Charlotte now
saw the man on whose account she had already suffered
so much in her heart, seated in front of her in the half-
light, propelling the vessel by the use of the two oars
in any direction they might choose. She had a sense of
deep sadness that she seldom experienced. The circling
of the boat, the splashing of the oars, the wind breathing
over the water's surface, the rustling of the reeds, the
last hovering of the birds, the gleaming of the first stars:
everything had a ghostly appearance in this general
stillness. It seemed to her as if her friend were taking
her afar off in order to cast her away and leave her
alone. There was a strange movement within her, and
she could not weep.

In the meantime the Captain was describing to her
how he thought the gardens should be laid out. He
praised the good qualities of the boat, particularly that
it could easily be moved and steered by one person with
two oars. She would learn this herself, he said, it was a
pleasant sensation to be swimming along on the water,
often alone, and to be one's own ferryman and helms-
man.

At these words Charlotte recalled the coming separation. 'Is he saying that deliberately?' she thought to

herself. 'Does he already know about it? Does he suspect it? Or is he saying it accidentally, so that he is unconsciously predicting my fate?' She was seized by a great melancholy and impatience; she asked him to land as soon as possible and to return with her to the castle.

It was the first time that the Captain had sailed on the pools, and although he had a general idea of their depth, there were nevertheless isolated places which were unknown to him. It began to grow dark; he directed his course to where he thought there might be an easy spot for disembarking and where he knew the footpath to the castle could not be far away. But he was to some extent led away even from this course when Charlotte, with a kind of fearfulness, repeated her wish to be on land soon. He approached the shore with renewed efforts, but realised that unfortunately the boat had become held up at some distance from the land; he had got stuck, and his efforts to get away again were in vain. What could be done? He had no alternative but to go into the water, which was shallow enough, and to carry his companion to dry land. He carried the dear burden across without mishap, strong enough not to stagger or cause her any worry; however, she had put her arms anxiously round his neck. He held her tight and pressed her to him. He did not put her down until he reached a grassy slope, and did so not without emotion and confusion. She still held her arms about his neck; he clasped her anew in his arms and kissed her passionately on the lips; but in that same moment he was at her feet, pressing his mouth against her hand and saying: 'Charlotte, will you forgive me?'

The kiss, which her friend had ventured to give and which she had almost returned, brought Charlotte to herself again. She pressed his hand, but she did not raise him from the ground. However, she bent down toward him and laid a hand on his shoulder, saying: 'We can't prevent this moment from being a decisive one in our lives; but whether it becomes a moment that is worthy of us, depends on ourselves. You must go, dear friend, and you will go. The Count is negotiating to improve your position; I am both glad and sorry because of it. I didn't want to say anything about it until it was certain; the present moment compels me to reveal this secret. Only to this extent can I pardon you and myself, if we are courageous enough to change our situation, since we can do nothing to change our state of mind.' She raised him up and took his arm for support, and in this way they walked silently back to the castle.

But now she was standing in her bedroom where she must have the feelings of being Edward's wife and to regard herself as such. In the midst of these contradictions she was helped by her character which was strong and had been tested by many experiences in life. As she had always been accustomed to be aware of her personality and to exercise self-control, it was not difficult for her even now to come close to the desired equanimity by the exercise of serious thoughts; indeed she could not help smiling at herself when she thought of the unusual visit of the previous night. Yet a strange foreboding quickly came upon her, a joyfully anxious trembling that dissolved into pious wishes and hopes. Feeling moved, she knelt down and repeated the promise that she had made to Edward at the altar. Joyful images of friendship, affection and resignation passed through her mind. She felt inwardly refreshed. Soon sweet tiredness seized her, and she went peacefully to sleep.

CHAPTER XIII

EDWARD for his part was in quite a different mood.
He had so little thought of sleeping that it did not even
occur to him to undress himself. He kissed the copy of
the document many times, especially the opening part
which was in Ottilie's shy handwriting; he scarcely
dared to kiss the latter part, for he believed that he
could recognise it as his own writing. 'If only it were
another document!' he said to himself; and yet it seemed
to him to be already the most beautiful assurance that
his dearest wish was fulfilled. After all, it was now in his
hands! And would he not always press it to his heart,
although it would be disfigured by a third person's
signature?

The waning moon rose from above the tree. The warm
night attracted him out of doors; he wandered about,
the happiest and most restless of all mortals. He walked
through the gardens; they were too narrow for him; he
hurried to the open fields, and they were too wide for
him. He was drawn back to the castle; he found himself
below Ottilie's windows. There he sat on one of the steps
of the terrace. 'Walls and bolts separate us now, but
our hearts are not separated,' he said to himself. 'If she
were standing in front of me, she would fall into my
arms, and I into hers, and what more is needed than
this certainty!' Everything around him was quiet, not a
breath of air could be felt; it was so quiet that he could
hear below the earth's surface the burrowing of busy
animals to whom day and night are one. Wholly wrapped
up in happy dreams, he fell asleep and did not wake

until the sun rose in splendid light and dispersed the early mists.

Now he found that he was the first to wake up on his estate. It seemed to him as if the workmen were too slow in arriving. When they came, he thought that there were too few of them and that the work planned for the day was too little. He asked for more workers; these were promised and found in the course of the day. But even these were not enough for him to see his intentions carried out quickly. The carrying out of the work no longer gave him pleasure; he wanted it to be finished and done with; and on whose account? The paths should be constructed so that Ottilie could walk easily, and the seats should be in place so that Ottilie could take her ease there. He hurried on the work at the new summer-house too, as far as he could; it was to be ready by Ottilie's birthday. There was no longer any moderation in Edward's thoughts and actions. The knowledge that he loved and that his love was returned impelled him beyond all bounds. How different all the rooms and all the surroundings appeared! He could not find his way about his own house. The presence of Ottilie was all consuming; he was obsessed by her, incapable of any other thought, deaf to conscience; whatever had been restrained in his nature now burst forth, and his whole being surged out towards Ottilie.

The Captain noticed this passionate activity and wanted to prevent its having unfortunate consequences. All these operations, which were now being forced ahead with one-sided vigour, he had thought of as a quiet, friendly piece of co-operation. He had completed the sale of the farm, the first payment had been made and Charlotte had taken charge of the money as agreed. But already in the first week she would have to exert an unusual degree of seriousness, patience and order; for the amount set aside would be in no way adequate, with this overhasty way of working.

Much had been started, and there was much to be done. How could he leave Charlotte in this situation! They conferred together and agreed that they would rather hasten the execution of the work planned and for that purpose take up money which was to be paid back by allowing for the instalments which had fallen short as a result of the sale of the farm. This could be done almost without any loss by ceding the titles, now they had a freer hand; since everything was in motion and enough workers were available, more could be achieved at once and their aims were accomplished with certainty and speed. Edward was glad to agree to this, because it coincided with his own intentions.

In her heart, however, Charlotte remained faithful to what she had considered and planned, and her friend the Captain supported her with manly loyalty. But their friendship only became more intimate in consequence. They both voiced their opinions about Edward's passion and conferred about it. Charlotte drew Ottilie nearer to herself, watched over her more strictly, and the more she became aware of her own feelings, the more deeply she saw into the girl's heart. She could see no salvation except through sending the child away.

At this time it seemed to her to be a happy chance that Luciane had received such outstanding praise at school; for when her great-aunt heard about it, she expressed the desire to take her into her home to have her about her and to introduce her to society. Ottilie could go back to the boarding-school, and the Captain could depart with good prospects; and everything would be as it was a few months ago, indeed even rather better than previously. Charlotte hoped to restore her own relationship with Edward soon, and she thought this all out in such a sensible manner that she became ever more confirmed in the illusion that it might be possible to return to their former, more limited way of living, and that forces which had been violently unleashed would let themselves be driven into a corner again.

But Edward felt very sensitively the obstacles that were being put in his way. He soon noticed that he and Ottilie were being kept apart, that it was being made difficult for him to speak to her alone or even to come near her, unless in the presence of others; and being angry about this, he also became irritable about a number of other things. When he could speak to Ottilie for a passing moment, he used the opportunity not only to assure her of his love but also to make complaints about his wife and the Captain. He did not feel that he himself was on the way to exhausting the funds by his impetuous hastening of the work; he blamed Charlotte and the Captain severely for having departed from the first agreement about the business, and yet he himself had consented to the second agreement, in fact it was he who had given the impetus to it and made it necessary.

Hate is partisan, but love is even more so. Ottilie also became somewhat estranged from Charlotte and the Captain. When Edward on one occasion complained to Ottilie that the Captain as a friend did not always behave quite honestly in such a position, Ottilie replied unthinkingly; 'I've been uncomfortable before now because he isn't quite straightforward with you. I once heard him say to Charlotte: "If only Edward would spare us his doodling on the flute! It will never come to anything and it's so wearing for the listeners." You can think how that grieved me, as I like accompanying you so much.'

She had scarcely said this when her better self told her that she should have kept silent; but she had let it out. Edward's face fell. He had never felt more irritated; he had been attacked in his fondest wishes, for he had been conscious only of a naïve striving without the least presumptuousness. Something that entertained him and gave him pleasure should surely be regarded considerately by his friends. He did not think how frightful it is for a third person to have his ears offended by performances of inadequate competence. He felt insulted and enraged and unwilling to forgive in his turn. He regarded himself as absolved from all obligations.

With each day the need to be with Ottilie, to see her, to whisper something to her and to confide in her grew. He decided to write to her and to ask her to conduct a secret correspondence. The slip of paper, on which he had written this request casually enough, lay on the writing-desk and was blown down by a draught when the valet came in to curl his hair. The man usually took up a scrap of paper from the floor in order to try out the heat of the iron; this time he picked on the note, screwed it up hurriedly and singed it. Noticing the mistake, Edward snatched it from his hand. Soon after he sat down in order to write it out again; it was not so easy for him to write it a second time. He felt some misgivings and anxiety, but he overcame them. The note was pressed into Ottilie's hand at the first opportunity when he could come near her.

Ottilie did not delay answering him. Without reading it he put the note in his waistcoat which, being short as was the fashion, did not conceal it well. It worked its way loose and fell to the ground without his noticing. Charlotte saw it, picked it up and handed it to him with a casual glance at it.

'Here is something in your writing which you might be sorry to lose,' she said. He was taken aback. 'Is she dissimulating?' he thought. 'Does she know the contents of the note, or has she made a mistake because of the similarity of the handwriting?' He hoped and believed it was the latter case. He had been warned, doubly warned, but these strange, chance signs, by means of which a higher Being seems to be speaking to us, were incomprehensible to his passion; rather the more he was led on by his infatuation, the more irksome seemed to him the constraint in which he felt he was being kept. Friendly sociability was lost. His heart was hardened, and when he was compelled to be with his friend and his wife, he did not succeed in discovering or rekindling in himself his former affection for them. The tacit reproach which he could not but level against himself in this connection made him feel uncomfortable, and he tried to get over this by recourse to a kind of humour which lacked his usual graciousness because it was without affection.

Charlotte was helped out of all these trials by her inner feelings. She remembered her earnest resolution to forswear an attractive and inspiring inclination that was not without fineness and nobility.

How she wished she could help those two! Distance, she now felt, would not in itself be sufficient to repair such damage. She made up her mind to talk about the matter with Ottilie, but could not; the memory of her own vacillation stood in her way. She tried to express herself about it in general terms; but such a reference would also be fitting to her own position, and this she was reluctant to express openly. Every hint that she would like to give to Ottilie pointed back to her own condition. She wanted to admonish and felt that she herself in fact might well need admonition.

She therefore continued silently to keep the loving couple apart, and the situation became no better in consequence. Gentle hints which occasionally escaped her had no effect on Ottilie; for Edward had convinced Ottilie of Charlotte's affection for the Captain, and had convinced her that Charlotte herself was desirous of a divorce which he was now considering putting through in a respectable manner.

Ottilie, carried along by the feeling of her innocence, believed that she was on the way to the most desirable happiness, and lived only for Edward. Strengthened in all that was good by her love for him, happier on his account in all that she did, more open towards other people, she was in a state of rapture.

Thus they all in their own ways carried on with their daily lives, either thoughtful or heedless; everything seemed to be going on in the usual way, and indeed we do go on living as if nothing unusual has occurred, even in terrible circumstances where all is at stake.

CHAPTER XIV

IN the meantime a letter had come to the Captain, in fact a double letter, with one section containing beautiful views into the distance which was to be shown round, and the other section making a definite offer for the immediate future of an important court administrative post with the rank of major, a good salary and other advantages; this he was asked to keep secret for the time being on acount of various accompanying circumstances. The Captain informed his friends only of his hopes and said nothing about what was so near at hand.

Meanwhile he carried on with his present occupations and made arrangements on the quiet for everything to proceed smoothly in his absence. He himself was now concerned that various operations should be completed by a specific date and that Ottilie's birthday should be a reason for hurrying the work along. The two men now worked happily together again, although without any express agreement. Edward was very satisfied that the funds were strengthened by taking up the money in advance; the whole venture was progressing most rapidly.

The Captain would have liked best now to advise them against converting the three pools into one lake. The lower dam needed strengthening, the middle ones had to be removed, and the whole business was important and needful of consideration in more than one sense. But both phases of the work, insofar as they could be fitted in together, had already been begun, and at this point a young architect, a former protégé of the Captain, came at the right moment: he encouraged and promised security and permanence to the operation, partly by appointing competent master-craftsmen, partly by giving the work out on contract wherever possible; the Captain was secretly pleased at this, because it meant that his departure would not be missed. For he had the principle that he could not leave unfinished a task that he had undertaken until he knew that he had been adequately replaced. Indeed, he was scornful of the sort of people who deliberately cause confusion in their sphere of activity in order to make their departure felt, and who in their crude selfishness would like to destroy anything which they can no longer work at.

Thus constant efforts were being made in order to celebrate Ottilie's birthday, without anyone saying so or even admitting it honestly to himself. From Charlotte's point of view, one not based on enviousness, it could not be made into a definite celebration. Ottilie's youth, her circumstances and her relationship to the family did not entitle her to appear as queen of one day. And Edward did not want to mention it, because everything was to appear as if of its own accord as a surprise and, naturally, a pleasure.

They consequently all came to tacit agreement about the pretext, as if this summer-house were to be completed on this particular day, without any further connections, and on this occasion the local people as well as their own friends could be informed of the celebration.

But Edward's love was unrestrained. As he desired to possess Ottilie, so too he knew no bounds in yielding or in giving presents and promises. For some of the gifts which he wanted to bestow on Ottilie on this day, Charlotte had made suggestions which were much too mean. He consulted his valet who looked after his wardrobe and was in constant touch with merchants and fashion-dealers. This man was not unfamiliar with the most superior gifts themselves, nor also with the best manner in which to present them; he at once ordered in the town the prettiest chest, covered with red morocco leather held down by steel nails and fitted with presents that were worthy of so elegant an exterior.

He suggested something else to Edward. There was a small set of fireworks available which they had repeatedly omitted to let off. It would be easy to augment those that were already there. Edward took up the idea, and the valet promised to see to the practical arrangements. The matter was to remain a secret.

Meanwhile, as the day drew closer, the Captain had made his policing arrangements which he regarded as so necessary whenever a crowd of people are summoned or attracted together. Indeed he had even taken full precautions with regard to begging and other unpleasantnesses which might disturb the agreeableness of the occasion.

Edward and his confidant on the other hand were chiefly occupied with the fireworks. They were to be set alight by the middle pool in front of the large oak-trees; the spectators were to stand opposite under the plane-trees, in order to view in safety and comfort the effect from a suitable distance, the reflection in the water, and those fireworks intended to float burning on the water.

Under another pretext Edward had the space under the plane-trees cleared of undergrowth, grass and moss, and now for the first time the magnificence of the trees' growth, both in height and breadth, became visible against the cleared ground. Edward felt overjoyed at this. 'It was about this time of year that I planted them. How long ago is it now?' he said to himself. As soon as he came home, he looked it up in old diaries which his father had kept in a very orderly way, especially when he had been in the country. It was true that this planting could not be mentioned in them, but another domestically important event on the same day, which Edward still clearly remembered, must inevitably be noted there.

He skimmed through a few volumes, and this particular circumstance was found. But how surprised and pleased Edward was when he came upon the most remarkable coincidence! The day and year of the planting of the trees was at the same time the day and year of Ottilie's birth.

CHAPTER XV

Aт long last the morning which Edward had eagerly anticipated arrived, and gradually a large number of visitors arrived; for invitations had been widely distributed, and a number of people who had missed the laying of the foundation-stone, about which much that was agreeable had been told, wanted to be all the surer not to miss this second celebration.

Before the mealtime the carpenters appeared with music in the courtyard of the castle, bearing their ornate wreath which was composed of many circles of foliage and flowers swaying one above the other in layers. They gave their spoken greeting and requested silk cloths and ribbons from the fair sex as their accustomed adornment. While the gentry were dining, they continued their merry procession, and after they had stayed for a time in the village and likewise deprived women and girls of many a ribbon, they at last came to the heights where the completed house stood, and were accompanied as well as awaited by a large crowd.

After the meal Charlotte restrained the company to some extent. She did not want a solemn, formal procession, and so they found their way to the spot in individual groups without rank or order. Charlotte held back with Ottilie and did not improve matters by this; for as Ottilie really was the last to arrive it did seem as if the trumpets and drums had only been waiting for her, as if the proceedings must begin immediately now that she had arrived.

In order to temper the raw appearance of the house, it

had been decorated artistically with green branches and
flowers, according to the Captain's instructions; but
without consulting him Edward had told the architect
to carve on the moulding the date with flowers. That
was just about tolerable; the Captain, however, only
arrived in time to prevent the name of Ottilie shining
forth from the pediment. He was able to scotch this plan
in a tactful way and to remove the flowered letters which
had already been finished.

The wreath was hoisted up and was visible far and
wide in the district. The ribbons and cloths fluttered
gaily in the air, and a short speech was for the most part
carried away by the wind. The solemnities were over,
and now dancing could begin on the space which had
been levelled and enclosed with green, in front of the
building. A neatly dressed carpenter's apprentice led a
smart peasant-girl up to Edward and invited Ottilie, who
was standing by, to dance. The two couples at once
found others to follow them, and quite soon Edward
changed partners, taking Ottilie and circling the floor
with her. The younger visitors mixed happily in this
folk-dance, while the older ones looked on.

Before separating to go for walks, the company agreed
to meet again by the plane-trees at sunset. Edward
arrived first, put things in order and consulted with the
valet who, together with a man experienced in fireworks,
had to look after the entertainment on the other side.

The Captain was unhappy when he noticed the
arrangements made in this connection; he was about to
have a word with Edward about the pressure of spectators that could be expected, when the latter asked him
rather brusquely to leave this part of the proceedings to
him.

The crowd had already pushed forward on to the dams
which had been cut at the top and denuded of their grass,
and where consequently the ground was insecure. The
sun set, twilight came, and while waiting for more

111

complete darkness the company under the plane-trees were served with refreshments. They declared it an incomparable spot and inwardly looked forward to a time when they could enjoy from here the view on to a lake that was both extensive and varied in shape.

A quiet evening with complete calm held out favourable promise for the nocturnal celebration, when all at once a dreadful shrieking arose. Large clods of soil had come apart from the dam, and a number of people could be seen falling into the water. The soil had given way under the movement and pressure of the ever-increasing crowd. Everyone wanted to have the best place, and now nobody could move backwards or forwards.

Everybody jumped up and went along, more to watch than to help; for what was there to be done, where nobody could reach the spot? The Captain hurried along, together with a few determined men, and they at once drove the crowd down from the dam to the banks of the water, so that they could make work easier for the helpful people who were attempting to pull out those who were in the water. Already they were all on dry land once more, partly as a result of their own efforts and partly through the efforts of others, with the exception of one boy who because of his over-anxious struggling had drifted some way from the dam instead of making towards it. He seemed to be losing strength, it was only fitfully that a hand or foot was stretched into the air. Unfortunately the boat was on the other side, fitted with fireworks which could only be unloaded slowly, and help was delayed. The Captain's mind was made up, he threw off his top clothes, all eyes were turned on him, and his efficient and strong figure gave confidence to all; but a cry of surprise came from the crowd when he dived into the water, and all eyes followed him when, swimming strongly, he soon reached the boy, and brought him to the dam, although it seemed as if the lad was dead.

In the meantime the boat came along, the Captain climbed in and asked particularly those who were present if in fact everybody had been saved. The surgeon came and took charge of the boy believed to be dead; Charlotte approached and asked the Captain simply to look after himself, to go back to the castle and get changed. He hesitated until reliable and sensible people who had stood quite close by and had themselves helped with some of the rescue work, assured him most solemnly that everyone had been saved.

Charlotte saw him go home, and it occurred to her that wine and tea and whatever else might be necessary were locked away, and that in such cases people usually do act the wrong way; she hurried through the confused company who were still underneath the plane-trees. Edward was busy persuading someone to stay, saying that he was thinking of giving the signal for starting the fireworks. Charlotte stepped up and asked him to put off an entertainment which was now out of place and could not give pleasure at the present moment; she reminded him what was owing to the boy who had been saved and to his rescuer. 'The surgeon will already be doing his duty,' Edward replied. 'He's got everything he needs, and our interference would be more of a hindrance than a help.'

Charlotte insisted on her point of view and made a sign to Ottilie who at once prepared to leave. Edward seized her hand and called: 'We don't want to spend the rest of today in a hospital! She's too good to be a sister of mercy. Those who seem to be dead will reawaken, and the living will dry themselves, even without us.'

Charlotte said nothing and went. Some people followed her, and others Edward and Ottilie; finally nobody wanted to be the last on the scene, and so they all followed. Edward and Ottilie were left alone under the plane-trees. He insisted on remaining, however urgently and anxiously she begged him to return to the castle with her. 'No, Ottilie!' he cried, 'extraordinary things don't happen in a smooth, commonplace way. This surprising event this evening is bringing us together more quickly. You are mine! I have already told you so and vowed it to you so often; let us make no more speeches and vows about it, now it must be made reality.'

The boat came across from the other side. It was the valet who asked with some embarrassment what was to be done with the fireworks now. 'Let them off!' he shouted to him. 'It was only for you that they were arranged, Ottilie, and now it shall only be you who will see them! Just let me sit by your side and enjoy them too.' In a tenderly unassuming manner he sat down by her, without touching her.

Rockets roared upwards, cannon-shots thundered, light-balls ascended, crackerjacks coiled around and exploded, catherine wheels hissed, at first singly, then in pairs, then altogether and ever more violently one after another and together. Edward, his heart aflame, followed this fiery spectacle with animated and satisfied eyes. To Ottilie's delicate and agitated feelings this tumultuous and flashing appearance and disappearance was disturbing rather than pleasant. She leaned shyly against Edward whom this approach and trust convinced that she belonged wholly to him.

Night had scarcely come into its own again when the moon rose and lit up the paths of the two on their way back. A figure, hat in hand, barred their way and begged for alms, saying that he had been prevented from participating in this festive day. The moon shone upon his face, and Edward recognised the features of the beggar who had been importunate on a previous occasion. But in his present happiness he could not be angry, nor did it occur to him that on this day especially begging had been strictly forbidden. He did not take long searching in his purse and handed over a gold coin. He would have been glad to make everybody happy, since his own happiness seemed to be unbounded.

Meanwhile everything at home had gone as well as could be desired. The surgeon's activity, the fact that everything necessary was ready, Charlotte's assistance, everything worked together, and the boy was restored to consciousness. The visitors dispersed, partly to have a look at something of the fireworks from afar, and partly also to be once more in their own quiet homes after such confused scenes.

After quickly changing his clothes, the Captain too had taken active part in the necessary first-aid; all had become quiet, and he found himself alone with Charlotte. With confiding friendliness he now declared that he would be leaving soon. She had gone through so much that evening that this news made little impression on her; she had seen how her friend sacrificed himself, how he saved life and had himself been saved. These strange events appeared to her to prophesy a future of some significance, but not an unhappy one.

The coming departure of the Captain was made known similarly to Edward, who came in with Ottilie. He suspected that Charlotte had already known the details earlier, but he was much too much concerned with himself and his own plans to take it amiss.

On the contrary, he listened attentively and with satisfaction to the account of the good and honourable position which the Captain was to take up. His own secret wishes uncontrollably anticipated the events. He already saw the Captain linked to Charlotte, and himself to Ottilie. No better present could have been made to him on the occasion of this festivity.

But how surprised Ottilie was when she entered her room and found the charming little chest on her table! She did not delay in opening it. There everything was revealed so beautifully packed and arranged that she did not dare to disarrange it, indeed, she scarcely ventured to lift the lid. Muslin, cambric, silk, scarves and lace vied with each other in delicacy, prettiness and costliness. Jewelry had not been forgotten either. She must have understood the intention of providing her with more than one change of clothing from head to foot; but it was all so costly and strange that she did not venture to think of it as her own.

CHAPTER XVI

THE next morning the Captain had disappeared, leaving for his friends a note filled with expressions of gratitude. The evening before he and Charlotte had taken leave of one another, though in incomplete and monosyllabic terms. She had a feeling of eternal separation and resigned herself to this; for the Count's second letter, which the Captain finally revealed to her, spoke also of the prospect of an advantageous marriage, and although he took no notice of this point, she took the matter as a certainty and renounced him purely and unreservedly.

On the other hand she now believed that she could expect of others the same rigid self-control that she had exercised over herself. It had not been impossible for her, and so it should be equally possible for others. She began talking to her husband on these lines, all the more frankly and confidently as she felt that the business would have to be settled once and for all.

'Our friend has left us,' she said, 'we now confront each other as before, and really now it is up to us to decide whether we would like to return completely to the old life.'

Edward, who heard only what was flattering to his passion, believed that Charlotte was referring with these words to her earlier life as a widow and that she was offering hope of a divorce, although speaking in a vague way. He therefore answered smiling: 'Why not? It would only be a matter of coming to an agreement.'

He therefore felt very much deceived when Charlotte

117

added: 'Just now we've only got to make the choice in order to find another place for Ottilie; for there is a double opportunity to provide her with surroundings which are desirable for her. She could return to the boarding-school, since my daughter has gone to her great-aunt's; or she could find a place in a reputable household where she could share with an only daughter all the advantages of a socially desirable education.'

'But Ottilie has become so spoilt in our friendly company that any other way of life would hardly be welcome to her,' Edward replied, in quite a controlled manner.

'We've all let ourselves be spoilt,' said Charlotte, 'not least yourself. Still this is a time that calls us to reflection and seriously admonishes us to think of what is best for all members of our little circle, and not to fall short if any sacrifice is demanded.'

'Anyway, I don't think it fair for Ottilie to be sacrificed, and that is what would happen if she were pushed among strangers at the moment,' Edward replied. 'Good fortune has caught up with the Captain here; we may let him depart from us with quiet and ease of mind. Who knows what is in front of Ottilie? Why should we be overhasty?'

'It's pretty clear what is in front of us,' Charlotte replied with some agitation, and, intending to speak out once and for all, she continued: 'You love Ottilie, you are getting used to her presence. Affection and passion are arising and developing on her side as well. Why shouldn't we put into words what every hour that passes admits and confesses to us? Should we not be sufficiently far-seeing as to ask ourselves what this is all leading to?'

'Even if we can't answer that immediately,' Edward replied, holding himself back, 'at least we can say this, that we ought first of all to wait and see what the future will bring us, if we can't say exactly what is to become of any matter.'

'It doesn't require any great wisdom to prophesy here,'

Charlotte said, 'and whatever happens, it can be said straightaway that neither of us is any longer young enough to go rushing blindly ahead to where we should not care or ought not to go. There is no longer anybody else to look after us; we must be our own friends and tutors. Nobody expects of us that we shall get lost in some extravagance; nobody expects to find us culpable or even silly in our behaviour.'

'Can you think it wrong of me,' Edward answered, who was unable to reply to the open, straightforward words of his wife, 'can you blame me for taking Ottilie's happiness to heart? And not some possible future happiness that cannot be predicted, but her present happiness? Can you honestly and without self-deception imagine Ottilie torn from our company and handed over to strangers? I at least don't feel sufficiently hard to demand such a change from her.'

Charlotte could not but be aware of her husband's determination behind his dissembling. Only now did she feel how far he had moved from her. It was with some emotion that she cried: 'Can Ottilie be happy if she separates us, if she deprives me of a husband and a father of his children?'

'I should have thought there was no need to worry about our children,' Edward said, smiling coldly; but in a rather more friendly manner he added; 'But who wants to think right away in terms of extreme measures!'

'Extreme measures go closely hand in hand with passion,' Charlotte observed. 'Don't refuse the good advice and help which I am offering to both of us while there is still time. On troubled occasions the one who sees most clearly must be active and helpful. This time I'm the one. Dear, dear Edward, do leave it to me! Can you expect me to give up my well earned happiness, my most delightful rights, in fact, to give up you?'

'Who's saying anything about that?' Edward put in with some embarrassment.

'You yourself,' Charlotte replied; 'when you wish to keep Ottilie close at hand, aren't you conceding everything that must result from it? I won't press you; but if you can't master yourself, at least you won't be able to deceive yourself much longer.'

Edward felt how right she was. A word that is spoken is terrible, if it speaks out all at once something that the heart has long permitted itself in secret; and in order only to avoid the issue for the moment, Edward replied, 'But I'm not even clear yet what you want.'

'My plan was to discuss the two suggestions with you,' Charlotte answered. 'Both have much to be said in their favour. The boarding-school would be most suitable for Ottilie when I consider what the child is like now. But the larger and wider sphere promises more when I consider what is to become of her.' She then expounded the two situations to her husband in detail, concluding with the words: 'I personally should prefer the house of that lady to the boarding-school for a number of reasons, in particular also because I don't wish to encourage the affection, indeed the passion of the young man there whom Ottilie has made a conquest of.'

Edward seemed to approve, but only in order to delay the matter a while. Charlotte, determined to do something definite, at once took the opportunity, seeing that Edward did not directly contradict, of arranging for Ottilie to depart in a few days' time, for she had already made all preparations for this without telling anyone.

Edward recoiled, believed that he had been betrayed, and thought that his wife's affectionate words had been artificially and deliberately calculated with a view to separating him for ever from his happiness. He seemed to be leaving the matter entirely to her; but already he had made up his mind within. Simply to recover his breath and to avert the imminent, incalculable disaster of Ottilie's absence, he decided to leave home; he did this not entirely without Charlotte's foreknowledge, which however he was able to deceive by saying that he did not wish to be present at Ottilie's departure and that he did not wish to see her from this moment on. Charlotte, believing that she had won, gave him all assistance. He ordered his horses, gave the valet the necessary instructions about packing and following after him, and in this way, as if on the spur of the moment, he sat down and wrote.

Edward to Charlotte

The evil that has befallen us, my dear, may be capable of being healed or not, but this I do feel: if I am not to despair now, I must find a respite for myself, for all of us. Since I am making a sacrifice, I can make a demand. I am leaving my house and shall only come back when prospects are more favourable, more peaceful. In the meantime you are to remain in possession, but with Ottilie. I want to know her with you and not among strangers. Look after her, treat her as has been usual up to now, indeed with ever more affection, friendship and tenderness. I give my word not to attempt any clandestine relationship with Ottilie. I would rather be left for a time in complete ignorance about how you live; I will imagine the best. Think the best of me too. There is only one thing that I do entreat of you in the most sincere, forcible tones: do not attempt to send Ottilie away or to place her in new surroundings! If she leaves the area of your castle and park and is entrusted to the hands of strangers, she belongs to me and I shall take possession of her. But if you respect my affection, my wishes, and my grief, if you flatter my illusions and my hopes, I for my part will not resist the power of healing, should it be offered to me.

The last phrase came from his pen, not his heart. Indeed, when he saw it on the paper, he began to weep bitterly. In some way or other he was to renounce the happiness, indeed the unhappiness, of loving Ottilie! Now he realised what he was doing. He was going away without knowing what could result from it. He was not to see her again, at least not for the time being; what security could he promise himself that he would ever see her again? But the letter had been written; the horses were waiting at the door; at any moment he had to fear that he might catch sight of Ottilie somewhere and at the same time see his plan made vain. He pulled himself together; he thought that after all it would be possible for him to return at any moment and through the very fact of his absence to come closer to a realisation of his wishes. As against that, he imagined Ottilie banished from the house if he stayed. He sealed the letter, hurried down the stairs and jumped on to his horse.

Riding past the inn, he saw the beggar to whom he had given so generously the night before sitting under the trees outside. The man was sitting comfortably over his midday meal; he stood up, and bowed respectfully, even admiringly to Edward. This was the man who had appeared before him yesterday when he led Ottilie by the arm; his presence now reminded him painfully of the happiest hour of his life. His sufferings became intensified; the feeling of what he was leaving behind was unbearable to him; he looked back again at the beggar: 'You don't realise how lucky you are!' he cried; 'you can still enjoy your yesterday's alms, but I can no longer benefit from my happiness of yesterday!'

CHAPTER XVII

OTTILIE went to the window when she heard someone riding away, and she could see Edward's back as he disappeared. It seemed strange to her that he should leave the house without seeing her, without giving her a morning greeting. She became restless and increasingly thoughtful when Charlotte took her with her on a long walk and talked about all kinds of subjects but did not mention her husband, and this, it seemed, was deliberate. She was doubly taken aback to find on returning that only two places had been laid at the table.

We do not like to miss customs that are apparently trivial, but it is not until matters of importance arise that we feel such losses as grievous. Edward and the Captain were absent, Charlotte had arranged the table herself for the first time for a long period, and Ottilie could not help thinking that she had been dismissed from her office. The two women sat facing one another; Charlotte spoke in a completely easy-going manner about the Captain's appointment and about how little hope there was of seeing him again soon. The only thing that consoled Ottilie in her present position was that she could believe that Edward had ridden after his friend to accompany him for some distance further.

But when they rose from the table they saw Edward's carriage by the window, and when Charlotte asked with some annoyance who had ordered the carriage to come here, she was told that it was the valet who wanted to pack up a few more things here. Ottilie needed all her self-control to be able to hide her surprise and grief.

The valet came in and requested one or two things more. There was the master's cup, a few silver spoons and various other things that seemed to Ottilie to point to a considerable journey and a fairly long absence. Charlotte refused him his request quite drily: she did not understand what he meant, for after all he had control over everything that was to do with his master. The smart fellow, whose only concern was really to have a word with Ottilie and therefore to entice her out of the room on some pretext or other, was able to make his excuses and insistently to repeat his request, which Ottilie too wished to grant; but Charlotte refused it, the valet had to leave, and the coach rolled away.

It was a terrible moment for Ottilie. She could not understand or fathom it; but she did sense that Edward had been torn from her for a considerable time. Charlotte understood her position and left her alone. We do not dare to describe her grief, her tears. She suffered infinitely. She only prayed to God that He should but help her over this day; she got through the day and the night, and when she had found herself again she believed that she was another being.

She had not learnt self-control nor had she acquiesced, but after having lost so much she was still there and still had more to fear. Her next worry, after clear consciousness of mind had returned to her, was that she herself might now be removed, as had been the men. She had no inkling of Edward's threats, which secured her staying with Charlotte; however, Charlotte's behaviour did serve to calm her to some extent. Charlotte tried to find occupation for the dear child and seldom left her on her own, if she could help it; and although she knew well enough that words cannot do much in opposition to a vehement passion, she was, however, familiar with the power of prudence and self-knowledge, and therefore introduced many topics of conversation between herself and Ottilie.

Hence it was a great comfort for Ottilie when Charlotte with calculated intent on one occasion made this wise remark: 'How deep is the gratitude of people whom we help quietly out of their emotional embarrassments! Let us continue joyfully and gaily with those things which the men have left incomplete; in this way we may prepare the prettiest panorama for their return by preserving and encouraging through our temperance what their stormy, impatient natures would have liked to destroy.'

'Since you are talking of temperance, dear aunt,' Ottilie replied, 'I can't hide the fact that I am reminded of the immoderacy of the menfolk, especially as far as wine is concerned. How often have I been troubled and worried when I could not fail to observe how pure reason, good sense, consideration for others, graciousness and charm are lost for several hours, and often, instead of all the good that a fine man can achieve and promote, evil and confusion threaten to break in! How often may violent strong-headed decisions be caused by this!'

Charlotte agreed with her, but did not pursue the conversation; for she felt only too well that here too Ottilie once more was thinking only of Edward who was accustomed to increase his pleasure, his talkativeness and his activity, by the occasional enjoyment of wine, not habitually certainly, but still more frequently than was desirable.

If that remark of Charlotte's had reminded Ottilie of the men again, in particular of Edward, it became all the more noticeable when Charlotte referred to a possible future marriage of the Captain as if it were a familiar and certain fact; this caused everything to have a different appearance from what she had liked to imagine after hearing Edward's earlier assurances. All this caused Ottilie to observe more closely each expression, gesture, action and step of Charlotte. Without knowing it, Ottilie had become clever, sharp and suspicious.

Meanwhile Charlotte saw with lucidity the individual problems connected with the surrounding landscape planning and played an active part there with a clear-minded adroitness; she always insisted on Ottilie taking part here. Without being niggling she cut down the household expenses; indeed, if she looked at everything in detail, she could take the flare-up of passion as a kind of happy ordinance of providence. For if they had continued as they had been doing up to now, they would have easily drifted into unlimited expense and might have seriously disturbed, if not destroyed, through their intrusive way of life and activity, the equable circumstances of their ample riches.

She did not disturb the work already going on in the gardens. On the other hand she ordered the continuation of that work which would be essential as a basis to future developments; but at this point this matter too would have to rest. Her husband was still to find ample pleasurable activity when he returned home.

During these operations and plans she could not find sufficient praise for the architect's management. Within a short time the lake lay spread out before her eyes and the newly devised shores looked attractive and varied with their plants and grass. All the rough work on the new summer-house was completed, what was necessary to conserve the building was done, and then she made a stop at that point where they could with some pleasure start again. During this activity she was calm and gay; Ottilie only seemed to be so; for she saw in everything nothing but signs as to whether Edward would be expected soon or not. This was the only consideration that interested her about the whole matter.

Consequently she welcomed an arrangement by which the peasant boys were summoned together for the purpose of keeping the park, which had become extensive, in a tidy condition. Edward had already cherished the idea. A kind of attractive uniform was made for the

boys which they put on in the evenings after they had
made themselves thoroughly clean and tidy. The clothing
was kept in the castle; the most sensible and careful of
the boys was entrusted with the supervision; the architect kept an eye on the whole affair, and within a very
short time all the boys had acquired a certain skill. They
were not difficult to train, and they carried out their job
efficiently. In fact it was a handsome and pleasing procession when they came along with their scraping irons,
garden knives, rakes, little spades and hoes, while others
came behind with baskets to remove weeds and stones,
or else were dragging behind them the big iron roller; the
architect noted a pleasant sequence of poses and activities for the frieze of a summer-house; Ottilie on the
other hand saw in it only a kind of parade which was
soon to greet the master on his return.

This encouraged her to think of welcoming him with
something similar. In recent times attempts had been
made to rouse up the village girls by means of sewing,
knitting, spinning and other womanly labours. These
virtues had also increased since the arrangement had
been made for keeping the village clean and attractive.
Ottilie also had collaborated, but more by chance than
by deliberately sought opportunity and inclination. Now
she thought of doing it more completely and consistently.
But a number of girls cannot be formed into a team as
a group of boys can. She followed her own good sense,
and without making it quite clear in her own mind,
she attempted no more than to teach every girl to be
devoted to her home, her parents and brothers and
sisters.

With many of the girls she succeeded. There were,
however, always complaints about one small, lively child
that she was clumsy and indeed unwilling to do anything
at all in the home. Ottilie could not dislike the girl, for
the latter was particularly friendly towards her. The girl
was drawn to Ottilie, walking and running with her if she

was allowed. Moreover she was active, gay and untiring. It seemed as if the child had need of an attachment to a beautiful mistress. At first Ottilie tolerated the child's company; then she herself developed an attachment to her; in the end they were inseparable, and Nanny accompanied her mistress everywhere.

Ottilie often took the path to the garden and derived pleasure from the fine way things were growing. The season for soft fruit and cherries was just over, though Nanny was particularly pleased to pick any remaining fruit. As far as the rest of the fruit was concerned, which promised such a rich harvest for the autumn, the gardener kept thinking of the master and always wished him back. Ottilie was so happy listening to the old man. He knew his work perfectly, and never tired of talking to her about Edward.

When Ottilie expressed gladness that twigs which had been grafted in the early part of the year had all come on so well, the gardener replied gravely: 'I only wish that the master may have much pleasure from them. If he were here this autumn, he would see what excellent varieties are still standing in the old castle-garden from the time of his father. Present-day gardeners are not so reliable as the Carthusians used to be. All you find in the catalogues are well-sounding names. You graft them and bring them on, and finally when they bear fruit, it isn't worth the trouble of having the trees in the garden.'

But what the faithful servant most repeatedly asked almost every time he saw Ottilie, was when was the master to return. And when Ottilie could not tell him this, the good man let fall to her, not without some quiet distress, that he believed she did not trust him, and the feeling of uncertainty which was brought home to her in this way distressed her. However, she could not separate herself from these flower beds and borders. What they had planted, in part together, was not in full bloom; it hardly needed any looking after except that

Nanny was always prepared to do some watering. With what emotions Ottilie regarded those late flowers which were just coming out, and whose brilliance and fullness were one day intended to be resplendent and to express her affection and gratitude on Edward's birthday, an occasion which she many a time promised herself she would celebrate! But the hope of seeing this occasion was not always equally bright within her. Doubts and care constantly presented themselves to the good child's mind.

It was also not likely that there could be real, frank agreement with Charlotte again. For indeed the position of the two women was very different. If everything stayed as before, if they returned into the groove of lawful living, Charlotte would gain additional happiness in the moment, and a happy prospect for the future would open up before her; Ottilie on the other hand lost everything, one may well say, everything; for it was with Edward that she had first found life and joy, and in her present condition she felt an unending emptiness of a sort she had hardly suspected existed before. For a heart that is seeking cannot but feel that something is lacking to it; a heart that has lost something feels its deprivation. Longing turns to discontent and impatience, and a woman who is accustomed by temperament to expecting and waiting, would like now to break outside her circle, become active and enterprising and do something for her own happiness.

Ottilie had not renounced Edward. How could she do so, even though Charlotte was clever enough to assume that it was taken for granted, against her own conviction, and to take as settled that a friendly, calm relationship between her husband and Ottilie was possible. How often, though, did Ottilie kneel down at night, when she had locked her door, before the opened chest looking at the birthday present, nothing of which had yet been used, cut up or made ready. How often did the good

129

girl hasten at daybreak out of the house, where she had previously found all her happiness, into the open air, into the country which formerly had meant nothing to her. Neither did she like to stay on dry land. She would jump into the boat and row into the middle of the lake; then she would take out a travel-book, allow herself to be rocked by the movement of the waves, dream herself into the far distance, and there she always found her friend; she had still stayed close to his heart, and he to hers.

CHAPTER XVIII

IT can well be imagined that Mittler, that curiously active man whom we have met already, was not reluctant to show his friendship and prove his skilfulness in this case, after he had received news of the misfortune that had broken out among these friends, although none of them had as yet asked him for help. But it seemed advisable to him to wait a while first; for he knew only too well that it is more difficult to help refined people in cases of moral confusion than uneducated ones. He therefore left them to themselves for a time; but in the end he could not restrain himself any longer and hastened to visit Edward, whose whereabouts he had soon traced.

His journey led him to a pleasant valley through whose delightfully green and wooded meadowland flowed by turns gently and turbulently the full waters of a river that still had something of the liveliness of a stream. Fertile fields and well tended orchards stretched over the gentle slopes. The villages did not lie too close to one another, the whole had a peaceful character, and individual parts seemed to be excellently suited for living in, though less ideal for an artist.

At last he noticed a prosperous farm with a clean, modest dwelling-house surrounded by gardens. He guessed this might be Edward's present quarters, and he was not mistaken.

We can say this much about our solitary friend, that while on his own he was giving himself over completely to his feelings of love and in this connection was thinking out all kinds of plans and cherishing all kinds of hopes.

He could not deny that he would like to see Ottilie here, that he would like to bring her, to entice her here, and that he did not suppress various other thoughts, permissible and illicit. Then his imagination flitted around all the possibilities. If he could not possess her here, rightfully possess her, then he would make over the ownership of the estate to her. There she could live quietly and independently; she was to be happy and, if his self-tormenting imagination led him further, to be happy perhaps with some other man.

In this way the days passed by for him in an incessant vacillation between hope and anguish, tears and gaiety, between intentions, preparations and despair. The sight of Mittler did not surprise him. He had long expected his arrival, and so his presence was in part welcome. If he thought he had been sent by Charlotte, he had already prepared himself for all kinds of excuses and delays and then also for more decisive suggestions; but if on the other hand he hoped to hear something of Ottilie, Mittler would be as welcome as a messenger from heaven.

Consequently Edward was annoyed and put out when he heard that Mittler had not come from the castle, but of his own impulse. His heart hardened, and conversation would not at first develop. But Mittler knew only too well that a mind that is preoccupied with thoughts of love has an urgent need to express itself and to pour out to a friend what is happening within, and after a certain amount of hedging he let himself depart from his usual role and act as confidant instead of mediator.

When, after this, he blamed Edward in a friendly manner for his lonely life, the latter replied: 'Oh I don't know how I should spend my time more pleasantly! I am always concerned with her, and always in her presence. I have the inestimable advantage of being able to imagine where Ottilie is, where she is walking or standing or resting. I can see her in my mind's eye acting and moving as usual, doing and plannings things, always admittedly,

those things which are most flattering to myself. But I
don't leave it at that; for how can I be happy away from
her! Now my imagination is turning over what Ottilie
should do in order to come close to me. I write myself
sweet, intimate letters in her name, I reply to her and keep
the letters together. I have promised not to take any steps
to approach her, and I want to keep this promise. But
what is to stop her from turning to me? For instance,
has Charlotte been so cruel as to demand from her a
promise or vow that she shan't write to me or give me
any news of herself? This is natural and probable, and
yet I find it preposterous, unbearable. If she loves me,
as I believe, as I know, why doesn't she decide and dare
to take flight and throw herself into my arms? She ought
to do this, I often think she could do it. Whenever there
is any movement in the hall, I look to the door. Let her
come in, I think and hope. Alas! And as the possible is
impossible, I imagine that the impossible must have
become possible. If I wake up at night, with the lamp
casting an uncertain gleam over the bedroom, it is her
figure, her spirit, or a premonition of her tuat should
hover near to approach and seize me, just for a moment,
so that I could have a kind of assurance that she is
thinking of me, and that she is mine.

'One single happiness still remains for me. When I
was near her, I never dreamt about her; but now that
we are apart, we are together in our dreams, and
strangely enough, it is since I have become acquainted
with other pleasant people round her, that her image
appears to me in dreams, as if she were trying to say:
"Only look around you! After all, you won't find anything more beautiful and more beloved than me." And
in this way her image is mingled into all my dreams.
Everything that happens between us becomes interlaced
and mingled. Sometimes we are signing a contract; there
her hand and mine, her name and mine are joined; both
cancel each other out and consume each other. Neither

are these delightful deceptions of fantasy without pain. Sometimes she does something that insults the pure idea which I have of her; it is then only that I realise how much I love her, when I am fearful beyond all description. Sometimes she teases and torments me in a way that is quite unlike her; but at once her image changes, her beautiful, round, divine little face is lengthened; she is someone else. But still, I remain tormented, dissatisfied and thrown into confusion.

'Don't smile, my dear Mittler, or rather, smile if you must! No, I'm not ashamed of this attachment—this foolish, mad infatuation, if you like. No, I had never been in love before; it's only now that I realise what love means. Before this my whole life had been only an anticipation, an amusement, a pastime, in fact a waste of time, until I met her and fell in love with her, loved her wholly and truly. People haven't actually said so to my face, but I know that they've criticised me behind my back, saying that in most things I'm only a dabbler and a bungler. It may be; but I hadn't then found what it is I can prove myself a master in. I'd like to see the man who can surpass me in the gift of loving.

'It is certainly a wretched gift, full of pain and tears; but it is so congenial and natural to me that I'm sure it would hardly be possible for me ever to give it up again.'

Edward had certainly relieved himself by this expression of lively, sincere feeling; but all at once every single feature of his strange predicament appeared clearly to his mind's eye, so that he was overwhelmed by the painful conflict and burst into tears which flowed all the more freely since his heart had become tender as a result of making these confidences.

Mittler could not resist his own quick nature and inexorable reasoning powers, much less so since he saw himself being deflected from the purpose of his journey by Edward's painful and passionate outburst, and he expressed his disapproval honestly and bluntly. Edward, he said, should pull himself together and consider what he owed to his manly dignity, and should not forget that it did a man the greatest credit to be composed in misfortune, to bear pain with equanimity and dignity and in this way to become highly respected, esteemed and regarded as a pattern to be followed.

Excited and permeated by the most distressing feelings, as Edward was, he could not help feeling that these words were hollow and vain. 'It's all very well for a man who is happy and comfortable to talk,' Edward flared up; 'but he would be ashamed if he could realise how unbearable he is to someone who is suffering. There is supposed to be such a thing as infinite patience, but infinite grief is something that your narrow, self-satisfied man won't acknowledge. There are cases— yes, really there are—where all consolation is mean, and despair is a duty. Isn't it a fact that a noble Greek, able also to describe heroes, in no way disdains to let his characters weep when grief overwhelms them. He even has a proverb saying that "men who weep easily are good." Let me have no contact with those whose eyes and heart are dry! I curse those fortunate people for whom the unhappy man is nothing more than a play to be watched. This man is supposed to go on behaving in a noble manner in the most terrible situations of physical and spiritual trouble, just so that he can gain their applause and be like a gladiator dying with decorum in front of their eyes. My dear Mittler, I'm grateful to you for your visit; but you would be doing me a great favour, if you would have a look round the garden or the district. We can meet again. I will try to become more composed and more like yourself.'

Mittler would rather have gone on with the discussion than broken it off, realising that he could not take up the conversation again so easily. It also suited Edward quite well to continue their talk, which in any case seemed to be moving towards its goal.

'Certainly, turning things over in one's mind and keeping on talking about them doesn't help at all,' Edward said; 'but while we've been talking I've realised for the first time in a definite manner what I should decide, what in fact I have decided. I see my present and my future life before me; all I have to choose between is wretchedness and happiness. My dear fellow, do arrange a divorce, which is something that is so necessary and has indeed already taken effect; get Charlotte's consent for me! I don't want to go into further details as to why I believe that her consent will be given. Do go there, my dear man, and calm us all down and make us happy!'

Mittler was silent. Edward continued: 'My fate and Ottilie's cannot be separated, and we are not going to be brought to destruction. Look at this glass! Our initials are carved in it. A man who was in a state of gaiety and jubilation threw it into the air; nobody was to drink out of it again, it was to be shattered on the stony ground; but someone caught it. I've bought it back at a high price, and now I drink out of it every day so that I can convince myself daily that all relationships which fate has decreed are indestructible.'

'Oh heavens!' Mittler cried, 'how patient I have to be with my friends! Now I've come up against superstition, which I always hate as the most injurious thing that can beset human beings. We are playing with prophecies and dreams and using them to make everyday life portentous. But when life itself becomes portentous, when everything round us moves and surges, the storm is only made still more terrible by these ghosts.'

'In the uncertainty of life between hope and fear,' Edward cried, 'do leave the needy heart some kind of guiding star to which it can look up, even if it can't steer by it.'

'I might accept that,' Mittler replied, 'if only a certain consistency could be hoped for, but I have always found that no one pays attention to warning symptoms, and attention is only given to the flattering and hopeful signs, and it is only in them that faith is really alive.'

As Mittler now saw himself being led right into those dark regions where he always felt more uncomfortable the longer he remained, he took up rather more readily Edward's urgent request that bade him go to Charlotte. For what in fact was it that he wanted to confront Edward with at this moment? What remained for him to do, according to his own views, was to gain time and to find out what the women's situation was.

He hurried to Charlotte, whom he found composed and serene as usual. She was glad to tell him about everything that had happened; for Edward's talk only allowed him to judge the effects of what had happened. He tactfully came in from his own side, but could not bring himself to pronounce the word 'divorce' even in passing. How surprised and amazed and, with his principles, how relieved he consequently was when Charlotte finally said to him, after mentioning much that was unpleasant: 'I must believe and hope that all will be well again and that Edward will come closer once more. Indeed, how can it be otherwise, since I am in this condition.'

'Do I understand you rightly?' Mittler interposed. 'Quite,' Charlotte added. 'May this news be blessed a thousandfold!' he cried, clapping his hands together. 'I know the strength of this argument on a manly heart. How many marriages have I seen hastened, made secure or restored in this way! So good an expectation is better than a thousand words, it is certainly the best hope that we can have. But,' he went on, 'as far as I am concerned, I might have every reason to be annoyed. In this case, I can see well enough, my vanity will not be flattered. With you people my activity can merit no

137

thanks. I seem to myself to be like a friend of mine, a doctor, whose treatment of poor people, which he did for nothing, always succeeded, while he seldom managed to cure a rich man who would have paid well. Fortunately in this case the business is settling itself, as my efforts and admonitions would have remained fruitless.'

Charlotte now asked him to take the news to Edward, to take with him a letter from her and to see what needed doing and what needed patching up. He was unwilling to agree to this. 'It's all been done,' he cried out. 'Just write! Any messenger will do as well as I would. After all, I must turn my steps to where I am more needed. I shall only come back to give my congratulations; I shall come to the christening.'

As already a number of times previously, Charlotte was discontented with Mittler on this occasion. His quick nature effected much that was good, but his precipitancy was responsible for many a failure. Nobody was more dependent that he was on preconceived notions that had been hastily decided upon.

Charlotte's messenger came to Edward, who received him half in terror. The letter could be equally decisive one way or the other. For a long time he did not dare to open it, and how astonished and petrified he was after reading it through, to read this passage at the end:

'Remember those hours by night when you visited your wife as a venturesome lover, drew her irresistibly to you and enfolded her in your arms as a lover or a bride. Let us respect this strange chance as a divine dispensation which has provided a new bond in our relationship at the moment when our life's happiness threatened to fall apart and disappear.'

It would be difficult to describe what went on in Edward's mind from that moment. In such a crisis it is old habits and likings that finally reassert themselves as a way of killing time and filling out life's course. Hunting and war are an ever ready resource of this type for a nobleman. Edward longed for external danger in order to hold the balance against danger from within. He longed for destruction because existence was threatening to become unbearable to him; indeed it was a comfort for him to think that he would no longer be there and that just because of this he would be able to make his friends and dear ones happy. Nobody opposed his intention, because he kept his resolve secret. He drew up his will with all formalities; it gave him a sweet sensation to be able to bequeath the estate to Ottilie. He made provision for Charlotte, the unborn child, the Captain, and the servants. The war, which had just broken out again, favoured his plan. In his youth he had had a lot to do with military trivialities; that was why he had left the service. Now it seemed magnificent to him to be setting out with a commander of whom he could say: 'under his leadership death is probable and victory certain.'

After hearing Charlotte's secret Ottilie was as taken aback as Edward, more so indeed, and she withdrew into herself. She had nothing further to say. She could not hope, and it would be wrong to desire. However, her diary, from which we hope to give some extracts, allows us a glimpse into her inner mind.

PART TWO

CHAPTER I

In everyday life we often encounter something that we are accustomed to praising in epic poetry as the poet's artistry; that is to say, when the chief characters move away, hide or sink into inactivity, their place is taken at once by a second or third person who has hardly been noticed up to now and, as he proclaims his whole activities to us, seems to us to be equally deserving of notice and sympathy, indeed of praise and commendation.

In this way, as soon as the Captain and Edward had gone, that architect, on whom alone the arrangement and execution of so much of the undertaking depended, became daily a more important person; in his work he proved himself to be exact, sensible and energetic, while at the same time he gave support to the ladies in various ways and was able to entertain them during quiet, dull hours. His external appearance in itself was of a nature to inspire confidence and to kindle affection. He was a young man in the full sense of the words, well-built, slim, possibly a little too tall, modest without being timid, confiding without being importunate. It was a pleasure to him to take on any responsibility or troublesome task, and as he could do accounts with great ease, the running of the household soon ceased to be a secret to him, and his beneficent influence made itself felt everywhere around. He was usually allowed to receive strangers, and he knew how to refuse an unexpected visitor or else at least to prepare the womenfolk in such a way that they did not suffer any inconvenience there-from.

Among others, there was one day a young lawyer who kept him very busy. He had been sent by a neighbour-ing nobleman to raise a subject which, although of no particular importance, nevertheless touched Charlotte closely. We must consider this incident, because it gave an impetus to various matters which might otherwise have lain dormant for a long time.

We can recall the alterations which Charlotte had undertaken with regard to the churchyard. All the grave-stones had been moved from their places and had been set up against the wall or against the base of the church itself. The rest of the space had been cleared. Apart from a broad path which led up to the church and then past it to the little gateway on the other side, all the remaining ground had been sown with various types of clover which looked very beautiful when green and in flower. The new graves were to be arranged according to a certain order from the end onwards, but the space was to be levelled again every time and then sown over. Nobody could deny that this arrangement provided a serene and dignified prospect when walking to church on Sundays and feast-days. Even the aged priest, who clung to old habits and at first was not particularly happy about the measure, now came to be pleased with it, when, like Philemon, he would sit quietly with his Baucis under the lime-trees by the back-door and could see in front of him a fine, gay carpet of clover instead of the uneven gravestones; what is more, the newly sown carpet would come to be useful in his own domestic economy, as Charlotte had provided that the use of this patch of ground would be guaranteed to the vicarage.

But for all that, quite a number of parishioners had already earlier expressed their disapproval that the indication of the place where their ancestors lay had been removed and that in consequence their memory had been blotted out, as it were; for the carefully pre-served grave-stones certainly indicate who is buried, but not where he is buried, and this latter is what really matters, many people maintained.

A neighbouring family was of the same opinion; several years ago they had claimed a space for them-selves and their descendants in the general cemetery and in exchange had made a small bequest to the church. Now the young lawyer had been sent out to countermand the bequest and to give notice that there would be no further payments, because the conditions according to which payments had previously been made had been unilaterally revoked and no attention had been given to all representations and protests. Charlotte, who was the cause of this change, saw the young man herself; he outlined his own and his principal's case in a lively, but not too forward manner, and gave the company quite a lot to think about.

After a short preamble which he used to justify his own presumptuousness, he said: 'You see, both the humblest and the highest person is concerned to indicate the place where members of his family lie buried. For the poorest farm-labourer who buries one of his children it is a kind of consolation to place a slight, wooden cross on the grave and to decorate it with a wreath in order to preserve the memory at least for as long as the grief lasts, even though such a sign, like mourning itself, is lost in the course of time. Prosperous people erect iron crosses instead of wooden ones, making them firm and protecting them in various ways, and this gives duration for a number of years. But since these crosses also even-tually sink down and become insignificant-looking, the well-to-do can think nothing more advantageous than to set up a stone which promises to last for several gener-ations and can be renewed and refurbished by their descendants. Yet what attracts us is not this particular

143

stone, but what is contained below it and entrusted to the earth beside it. It is not so much a question of the monument so much as of the person himself, of the present not of the past. I can embrace a loved departed one much more readily and more intimately in a sepulchral mound than in a memorial, for this latter means really very little to me; but after death the widow or widower, relations, and friends should meet again by such a monument as if it were a boundary-stone, and the principal mourner should retain the right to be able to turn away strangers and disgruntled individuals from beside his dear departed ones.

'That is why I think my principal is absolutely right to revoke the bequest; and this is surely reasonable enough, for the members of the family have been injured in a matter for which no restitution is conceivable. They are to be deprived of the bittersweet feeling of bringing to their dear one a sacrifice to the dead, and of the comforting hope that at some time they will rest directly beside them.'

'The matter is not so important that we should disturb ourselves by a law-suit on account of it,' Charlotte replied. 'I have no regrets about my arrangements, and I should be glad to make up to the church what it will be losing. There is only one thing that I must honestly confess to you: your arguments haven't convinced me. The pure feeling of a final general equality, at least after death, seems more consoling to me than this obstinate and stubborn continuation of our personalities, attachments and conditions of living. And what do you think about this?' She directed her question to the architect.

'I have no wish to argue in such a matter or to give a casting vote,' the latter replied. 'But I should like to say in all modesty what appeals to my training and my way of thought. Since we are no longer so fortunate as to be able to press the remains of a beloved one to our breast in an urn, nor preserve them undamaged in

144

large ornate sarcophagi, nor even to find room for ourselves and our dear ones in the churches, but are shown
out into the open air, we have every reason to approve
of the approach which you, Madam, have introduced.
When members of a community lie side by side, they
are resting with as well as below their own folk; and if
the earth is to receive us one day, I can find nothing
more natural and nothing tidier than for the mounds,
which arose by chance and are now gradually subsiding,
to be levelled out straightaway, so that the covering
which lies over them all can be made lighter for each.'

'And all those people are to pass on without any
indication of a memorial or anything to help to remember
them by?' Ottilie put in.

'Oh no!' the architect continued: 'it's a question not
of breaking away from the memorial, but only from the
actual place. Architects and sculptors are particularly
interested that man should expect from the art of their
hands a perpetuation of his life: and on that account I
should like to have well planned and well executed monuments that are not scattered about singly and by chance,
but are erected at a spot where they can expect perman-
ency. As even the pious and those of high station forego
the privilege of being laid to rest in person in the
churches, let us at least erect tokens of remembrance
and written memorials in the churches or in beautiful
halls near the burial grounds. There are thousands of
forms that could be prescribed for them, thousands of
ways in which to decorate them.'

'If the artists are so rich in ideas,' Charlotte said,
'will you tell me how it is one can never get away
from the form of a little obelisk, a truncated column
and a funeral urn? Instead of the thousand inventions
which you boast of, I have seen only thousands of
repetitions.'

'That may well be, so far as we are concerned,' the
architect answered, 'but not everywhere. And altogether

it can be a peculiar business as far as invention and suitable application are concerned. In this particular case it is particularly difficult to brighten up a serious subject, and not to produce something that is unpleasant when dealing with an unpleasant subject. As far as monuments of all kinds are concerned, I have collected a good number and occasionally I show them to people; but a man's own portrait always remains his most beautiful memorial. A portrait gives better than anything else an idea of what he used to be; it is the best words to the music, whether there is much or little of this latter; the only thing is that the portrait should be painted during the best years of a person's life, and this is usually forgotten. Nobody thinks of preserving living forms, and when it does happen, it happens in an inadequate manner. A death-mask is hastily taken and put on a block, and that's what they call a bust. How seldom it is that an artist can give a sense of life to such a bust!'

'You've turned the conversation entirely in my favour, perhaps without knowing it or intending to,' Charlotte added. 'A man's portrait is after all so independent; whoever it may be, it stands in its own right, and we shan't ask that it shall mark the actual gravestone. But may I confess to you a strange feeling I have? I have a kind of dislike even of portraits, for they always seem to me to be making a silent reproach; they are pointing to something distant and finished, and remind me how difficult it is to show true reverence to the present. How do we feel when we think how many people we have seen and known, and when we confess how little we have meant to them, and they to us! We meet the wit without enjoying conversation with him, we meet the man of learning and the much-travelled man without being instructed by them, we meet an amiable man without showing him some kindness in our turn.

'And unfortunately this doesn't merely happen with passing acquaintances. Whole societies and families behave in this way towards their dearest members, whole towns towards their worthiest citizens, people towards their princes, nations towards their finest men.

'I once heard somebody ask why one says good things of the dead so unreservedly, but always speaks of the living with a certain caution. The answer given was that we have nothing to fear from the former, whereas the latter could still conceivably get in our way. So impure is our care for the memory of others; for the most part it is only an egoistic joke, while on the other hand it would be a matter of great seriousness for a man to keep his relationship with a dead person's surviving family constantly alive and active.'

CHAPTER II

STIRRED up by the incident and by the discussions it had initiated, they went next day to the graveyard, and the architect made a number of happy suggestions for adorning and brightening it. His efforts were to be directed to the church itself as well, a building that had attracted his attention right from the start.

The church had been standing for several centuries, having been constructed in good proportions according to the German manner and art, and felicitously ornamented. One could understand that the architect of a nearby monastery had also lavished his skill on this smaller building with insight and affection, and the church continued to make a dignified and pleasant impression on the observer, although the newer interior arrangements for the Protestant service had deprived it of something of its calm and majesty.

The architect did not find it difficult to obtain from Charlotte a moderate sum which he thought of using to restore the exterior as well as the interior in accordance with its original appearance and to bring the front of the graveyard into harmony with it. He himself was clever with his hands, and it was gladly agreed to keep on some of the workmen who had been concerned with the building of the house until this pious work as well should be completed.

They were now in a position to be able to examine the building itself with all its surroundings and adjuncts, and to the great astonishment and delight of the architect they found a little side-chapel that had hardly been

148

noticed; its proportions were even more ingenious and more delicate, its adornments even more pleasing and more conscientiously carried out. Moreover, the chapel contained many carved or painted remains from the older forms of worship which indicated the various feast-days by means of various pictures and objects and celebrated each day in its own way.

The architect could not resist at once including the chapel in his plan and, particularly, restoring this small room as a monument to a bygone age and taste. He was thinking of decorating the plain surfaces according to his own inclination and was looking forward to practising his talent as a painter in this way; but for the time being he kept it a secret from the others in the house.

According to his promise, he first of all showed to the ladies the various models and plans of old tombs, urns and other objects of a like kind, and when conversation turned to the simpler grave-mounds of the Nordic people, he brought out his collection of various kinds of weapons and objects which had been found in such graves. He had everything set out in a very tidy and handy manner in drawers and compartments placed on carved boards which were covered by a cloth; consequently these old, portentous objects took on a certain stylishness as a result of his treatment, and one could look at them with pleasure, as if at the show-cases of a fashionable shop. And as he had once begun this showing and as solitude required some entertainment, he regularly appeared every evening with a part of his collection. For the most part they were of German origin; bracteati, double coins, seals and anything else of a comparable nature. All these objects directed the imagination back to the past, and as he finally illustrated his talks with early printing, wood-cuts and the oldest engravings and as the church day by day, in the same spirit, grew back to the past in colour and other decorations, it was almost necessary to ask oneself, if one really were living in modern times or if it were not a dream, and that one really was now placed among quite different customs, habits, ways of life and convictions.

After such preparations, he achieved his best effect with a fairly large brief-case which he brought out last. Admittedly it contained mostly only sketched figures, but as they had ben traced on to the paper they had completely preserved their old-world character, and how attractive the observers found this character to be! Only the purest way of living was revealed in all the figures; one had to acknowledge if not the nobility, at least the goodness of them all. Serene composure, glad acknowledgement of One above us Who is to be revered, quiet devotion in love and expectation were expressed on all faces and in all gestures. The old man with the bald head, the boy with hair in abundant locks, the cheerful youth, the serious man, the transfigured saint and the hovering angel, all seemed blessed in innocent contentment and pious anticipation. The most ordinary thing that happened had a touch of heavenly life, and action in a spirit of worship seemed fitting to the nature of each of them.

Most people look to such a sphere as if to a lost golden age, a lost paradise. Perhaps Ottilie alone was in the position of feeling that she was among her own sort of people.

Who could now have resisted the architect's offer to paint the spaces between the arches of the chapel according to the model of these ancient pictures, and in this way to preserve his own memory at a place where he had been so happy. It was with some melancholy that he explained how he felt about this; for he could indeed see from the way things were that his stay in such accomplished society could not last for ever, and in fact that it might have to be broken off soon.

For the rest, although these days were not rich in events, they were full of occasions for serious conversation. We are therefore taking the opportunity of imparting something of what Ottilie noted of these conversations in her diary, and we can find no more fitting bridge to this than in a simile that thrusts itself on our attention as we look through the beloved pages.

There is said to be a special device of the British navy. All the ropes of the royal fleet, from the strongest to the thinnest, are spun in such a manner that a red thread runs through the whole which cannot be removed without unravelling everything, and by means of which even the smallest pieces are recognisable as belonging to the crown.

Similarly there is running through Ottilie's diary a thread of affection and attachment which unites and characterises the whole. Thereby these notes, observations and selected aphorisms and whatsoever may be found here, become peculiarly characteristic of their writer and meaningful to her. Each single part that we have selected and communicated gives the most definite testimony of this.

From Ottilie's Diary

To be buried one day by the side of those whom one loves is the pleasantest thought that man can imagine, if once he thinks beyond this life. 'To be gathered to one's fathers' is such a heartfelt expression.

There are many kinds of memorials and signs which draw us closer to those who are far away or dead. None of these is more important than the portrait. The presence of a much loved portrait, even when it is a poor resemblance, has something exciting about it, just as there is something exciting about arguing with a friend. You feel in a pleasant way that there are just two of you, and yet that you can't be separated.

Occasionally a real person keeps us company in the same way that a portrait does. He need not talk, look round or occupy himself with us; we see him and feel our relationship to him and can indeed see our own personal relationships extending without his doing anything about it or having the feeling that he is behaving to us merely like a portrait.

One is never satisfied with a portrait of somebody whom one knows. That is why I have always felt sorry for portrait painters. It is not often that one asks people for what is impossible, and it is precisely from portrait-painters that this demand is made. They are expected to incorporate into their portrait everyone's attitude to the subject and picture, their likes and dislikes; they are asked not merely to depict how they conceive someone, but how everybody else would conceive him. I am not surprised when such artists gradually become hardened, indifferent and wilful. Anything might come of this, so long as one did not have to be deprived in consequence of the pictures of so many dearly loved people.

It is indeed true that the architect's collection of weapons and old objects, which were put by the dead body with high mounds of earth and pieces of rock, testifies to us how unnecessary are man's provisions for the preservation of his personality after death. How inconsistent we are! The architect admits that he has himself opened such tumuli of previous generations, and still continues to occupy himself with monuments for those who are to come after us.

But why should one take it so seriously? For is everything that we do intended for eternity? Do we not get dressed in the morning, in order to get undressed again in the evening? Do we not travel away in order to come back? And why should we not wish to be laid to rest with our own people, even if it were only for a hundred years?

When one sees the many sunken gravestones that have been worn down by churchgoers and even the churches that have collapsed over their own sepulchres, one can still continue to think of life after death as a second life, into which one now enters through a portrait or through a superscription and in which one may stay longer than in actual, living life. But even this picture, this second existence, is extinguished sooner or later. Time will not be deprived of its rights over memorials any more than over people.

CHAPTER III

It is such a pleasant sensation, to occupy oneself with
something that can only be done by halves, that nobody
should scold the dilettante who spends his time on an
art that he will never learn, or blame the artist if he has
the wish to go beyond the limits of his art and wander
across into a neighbouring field.

With fair-minded thoughts such as these do we observe
the architect's preparations for painting the chapel. The
colours were prepared, the measurements taken, the
sketches drawn; he had given up any claim to free invention; he kept close to his plans: his only aim was to
disperse the sitting and hovering figures in a clever
manner and with taste to decorate the space with them.

The scaffolding was erected, the work progressed, and
as something that attracted the eye had already been
achieved, he could not object to Charlotte coming to
visit him with Ottilie. The living faces of the angels and
their lively garments against the blue background of
heaven were a delight to the eye, while their quiet, pious
demeanour called the observer's mind to stillness and
brought forward an effect of great delicacy.

The women climbed up to him on the scaffolding, and
Ottilie scarcely noticed with what calculated lightness
and ease everything went, when what she had learnt
in her lessons earlier seemed to develop all at once and
she could reach out for paints and brush and, having
been given directions, could paint a robe that was complex in its folds with neatness and skill.

Charlotte, who was glad to see Ottilie occupying and

entertaining herself in any way, left the couple to it, and went away to lose herself in her own thoughts and work out for herself the preoccupations and worries that she could not share with anyone else.

If ordinary people cause us to smile pityingly when they are aroused to passionate and anxious behaviour by everyday embarrassments, it is with reverence on the other hand that we consider a mind in which the seed of a great fate has been sown, and which must await the growth of this conception, and which may not and cannot hasten either the happiness or misfortune that is to develop from it.

Edward had given a reply to Charlotte's messenger whom she had sent to him in his solitude; it was friendly and sympathetic, but controlled and serious rather than confiding and affectionate. Shortly afterwards Edward had disappeared, and his wife could obtain no news of him until finally she found his name by chance in the gazettes, where he was cited with honours among those who had distinguished themselves in an important incident of the war. She knew now the path he had chosen, and she learnt that he had escaped from great dangers; but she was at once convinced that he would seek out greater ones, and she could see only too clearly from this that he would hardly let himself be restrained from extreme measures, in any sense of the phrase. She kept these cares to herself; they were always in her thoughts, and however she might argue for or against, she could find no peace of mind, whatever view she took.

Not having any inkling of all this, Ottilie in the meantime had developed a strong attachment to the work she had taken up, and Charlotte had very gladly granted her permission to continue with it regularly. Now rapid progress was being made, and the azure heaven was soon populated with inhabitants worthy of it. As a result of continuous practice Ottilie and the architect attained more freedom of style in the later pictures; they were an obvious improvement. The faces too, which were left for the architect to paint by himself, gradually came to show a most peculiar trait; they all began to resemble Ottilie. The presence of the delightful girl could not but make so vivid an impression on the young man's mind that he gradually became able to depict with his hand what his eye had seen in such a way that nothing was lost in the process, until finally hand and eye worked in full harmony. Indeed, one of the last of the little faces was completely successful, so that it seemed as if Ottilie herself were looking down from the heavenly spaces.

The vaulting was now finished; it had been decided to leave the walls plain and simply to give them a coat of a brighter, brownish colour; the delicate columns and the artistically sculptured decorations were to be picked out in a darker colour. But as one thing always leads to another in such matters, it was decided to include flowers and hanging fruits which were, so to speak, to link heaven and earth together. Now here Ottilie was quite in her element. The gardens provided the finest models, and although the garlands were very richly decked out, it was possible to finish the work sooner than expected.

But it all still looked disorderly and messy. The scaffolding was still up, pranks thrown on top of each other, and the uneven floor was even more disfigured by the different coloured paints which had been spilt there. The architect now asked the ladies to give him a week and during that time not to enter the chapel. He then requested them both to appear there one fine evening; however, he would rather not accompany them, and he took his leave forthwith.

'I don't know what kind of surprise he has thought out for us,' Charlotte said, after he had gone, 'but I just don't feel like going down there at the moment. You go there on your own and tell me about it. I'm sure he's arranged something pleasant. I shall enjoy it first of all through your description and then in reality.'

Ottilie knew well enough that Charlotte was cautious in many respects and avoided all emotional excitement, in particular that she did not like being taken by surprise; she went forthwith alone and involuntarily looked round for the architect, who, however, was nowhere to be seen and must have hidden himself. She entered the church, which she found open. Work there had already been completed, and it had been cleaned and consecrated. She went up to the church door, which opened easily, for all the heaviness of its brasswork, and was surprised by an unexpected sight in a familiar room.

A steady, brightly coloured light fell through the one high window, gracefully fashioned of stained glass. The consequence of this was that the whole interior was given a strange atmosphere peculiar to itself. The beauty of the vaulting and the walls was enhanced by the decorative floor, which consisted of specially shaped bricks that had been laid according to a pleasant pattern and joined together by plaster-work. These bricks as well as the coloured window-panes had been prepared in secret by the architect, who had managed to put everything together in a short space of time. Seats had been thought of, too. A few finely carved choir-stalls which had been found among the antiquities of the church now stood very appropriately against the walls.

Ottilie was pleased to see familiar parts brought together before her as an unknown whole. She stood still, walked up and down, saw and inspected; finally she sat down in one of the choir-stalls, and it seemed to her, as she looked around and above her, as if this might all vanish before her eyes, and she herself as well; and only when the sun disappeared from the window which had just been so vividly lit up, did Ottilie come to herself again and hurry back to the castle.

She was not unaware that this surprise had come at a

strange time. It was the evening before Edward's birthday. She had certainly hoped to celebrate it in a very different manner. How everything was to have been decorated for this festivity! But as it was, the whole wealth of autumn flowers stood unpicked. The sunflowers still turned their faces towards the sky, the asters still stared quietly ahead and those flowers that had been made into wreaths looked as though they might have been put for the useful purpose of decorating a communal burial-place.

She could not help remembering the bustling activity with which Edward had celebrated her own birthday; her thoughts turned to the new house, beneath whose roof so much that was friendly had been promised. Indeed, the fireworks roared once more before her eyes and in her ears; the lonelier she was, the more part her imagination played; but she only felt the more solitary in consequence. She could no longer lean on his arm, and had no hope of ever finding support in him again.

From Ottilie's Diary

I must make a note of a young artist's remark: 'One can see most clearly from the craftsman and the artist that man is least able to make something his own when it belongs specially to himself. His works leave him just as birds leave the nest where they have been hatched out.'

The architect especially has the strangest of fates in this respect. How often he makes use of his full mind and affection in order to design rooms from which he himself must be excluded! Royal reception-rooms owe their brilliance to him, but he cannot take part in their moments of greatest effectiveness. In temples he draws a line between himself and the holy of holies; he no longer may walk up the steps which he put into place for the sake of a solemnity that lifts our hearts, while the goldsmith can only worship from a distance the monstrance whose blending of colours and precious

157

stones he has ordered. The architect hands over to the rich man the key of his palace and all its comfort and ease, without enjoying anything of it himself. Must not the art gradually be separated from the artist in this manner, when the work, like a daughter provided with her dowry, can react no longer upon the father? How well art could further its own ends when it was almost entirely designed to be concerned with what was public and belonged to everybody, including the artist too.

One idea cherished by primitive people is solemn and can appear as terrible. They thought of their ancestors as sitting on their thrones in circles in great caverns, in silent communication. If a newcomer were worthy enough, they stood up and bowed welcomingly to him as he entered. Yesterday, as I was sitting in the chapel and saw a number of seats facing my own carved chair, this idea seemed to me quite a friendly and pleasant one. 'Why can't I go on sitting here?' I thought to myself, 'go on sitting here quietly and turned in upon myself, a long, long time, until at last my friends come and I stand up for them and show them their places with a friendly bow.' Coloured glass makes day into solemn twilight, and somebody ought to present an ever-burning lamp so that the night too should not be wholly dark.

We may imagine whatever we will, but we always think of ourselves as having sight. I believe man only dreams in order not to stop seeing. It might well be that the inner light would one day step outside us so that we should need no other.

The year is on the decline. The wind blows over the stubble, no longer finding anything there to move; there are only the red berries of those slender trees which seem to want to remind us of something gayer, just as the regular beat of the thresher awakens in us the thought that so much is nourishing and vital lies hidden in the scythed grain.

CHAPTER IV

AFTER such happenings, and this compelling sensation of transience and passing away, how strangely Ottilie was affected by the news, which could not be concealed from her any longer, that Edward had delivered himself over to the changeable fortunes of war. Unfortunately she could not elude any of the thoughts which she had reason to have under the circumstances. Happily, man can only comprehend a limited degree of misfortune; what exceeds this measure either destroys him or leaves him indifferent. There are situations where fear and hope become one, or cancel each other out and are lost in a dark numbness. How otherwise could we know that our distant loved ones are in hourly danger and yet go on with our ordinary daily lives.

It was therefore as if a good spirit were taking care of Ottilie when all at once a wild throng of young people invaded the quietness in which she seemed to be sinking in her lonely and idle state; she was given enough to do from outside and taken out of herself, while at the same time she was aroused to a feeling of her own power.

Charlotte's daughter Luciane had scarcely left the boarding-school and come out into society, where in her aunt's house she was soon surrounded by many people, when her desire to attract really did attract someone, and a very rich young man soon longed passionately to make her his own. His considerable wealth gave him the right to have the best of everything for himself, and it seemed to him that the only thing he lacked was a perfect wife,

159

on whose account he would be generally envied, as he was already on account of everything else.

It was this family affair that had given Charlotte so much to do up to now; she had devoted to it all her thoughts and her correspondence, except when she was endeavouring to obtain more news of Edward; for this reason too Ottilie had been more alone lately than usual. She knew about Luciane's coming; she had taken the most essential steps in the house on that account; but it was difficult to imagine that the visit was so imminent. They still wanted to write, discuss, and make more detailed arrangements when the storm broke all of a sudden on the castle and on Ottilie.

Maids and men-servants, baggage-carts with trunks and chests now arrived; one might have thought that two or three sets of guests were already in the house; but the guests were only now arriving: the great-aunt with Luciane and some girl-friends, and the young man, who was similarly not unaccompanied. The entrance hall was now full of cases, portmanteaux and other leather containers. With some difficulty the many small boxes and cases were sorted out. There was no end to the baggage and its movements. Meanwhile it poured with rain, and this caused much discomfort. Ottilie dealt with these turbulent doings in a spirit of equable activity, indeed her serene character showed itself in its finest radiance; for it was only a short time before everything was sorted out and put in its place. Everybody was found a room, all were comfortable in their own way, believing themselves to be well looked after because they were not prevented from looking after themselves.

Now they would all have been glad to have enjoyed a certain amount of quiet after a most tiresome journey; the betrothed young man would have liked to come closer to his future mother-in-law in order to assure her of his affection and good will: but Luciane could not be still. She had at last reached the happy stage when she

was allowed to ride. Her fiancé had fine horses, and
there was nothing for it but to mount them right away.
The weather—wind, rain and storms—was not taken into
account; it seemed as if the only purpose in life was to
get wet and then dry again. If she took it into her head
to go out on foot, she did not trouble what clothes or
footwear she might have on: she simply had to view the
gardens, about which she had heard so much. What
was not accessible on horseback had to be hastily visited
on foot. It was not long before she had seen everything
and passed judgement on it. With her liveliness of
manner, it was not easy to contradict her. The household
had a lot to put up with, especially the maids who were
never finished with washing and ironing, mending and
sewing.

She had hardly exhausted the attractions of the house
and its surroundings before she felt obliged to pay visits
in the neighbourhood. As she and her companions rode
very quickly, whether on horse-back or in a carriage,
the term neighbourhood extended a considerable distance. The castle was inundated with visitors in return,
and soon definite dates were arranged so that people
should not miss each other.

While Charlotte was concerned to establish close connections with the aunt and the agent of the young man,
and Ottilie with her subordinates were seeing to it that
nothing should be lacking with so great a concourse of
people, for huntsmen, gardeners, fishermen and sales-
men had all been given employment, Luciane still
showed herself like a burning comet with a long tail
behind it. She soon found the usual visiting quite insipid.
She almost begrudged the oldest guests their quiet at the
card-table: anyone who was at all mobile—and who
would not be set into action by her charming importunity?—had to join in, if not in dancing, then certainly
in lively party-games. And although the games were all
centred upon herself, and the subsequent redemption of

forfeits too, on the other hand there was nobody, particularly if he was a man of any kind, who was allowed
to be entirely overlooked; in fact she succeeded in
winning the favour of a number of older people of some
importance by finding out their birthdays or name-days
and then arranging a special celebration, if the dates
fitted in. She showed a skill entirely her own in this sort
of thing, with the result that, while everybody found
themselves favoured, each individually thought that he
was the most favoured person: this was a weakness to
which in fact the oldest man in the company was most
obviously prone.

It seemed to be her plan to win the favour of men of
rank, reputation, honour or some sort of distinction in
general, while showing contempt for wisdom and
restraint; to gain the esteem even of cautious people for
her own uncontrolled and strange behaviour. At the same
time the young people were not neglected; each of them
had his allowance, his day or hour when she made it her
business to attract and charm him. Consequently she
soon had her eye on the architect, who, however, had
such a straightforward look beneath his black, long
hair and stood at a distance so erectly and quietly,
answering all questions briefly and sensibly but without
showing any inclination to take matters any further,
that at last she decided, with mixed motives of resent-
ment and cunning, to make him the hero of the day and
thereby to win him as one of her admirers.

Not for nothing had she brought so much luggage with
her, in fact a considerable quantity had come after her
as well. She was provided with never-ending changes of
clothes. She took pleasure in changing her clothes three
or four times a day, so that there was always variety in
her ordinary clothes, the ones which would be usual in
company, from morning till night; but in between she
would also appear in real fancy-dress, as a peasant
woman or fisherwoman, or as a fairy or flower-girl. She

did not shrink from disguising herself as an old woman, so that her young face would peep out the more freshly from her cowl; and she did in fact confuse what was real and what was imaginary to such an extent that people thought she must be related to the Nymph of the Hall.[1]

But she used these disguises mostly for miming tableaux and dances, for she was clever at depicting various characters in these ways. One of the young men from her following had so arranged things that he could accompany her movements on the piano with what little music was necessary; all that was needed was a brief discussion, and they were at once in harmony to give such a performance.

One day when someone had asked her apparently on the spur of the moment, though in fact at her secret suggestion, during the interval of a lively dance, she seemed embarrassed and surprised, and contrary to her usual custom had to be asked repeatedly. She showed herself undecided, left the choice open, asked for a theme as if she were improvising, until finally her piano-playing assistant, with whom the matter had been pre-arranged, sat down at the instrument, began to play a funeral march and invited her to perform the part of Artemisia, which she had studied so well. She allowed herself to be persuaded, and after a short pause she reappeared, to the delicately sad notes of the funeral march, in the figure of a royal widow, carrying in front of her with measured step a funeral urn. Someone came along in the rear bearing a large blackboard and a well-pointed piece of chalk fixed in a gold drawing-pen.

One of her admirers and assistants, to whom she whispered something, went at once to the architect who was invited, indeed pressed and to some extent pushed along, to show himself as an architect and draw the grave of Mausolos; he was thus to be a serious participant in

[1] The reference is to an adaptation made in 1792 for the Weimar stage of an operetta, *Das Donauweibchen* ('The Danube Fairy'), by K. F. Hensler.

the tableau, not merely a supernumerary. Although the architect was obviously embarrassed—for his black, tight-fitting, modern civilian clothes made a strange contrast to all the many coloured gauze and crepe fringes, tassles and crowns—he at once restrained himself, though it was in consequence an even stranger sight. With great seriousness he stood before the large blackboard, which was held by a few page-boys, and with much deliberation and exactitude he drew a sketch of a tomb which indeed would have been more fitted to a Lombardian King than to a king of Caria, but which was so well proportioned, with its various parts earnestly thought out and its decoration so intelligently conceived, that people could take pleasure in watching the drawing take shape and could admire it when it was finished.

During all this time he had hardly turned towards the Queen at all, devoting all his attention to his task. When at last he bowed to her and indicated that he believed he had now carried out her commands, she now held out the urn to him, indicating her wish to see it sketched in above the tomb. He did so, although with reluctance, since the urn did not fit into the character of the rest of his drawing. As far as Luciane was concerned, she was at last released from her impatience; for it was by no means her intention to receive from him a conscientious drawing. If he had just sketched in with a few strokes something roughly resembling a monument and had spent the rest of his time with her, that would have suited and pleased her better. But his behaviour embarrassed her greatly; for although she tried to vary her manner by means of her grief, her arrangements and hints, and her approval of the design as it gradually emerged, and although she almost pulled him about once or twice in her efforts to establish some sort of relationship with him, he still remained too stiff, with the result that she had to have a recourse to the urn all too often, pressing it to her and looking up to heaven, until in the end, since this

164

sort of situation can only become more exaggerated, she looked more like a widow of Ephesus than a queen of Caria. The performance consequently became rather long drawn-out; the piano-player, usually patient enough, could not tell into what key he was supposed to be modulating. He thanked God when he saw the urn standing on the pyramid, and when the Queen was about to express her gratitude, he unwittingly played a hilarious tune, with the consequence that, even if the performance lost its character, the audience was completely cheered up and divided its attentions between the lady and the architect, expressing a pleased admiration of the former for her excellent expressiveness and the latter for his artistic and graceful drawing.

Luciane's fiancée was particularly interested in conversing with the architect. 'I'm sorry,' he said, 'that your sketch is of such a transient nature. But at least you will allow me to take it up to my room and to talk with you about it.' 'If you're interested,' the architect said, 'I can show you some careful drawings of buildings like this and monuments, of which this is only a chance, fleeting sketch.'

Ottilie was standing nearby, and she stepped up to them. 'Don't forget to let the Baron see your collection some time; he is keen on art and antiquities; I should be happy if you were to become better acquainted.'

Luciane came rushing by and asked, 'What are you talking about?'

'An art collection which this gentleman possesses and which he will be happy to show us when there is an opportunity,' the Baron answered.

'Let him bring them straight away!' Luciane cried. 'You will bring them straight away, won't you?' she added flatteringly, catching hold of the architect with both hands.

'I don't think it's really a good time,' the architect replied.

'What!' Luciane cried in a commanding voice. 'You are unwilling to obey your Queen's orders?' Then she changed to playful pleading.

'Don't be obstinate!' Ottilie said in a half-whisper.

The architect bowed and went away; his gesture was neither one of acceptance nor of refusal.

He had hardly left before Luciane began racing around the room with a greyhound. 'Oh!' she cried, as she accidentally ran into her mother, 'How miserable I am! I didn't bring my monkey; I was advised not to; but it's only my servants' laziness that is depriving me of this pleasure. Still, I'll have him sent on, somebody can go and fetch him for me. If I could only see his portrait, I should feeel happy. But I really will have his portrait painted, and I won't let him go from my side.'

'Perhaps I can console you by sending to the library for a whole volume full of the strangest pictures of monkeys,' Charlotte replied. Luciane cried out loud with joy, and the folio volume was fetched. She was greatly delighted at the sight of these repulsive creatures which resemble human beings, and which in this case had been made even more human by the artist. But she felt completely happy when she could find in the case of each of these animals a resemblance to people she knew. 'Doesn't that one look like Uncle?' she cried mercilessly, 'that one like M—, the dealer in fancy goods, that one like Pastor S—, and this one is So and So, and he's — himself. As a matter of fact these monkeys are really French dandies, and it is incomprehensible that they should be excluded from the best society.'

She said this in the best society, but nobody took it amiss. People were so used to making her plenty of allowances because of her charm, that they finally came to condone her bad manners.

Meanwhile Ottilie was talking to Luciane's fiancé. She hoped that the architect would come back, for his more serious collection which was in good taste would set the company free of this monkey-business. In anticipation of this she had entered into discussion with the Baron and had drawn his attention to various things. But the architect was missing, and when he at last returned, he hid himself among the company without bringing anything and by behaving as if no request had been put to him. For a moment Ottilie was—how shall we say?—annoyed, impatient and surprised; she had appealed to him with well meant words, and she did not begrudge Luciane's fiancé spending a pleasant hour in a way that he would like; for he seemed to be suffering somewhat from her behaviour in spite of his infinite love for her.

The monkeys had to give place to supper. Party games, yet again dancing, and finally sitting around in a bored manner, and attempts to whip up a mood of pleasure that had already gone, all this went on, as it had done on previous occasions, until well after midnight. For Luciane had already got into the habit of not being able to get out of bed in the morning nor to get into bed at night.

There are fewer events noted in Ottilie's diary at this time, but more frequently there are maxims and mottoes concerning life in general. But as most of them cannot have been the product of her own thought, it is likely that someone passed on to her a volume from which she copied out what appealed to her. It will be possible to recognise much that is her own more intimate and personal thought by the red thread running through.

From Ottilie's Diary

We like to look towards the future because we should be so glad to deflect by our wishes the chance happenings that move this way and that to suit our own purposes.

We do not often find ourselves in a great gathering

without thinking that chance, which brings so many people together, should also lead our friends to us.

However retiringly one lives, before one realises it one is either a debtor or a creditor.

If we meet somebody who owes us a debt of gratitude, we at once remember it. How often we can meet someone to whom we owe thanks, without thinking about it!

It is natural to open one's heart to others; to receive confidences in the spirit in which they have been given requires refinement and education.

Nobody would say much in company if he realised how often he misunderstands others.

The only reason why other people's speeches are altered when someone repeats them is because they have not been understood.

A man who talks to other people a long time on his own without flattering them arouses antipathy.

Every word that is spoken can arouse misconstruction.

Contradiction and flattery both make bad conversation.

The pleasantest types of social intercourse are those where a cheerful respect of the individuals one to another predominates.

People define their own characters most clearly by the things they find ridiculous.

Something ridiculous originates in a moral contrast which is made evident to our senses in a harmless manner.

The man who lives by sense-impressions often laughs when there is nothing to laugh at. Whatever the stimulus may be, his inner complacency becomes obvious.

The matter-of-fact rationalist finds almost everything ridiculous, the wise man almost nothing.

A man of advancing years was criticised for still troubling about young women. 'It is the only way to become rejuvenated,' he said, 'and after all that is what everybody wants.'

One can listen to accounts of one's faults, one

accepts punishment and is willing to suffer much with patience on this account; but one becomes impatient if one is supposed to overcome these faults.

Certain shortcomings are essential to the well-being of the individual. It would be unpleasant for us, if old friends were to throw off certain of their peculiarities.

People say: 'He will die soon,' if someone acts contrary to his usual habits.

What faults may we retain, even encourage in ourselves? Those that flatter other people rather than hurting them.

Passions can be either faults or virtues, but they are exaggerated forms.

Our passions are true phoenixes. As the old one burns, a new one rises at once from the ashes.

Great passions are illnesses without hope of recovery. What might heal them, does in fact make them really dangerous.

Passion is both raised up and purified by confession. The middle of the road is perhaps nowhere more desirable than in trust and reticence towards those we love.

CHAPTER V

THUS Luciane whipped up the life around her into a
frenzy of sociability. Her court grew daily, partly
because her activity aroused and attracted so many
people, partly because she knew how to attach other
people to her by being pleasant and obliging. She was
generous to an extreme degree; for, as the affection of
her aunt and her fiancé had caused so many beautiful
and precious gifts to be made to her, it seemed as if she
possessed nothing that was really her own and as if she
did not know the value of the things that had piled up
around her. Thus she did not hesitate a moment to take
off a costly shawl and to slip it round the neck of a
woman who seemed to her to be poorly dressed by comparison with others, and she did this in such a light-
hearted and adroit manner that nobody could refuse
such a gift. One of her companions always carried a
purse and was instructed in the various places which
they visited to ask for the most aged and most sickly
people and to ease their condition, at least for the
moment. As a result of this she acquired throughout the
district a reputation for excellence which, however,
became uncomfortable sometimes, because it attracted
too many importunate needy folk in her wake.

There was, however, nothing which added more to her
reputation than her striking, but good and consistent
behaviour towards an unfortunate young man who fled
from society because, while being handsome and well
proportioned in general, he had lost his right hand,
though in an honourable way, in battle. This mutilation

caused him to be particularly ill-humoured and irritable because every new person he met had to be acquainted with the details of his misfortune, and so he preferred to go into hiding and to devote himself to reading and other studies, and once and for all not to have anything to do with society.

The existence of this young man did not remain unknown to her. He was to join them firstly in a small group, then in a larger one, then in the largest. She behaved more pleasantly towards him than towards anyone else; in particular she was able to make him realise the value of what he had lost by her officious obligingness, for she busied herself in making up the loss for him. At table he had to sit by her; she cut up his food, so that he only had to use the fork. If older, more highly ranking people took the place at her side from him, she paid attention to him across the whole table, and the hurrying servants had to perform the service that she was too far off to do. Eventually she encouraged him to write with his left hand; all his attempts at writing had to be addressed to her, and consequently, whether near or far, she was always in touch with him. The young man did not know what had happened to him, and really he began a new life from this time on.

One might perhaps think that such behaviour would displease her fiancé; but the opposite was the case. He thought highly of her for these efforts, and was all the more fully reassured about them since he was familiar with her exaggerated peculiarities which enabled her to reject anything that appeared in the least improper. She would jump around with anyone as it suited her fancy, and everybody was in danger of being pushed or dragged about by her at some time, or teased in some way; but nobody might allow himself anything comparable towards her in return, nobody might touch her casually, nobody might reply in the same spirit when she allowed herself liberties; and thus she restrained the others within the strictest propriety in their relationship with her, although she appeared to be on the point of overstepping the mark at any moment in her dealings with others.

Altogether one might have thought that she made it her principle to expose herself in equal measures to praise and blame, affection and repugnance. For whenever she attempted in various ways to win people over to her, she usually spoiled the effect again with her malicious tongue which spared no one. Thus whenever a visit was paid to someone in the neighbourhood, or she and her companions were received hospitably in some castle or house, she could not avoid making uninhibited comments on the way back which indicated how she was inclined to look at all human situations from the ridiculous side. Here were three brothers who, through politely waiting for one of them to be the first to get married, had been overtaken by old age; there was a small, young wife, with a tall, old husband; elsewhere again a cheerful little husband married to a clumsy giantess. In one house they stumbled over a child at every step; a second house did not seem properly full to her, even with a great assembly of people, because there were no children present. She thought that old husbands should get themselves buried without delay, so that someone in the house could at last have a good laugh again, since there were no lawful heirs. Young married couples should travel, because domesticity did not suit them at all. And just as she criticised people, she did the same with inanimate objects, whether buildings, furniture or table-requisites. Wall decorations of any kind aroused her in particular to witty comments. Gobelin tapestry or the latest style in wall-paper, the most venerable family portrait or the most frivolous modern copper-plate, all had to suffer and be pulled to pieces, as it were, by her mocking remarks, so that one might have wondered how it was that anything managed to survive within a radius of five miles.

There was not perhaps actual malice in this negative tendency of Luciane's; usually she would be egged on by selfish wilfulness; however, real bitterness had developed in her relationship to Ottilie. She looked down contemptuously at the dear child's quiet, steady activity, which was noticed and praised by everyone; and when conversation turned upon Ottilie's great interest in the gardens and hot-houses, she not only made fun of it, by appearing to be surprised that there was so little fruit or so few flowers to be seen, not allowing for the fact that they were living in the depths of winter, but she made a point from now on of fetching as much greenery as she could, branches and anything that was showing new leaf, and using it lavishly for daily decoration of the rooms and the table, until Ottilie and the gardener were not a little hurt to see their hopes for the coming year and perhaps for a longer period, destroyed.

She was just as reluctant to concede to Ottilie the quiet of her domestic supervision, where she could move about in an easy manner. Luciane insisted on Ottilie's coming on all the pleasure outings and skating expeditions, and joining in the balls which were organised in the neighbourhood; why should she be afraid of snow or cold or violent storms at night, as, after all, so many other people did not die from them; for although Ottilie went dressed in very simple fashion, she was still the most attractive woman or at least she seemed to be so to the men. A gentle attraction drew all the men to her, whether she was in the first or the last seat in the big assembly rooms; indeed, Luciane's fiancé himself often talked to her, and all the more as he desired her advice and co-operation in a matter which concerned him.

He had become more closely acquainted with the architect and had conversed with him a lot about historical matters in connection with his art collection and on other occasions too, particularly when viewing the chapel, and he had come to appreciate his talent. The Baron was young and rich; he was a collector and wanted to build; his enthusiasm as an amateur was lively, but his knowledge was weak; he believed he had found in the architect a man with whose help he could achieve more than one object at the same time. He had told his fiancé of this intention; she praised him because of it and was highly pleased with the suggestion, though possibly more because she might deprive Ottilie of this young man—for she thought she could observe something like affection for her on his part—than because she had been thinking of using his talent for her own ends. For although he had shown himself to be very active in her extempore festivities and had offered his various resources on this or that occasion, she nevertheless continued to believe that she knew better; and as her ideas were usually commonplace, all that was needed in order to execute them was the skill of a clever footman, which was just as effective as that of the most distinguished artist. If she was thinking of paying anyone a festive compliment on their birthday or on some other memorable day, her imagination could not rise above an altar for sacrificing on and a head, either of plaster of Paris or else a living one, for crowning with wreaths.

Ottilie was in a position to give Luciane's fiancé the most accurate information about the architect's present situation in the house. She knew that Charlotte had already earlier been looking for a position for him; if the company had not come, the young man would have departed as soon as the work on the chapel was finished, because all building was to stop, indeed had to, during the winter; and it was therefore very much to be desired that the skilful artist should be employed and helped along by a new patron.

The personal relationship between Ottilie and the architect was quite pure and straightforward. His pleasant and lively presence had occupied and pleased her like the proximity of an elder brother. Her emotions regarding him remained on the quiet, passionless level of blood relationship; for her heart had no more room for love, since it was completely filled with her love for Edward, and only the divinity which permeates all things could possess this heart jointly with him.

Meanwhile, the more deeply winter settled, the wilder the weather became and the more inaccessible the roads, the more attractive did it seem to spend the days as they shortened in such good company. After short ebb-tides a whole crowd flooded into the house periodically. Officers from fairly distant garrisons arrived, the educated ones to their own great advantage, the coarser ones to the discomfort of the company; there was also no lack of civilians, and quite unexpectedly the Count and Baroness came driving in together.

Their presence seemed to bring for the first time a real court-like atmosphere. The men of class and breeding surrounded the Count, and the women paid due justice to the Baroness. One did not have to wonder for long why they were together and looking so happy; for it was disclosed that the Count's wife had died and that a new marriage would be celebrated as soon as the proprieties allowed. Ottilie recalled that first visit and every word that had been spoken about marriage and divorce, union and separation, hope, expectation, deprivation and resignation. Both persons, who had at that time still been wholly without prospects of marriage, now stood before her so close to the happiness they hoped for, and an involuntary sigh escaped from her breast.

As soon as Luciane heard that the Count was fond of music she began to organise a concert; she wanted to be heard singing to a guitar. And so it was. She played the instrument by no means clumsily, and her voice was pleasant; but as far as the words were concerned, she could be no better understood than any other German beauty singing to a guitar. However, somebody assured the company that she had sung very expressively, and she could be satisfied with the loud applause. Only one strange piece of bad luck befell her on this occasion. Among the visitors was a poet whom she particularly hoped to interest in herself because she would have liked him to direct some songs towards herself, and in consequence this evening she sang mostly his own songs. Like everybody else, he was generally polite to her, but she had expected more. She had spoken to him about it a few times, but had heard nothing more from him until at last in her impatience she sent one of her courtiers to sound him as to whether he had not been delighted to hear his excellent poems so excellently sung. 'My poems?' he asked in astonishment. 'Excuse me, sir,' he added; 'I only heard vowels and not even all of those. However, it is my duty to show how indebted I am for such a well-meaning intention.' The tutor was silent and kept the matter dark. The other tried to withdraw from the affair by making a few pleasant compliments. Luciane dropped a rather obvious hint that she would like to have a piece of verse written specially for herself. If this had not been too unfriendly, he might have handed over to her the alphabet, so that she could imagine any adulatory poems she pleased and put it to any melody she liked. But she was not to escape from this incident without some injury to her feelings. A short while after she heard that he had written that very same evening a delightful poem to go with one of Ottilie's favourite melodies, and that the poem was more than mere politeness.

Like all people of her type, who always confuse what is advantageous to them and what is disadvantageous, Luciane now wanted to try her luck in recitation. Her memory was good, but, to put it bluntly, her execution was unintelligent and impetuous, and without feeling. She recited ballads, tales and anything else that customarily occurs in such declamations. At the same time she had acquired the unfortunate habit of accompanying her recitation with gestures, and in this way what is really epic and lyrical is confused—one cannot say united—in and unpleasant way with what is dramatic.

The Count, a discerning man, who very soon took in the nature of the company, its likings, enthusiasms and entertainment, gave Luciane, either fortunately or unfortunately, the idea of a new type of performance which was well suited to her personality. 'I see so many well proportioned persons here,' he said, 'who are certainly not lacking in the ability to imitate picturesque movements and postures. Can they by any chance not have attempted before now to depict real, well-known pictures? Such a form of tableau making, even though it requires a lot of troublesome arrangement, does on the other hand also provide undreamt-of attractions.'

Luciane quickly realised that she would be quite in her element here. Her fine proportions, her full figure, her regular but not insipid features, her light-brown plaits of hair and her slender neck were all as if already calculated for a portrait; and if she had known too that she looked more beautiful when she stood still than when she moved about, because in the latter case often a certain disagreeable, ungraceful element became perceptible, she would have given herself over with even greater zeal to these *tableaux vivants*.

There was now a search for copperplate reproductions of famous paintings; the first to be chosen was Van Dyck's Belisarius. A big, well-made, middle-aged man was to represent the sitting blind general, the architect was to be the warrior standing sadly and sympathetically by him, and in fact he did look rather like him. Half modestly Luciane had chosen for herself the part of the young woman in the background who is counting out into an open hand generous alms from a purse, while an old woman seems to be warning her against it, and explaining that she is doing too much. Another female figure, who really is giving alms, was not forgotten.

177

They occupied themselves very seriously with these and other pictures. The Count gave the architect a few hints about the type of arrangement that would be suitable, and the latter at once erected a stage for the purpose and looked after the necessary lighting. It was not until they had become deeply involved that they realised that such an undertaking would demand considerable expenditure and that many of their requirements could not be fulfilled in the country in midwinter. For this reason Luciane allowed almost all her wardrobe to be cut up, so that there would be no delays, to provide the various costumes which those artists had indicated arbitrarily enough.

The evening came, and the performance was given before a large company, arousing general applause. Solemn music heightened the sense of expectancy. The Belisarius picture provided the opening scene. The figures were so suitable, the colours so happily placed and the lighting so ingenious that one might well have believed that one was in another world, were it not that the presence of reality instead of appearance occasioned a kind of anxious feeling.

The curtain fell and was raised again more than once by request. A musical intermezzo entertained the audience whom one wished to surprise by a picture of a more exalted nature. It was Poussin's well-known representation of Ahasuerus and Esther. This time Luciane had calculated her effects better. She concentrated all her charm in the figure of the unconscious prostrate queen, and had cleverly picked out none but pretty and neat persons to act as the maidens surrounding and supporting her, though none of them could compare with herself at all. Ottilie was excluded from this tableau as from the others. They had chosen the most robust and handsome man of the party to represent the Zeus-like king on his golden throne, so that this tableau really achieved an incomparable perfection.

178

For their third they had chosen Terborch's so-called 'Paternal Admonition,' and who is not familiar with Wille's magnificent print of this painting! A noble, knightly father sits with one leg over the other and seems to be giving his daughter standing in front of him a talking-to. The latter, a magnificent figure in a white satin dress with abundant folds, is indeed only seen from behind, but her whole personality seems to indicate that she is making an effort to restrain herself. The father's face and gestures make it clear that the admonition is not vehement and humiliating; and as far as the mother is concerned, she appears to be concealing a slight embarrassment by looking into a glass of wine which she is just about to drink up.

On this occasion now Luciane was to appear in her greatest brilliance. Her plaits, the shape of her head and neck were exceptionally beautiful, and her figure, hardly discernible in women's modern classicist fashions, was dainty, slim and light and thus showed itself to extreme advantage in the older type of costume; and the architect had taken care to place the rich folds of white satin in the most artistic manner, so that without any question this living copy was far superior to the original painting, and it aroused delight generally. There was no end to the *encores*, and the wholly natural wish to see so beautiful a person, whom one had seen sufficiently from the rear, face to face as well, gained ground to such an extent that one impatient wag called out the words which are often written at the bottom of a page: 'Tournez s'il vous plaît,' and aroused general approval. The performers, however, recognised their advantage only too well and had grasped the meaning of these representations too clearly to let themselves yield to the general demand. The shamefaced looking daughter remained motionless, without betraying to the spectators her facial expression; the father remained seated in his admonitory posture, and the mother kept her nose and eyes fixed upon the

179

transparent glass where the quantity of the wine did
not diminish although she appeared to be drinking.
Why should we say yet more about the subsequent little
pieces, for which Dutch scenes from inn and market-
place had been chosen!

The Count and the Baroness departed, promising to
return in the first, happy weeks of their approaching
marriage, and Charlotte now hoped at the same time
to be rid of the rest of the company, after two months
which she had endured with difficulty. She was assured
of her daughter's happiness, once the girl had passed
through the first youthful restlessness of her engagement;
for her fiancé thought himself the happiest man in the
world. With his great wealth and moderate temperament
he seemed in a strange way to be flattered by the advantage of possessing a woman who could not but please
everyone. He had such a peculiar way of thinking of
everything in terms of his fiancée and of thinking of
himself only after this, that it disturbed him if a newcomer did not at once direct himself with his whole attention to her and sought a closer relationship with himself,
without troubling very much about her, as often
happened, especially in the case of older people, because
of his good qualities. Matters were soon settled with
regard to the architect. In the New Year the latter was
to follow him and spend the carnival season in the town,
where Luciane promised herself the greatest bliss from
the repetition of the so finely prepared tableaux and from
a hundred other things, all the more so as her aunt and
fiancé seemed to baulk at none of the expense which
would be necessary to her pleasure.

Now it was time to part, but this could not happen in
an ordinary manner. On one occasion there was some
rather loud joking to the effect that Charlotte's winter
supplies would soon be finished now; at this the good
man who had played the part of Belisarius and who was
certainly rich enough, carried away by Luciane's

charms, to which he had been paying homage so long now, cried out impulsively: 'Well, let's do things in the Polish manner! Come on now and finish up my supplies! And then we can go on to others in turn.' No sooner said than done: Luciane agreed. The next day they packed, and the crowd descended upon another estate. There too they had space enough, but less comfort and fewer amenities. Their way of life became increasingly rough and wild. *Battue* hunting expeditions in deep snow were arranged, and anything else of an uncomfortable nature that could be thought up. Women were not allowed to excuse themselves from these any more than men; and so they went hunting, riding, tobogganing and shouting from one estate to another, until they finally came near to the capital city, where news and reports about entertainment at court and in the town gave their imagination another turn and irresistibly drew Luciane and her entire entourage into another social circle, to which her aunt had already gone on in advance.

From Ottilie's Diary

In society everyone is esteemed at the value he puts on himself; but he has to make himself out to be something. Importunate people are tolerated more willingly than insignificant ones.

One can persuade a social circle to any measure, so long as it has no consequences.

We do not get to know people when they visit us; we must go to them to learn how things are with them.

I find it almost second nature that we find all sorts of faults with visitors, and that, after they have gone, we at once criticise them by no means in the kindest way; for we have the right, as it were, to measure them by our standards. Even sensible and fair-minded people do not restrain themselves in such cases from sharp comments.

On the other hand, if one has been at other people's houses and has seen them in their environment and habitual way of life, in their necessary and unavoidable circumstances, in their ways of reacting upon their circle or conforming to it, it would need stupidity and ill-will to find something ridiculous which in more than one sense should seem to us to be worthy of respect.

The aim of what we call refinement and good manners is to achieve something that can only be attained otherwise by force.

Social relations with women are the essence of good manners.

How can character, that which is the peculiarity of each individual, be reconciled with manners?

The individual characteristics should be emphasised, and this in particular can be achieved by good manners. Everyone wishes to have special qualities, but not if they are of an uncomfortable nature.

A soldier of breeding has the greatest advantages in society, as in life generally.

Crude military folk do at least remain in character, and as for the most part good nature lies concealed behind their strength, one can get on with them in case of need.

Nobody is more boring than an awkward civilian. One is entitled to expect refinement from such a man, as he does not have to occupy himself with what is gross.

When we are living with people who have a delicate feeling for what is proper, we become anxious on their account if anything improper occurs. Consequently I always feel for and with Charlotte when anybody rocks backwards and forwards on a chair, because she finds that unbearable.

Nobody would come into a boudoir wearing glasses if he knew that we women immediately lose all wish to look at him and converse with him.

Familiarity in the place of respect is always ridiculous. No one would put his hat down as soon as he had made his bow of greeting, if he knew how comic that looks.

There is no outward mark of politeness that does not have a deep ethical basis. The right education would be that which transmitted both the outward mark and the ethical basis at once.

Behaviour is a mirror in which everyone shows his image.

There is a politeness of the heart, related to love. It gives rise to the easiest form of politeness of outward behaviour.

Voluntary dependence is the most delightful state, and how would it be possible without love?

We are never further from our wishes than when we imagine we possess what we wish for.

Nobody is more a slave than the man who imagines himself to be free without being so.

A man has only to declare himself free, and he feels himself at that moment to be limited. If he ventures to declare himself limited, he feels free.

There is no salvation against the great advantages of another person except love.

There is something terrible about an excellent man of whom stupid people are proud.

The valet has no hero, they say. But that is merely because the hero can only be appreciated by a hero. But the valet will presumably be able to esteem someone of his own sort.

There is no greater consolation for mediocrity than that genius is not immortal.

The greatest men are always linked to their century by a trait of weakness.

One usually takes people for more dangerous than they are.

Fools and clever people are equally harmless. It is the half-fools and half-wise who are the most dangerous.

One cannot evade the world more effectively than by art, nor can one link oneself to the world more effectively, than by art.

We need the artist, even in the moments of greatest happiness and greatest trouble.

Art is concerned with what is difficult and good.

The sight of a difficult task accomplished lightly gives us the sense of the impossible.

Difficulties increase the nearer one comes to the goal.

Sowing is not so troublesome as reaping.

CHAPTER VI

THE great disturbance which this visit caused Charlotte was compensated for her by the fact that she had learnt to understand her daughter fully, her knowledge of the world being a great help to her in this. It was not the first time that she encountered so strange a character, although such a one had never previously appeared to her at this level. And yet she knew from experience that such persons, when moulded by life, by many kinds of happenings and by relationship with their parents, can attain a very pleasant and amiable maturity when their selfishness is tempered and their enthusiastic activities receive a definite direction.

Charlotte allowed herself as a mother to tolerate rather more readily an exhibition of behaviour which was perhaps unpleasant to others more than to herself, since it is fitting for parents to hope, whereas strangers only wish to enjoy or at least not to be bothered.

Charlotte was, however, to receive a blow in a peculiar and unexpected manner after her daughter's departure, since the latter had left behind her a bad reputation both by what was culpable in her behaviour and by what one might have been able to regard as praiseworthy about it. Luciane seemed to have made it a rule not only to rejoice with the merry but also to mourn with the sad and, fully to exercise the spirit of contradiction, on occasions to annoy the merry and to cheer up the sad. In every family where she came she enquired about the sick and the weak, who could not appear in company. She visited them in their rooms, played the doctor and pressed upon them all sorts of strong physic from her travelling medicine-chest which she always had with her in her carriage; and such cures, as may be imagined, succeeded or failed as chance would have it.

She was quite ruthless in this kind of philanthropy and would not let herself be dissuaded, as she was firmly convinced that she was acting admirably. But there was one experiment which went wrong from the moral point of view, and it was this that gave Charlotte a lot of trouble because it had consequences and everyone came to talk about it. It was not until after Luciane's departure that she heard about it; Ottilie, who had happened to be present at that gathering, had to give her a detailed account of it.

One of the daughters of a highly respected family had had the misfortune to be responsible for the death of one of her younger brothers and had not been able to console herself about it or to regain composure. She lived in her room quietly and busily occupied, and could only bear the sight even of her own relations if they came to her singly; for she suspected at once, if several came together, that they were discussing her and her condition amongst themselves. She would talk sensibly to each one on his own and converse for hours with him.

Luciane had heard about this and had immediately made up her mind on the quiet that she would perform a miracle, as it were, when she came into the house, and restore the girl to society. She behaved herself more carefully than usual in this connection, arranged to be introduced to the sick person on her own and to gain her confidence by means of music, as far as could be judged. It was only at the end that she made a mistake: for, just because she wanted to arouse attention, she brought the pale, beautiful child one evening into the gay, brilliant assembly, thinking that she had prepared her sufficiently; and perhaps this would have succeeded, had not the company itself behaved clumsily in its curiosity and apprehension, crowding round the sick girl, then avoiding her and making her confused and excited by whispering and putting their heads together. The highly strung girl could not bear this. She fled, emitting terrible cries which seemed to be expressive of some sort of terror of something monstrous that was thrusting itself on her. The company scattered in fright in all directions, and Ottilie was one of those who brought the girl back to her room in a state of complete collapse.

Meanwhile Luciane had strongly reprimanded the company in her own way, without thinking in the least that she alone was responsible and without letting herself be deflected by this failure and by others from her activity.

After this the sick girl's condition had become more serious, indeed the malady had become so intensified that the parents could not keep the poor child at home, but had to transfer her to a public institution. All Charlotte could do was to mitigate a little the grief that her daughter had occasioned by behaving with particular consideration to that family. The business had made a deep impression on Ottilie; she was all the sorrier for the poor girl since she was convinced, as she did not deny to Charlotte, that the sick girl would certainly have been capable of being cured if she had been treated with consistency.

It happened also that a little misunderstanding came to be discussed (since people do usually talk more about unpleasant happenings in the past than pleasant ones) that had arisen between Ottilie and the architect on that evening when he had been unwilling to show his collection, although she had requested him in so friendly a manner. This refusal had remained fixed in her mind, she herself did not know why. Her feelings were justified; for a young man like the architect should not refuse any request that a girl like Ottilie can make. But after hearing her occasional gentle reproaches, he brought forward reasonably acceptable excuses.

'If you knew how crudely even educated people react towards the most precious works of art, you would pardon me for not wishing to show mine to the crowd,' he said. 'None of them knows how to hold a medallion at the edges; they finger the most beautiful impression, the purest base, and let the rarest specimen slide between thumb and index-finger as if this were the way to examine artistic productions. Without thinking that a large piece of paper must be grasped in two hands, they reach out one hand for some invaluable engraving or irreplaceable sketch like an arrogant politician seizing a newspaper and giving his judgement in advance on world affairs by the way he crumples up the paper. It doesn't occur to anybody that it only wants twenty people one after another to treat a work of art in this way and the twenty-first wouldn't have much left to look at.'

'Haven't I too sometimes put you in such a predicament?' Ottilie asked. 'Perhaps I have occasionally damaged your treasures without realising it.'

'Never,' the architect replied, 'never! You couldn't do such a thing; you have an instinct for what is fitting.'

'In any case,' Ottilie added, 'it wouldn't be a bad idea to insert in the future a really detailed chapter about how to behave when looking at art collections and museums into the books on etiquette, after the chapters on how to eat and drink in society.'

'There's no doubt that museum custodians as well as private collectors would then be happier to show their precious things.'

Ottilie had forgiven him long ago: but as he seemed to take the reproach very much to heart and repeatedly emphasised that he really did like showing his things and being active for his friends, she felt that she had hurt his sensitive spirit and that she was in his debt.

Therefore when he made a request to her as a consequence of this conversation, she felt that she could not refuse it out of hand, although her own feelings in the matter were such that she did not see how she could grant him what he wished for.

It was like this. He had been extremely hurt that Luciane's jealousy had excluded Ottilie from the tableau; he had likewise noticed with regret that Charlotte had only been able to be present at these highlights of the social entertainment for part of the time, as she had not been feeling well. He did not want to leave now without showing his gratitude in one way by arranging a much finer tableau than the previous ones as a token of respect to the one lady and as an entertainment to the other. Perhaps a further secret motive played a part without his realising it: it was so difficult for him to leave this house and family, indeed he did not know how he could part from Ottilie, for the quiet, friendly glances from her eyes had been almost his only food and drink lately.

Christmas was approaching, and it occurred to him all at once that in fact those pictorial representations with living figures had originated in the nativity play, that pious performance which is devoted during this holy season to the divine mother and child and the way they are worshipped in their apparent lowliness firstly by the shepherds and then by the kings.

He had fully thought out how such a picture could be made possible. A fine, healthy baby boy was found; there could be no shortage of shepherds and shepherdesses; but the idea could not be carried out without Ottilie. The young man had elevated her in his mind to the part of Mother of God, and if she were to refuse, he felt without doubt that the undertaking would have to be dropped. Ottilie was half embarrassed at his proposal, and referred him to Charlotte. The latter gladly gave him permission and she also succeeded in a friendly

189

way in overcoming Ottilie's reluctance to assume that holy figure. The architect worked day and night so that nothing should be missing on Christmas Eve.

Day and night it was, literally. In any case he had few needs, and the presence of Ottilie seemed to suffice him in place of all refreshment; working for her, it was as if he needed no sleep, and doing things on her behalf, as if he needed no food. Consequently everything was ready and prepared for the solemn evening hour. He had succeeded in assembling some sonorous wind instruments to form an introduction and to evoke the desired atmosphere. When the curtain was raised, Charlotte was really surprised. The picture presented to her had been so often repeated throughout the world that one could scarcely expect to have a new impression from it. But in this case reality as a picture had particular advantages. The whole room was closer to night than to twilight in its lighting, and yet there was nothing obscure in the details of the surroundings. The artist had been able to use a clever lighting device to realise the insurpassable idea of letting all the light come from the child; the lighting was concealed by the shadowy figures in the foreground who were only lit up by accidental lights. There were many girls and boys standing round, their fresh faces sharply lit up from beneath.

Fortunately the child had fallen asleep in the most attractive position, so that nothing disturbed one's observation when one's glances lingered upon the figure of the assumed mother, who with boundless grace had lifted a veil in order to reveal the hidden treasure. The picture seemed to be held fast and petrified at this moment. The surrounding people, physically dazzled and surprised in mind, seemed to have been making a move to turn away their eyes and then to be blinking in that direction with curiosity and happiness, showing surprise and pleasure rather than admiration and reverence, although this last was not forgotten and its expression had been transferred to some of the older figures of the tableau.

But Ottilie's figure, gestures, the expression of her face and glance of her eyes surpassed anything that a painter has ever depicted. A sensitive connoisseur, seeing this vision, would have become anxious lest something should move; he would have stood there troubled, wondering if anything could ever give so much pleasure again. The architect alone, looking down as a tall thin shepherd from the side at the kneeling figures, certainly had the greatest pleasure from it, although he was not in precisely the best position. And who shall describe also the mien of the newly created queen of heaven? Purest humility and the most attractive feeling of modesty in face of a great honour that she felt she had not deserved, and in face of a piece of luck that seemed to her to be incomprehensible and immeasurable, formed themselves in her features, which were expressive of her own feelings as well as of her conception of the part she was playing.

The beautiful tableau pleased Charlotte, though it was chiefly Ottilie who affected her. Her eyes streamed with tears, and she imagined in the most lively fashion how she was hoping soon to have a similar dear child of her own to nurse.

The curtain was lowered, partly to give some relief to the players and partly to introduce some change in what was being shown. The artist had planned to transform the first picture, of lowliness by night, into a picture of daylight and glory, and with this in view he had prepared a great increase of illumination which in the meantime was being lit.

Up to now Ottilie in her half-theatrical pose had been greatly relieved that apart from Charlotte and some members of the household nobody had seen this pious artistic mummery. She was therefore somewhat taken aback to hear in the interval that a stranger had arrived and that he had been welcomed in a friendly manner by

Charlotte in the hall. No one could tell her who it was. She made no objection, in order not to cause any disturbance. Lights and lamps were burning, and a boundless brightness surrounded her. The curtain went up, and for the audience it was a surprising view: the whole scene was full of light, and in place of the shadow, now completely gone, there were left only colours which through their clever selection produced an effect of sweet moderation. Looking in front of her from below her long eyelashes, Ottilie noticed a man sitting near Charlotte. She did not recognise him, but she believed she could hear the voice of the assistant from the boarding-school. A strange feeling took hold of her. How much had happened since she last heard the voice of this faithful teacher! Like forked lightning the succession of her joys and sorrows flashed quickly before her mind's eye, impelling her to ask: 'May I admit and confess everything to him? And how little worthy I am to appear before him in this holy shape, and how strange it must seem to him to see me, whom he has only seen in natural shape, in a disguise!' With incomparable rapidity feeling and thought reacted one against the other within her. Her heartbeats came with difficulty, her eyes filled with tears, while she forced herself to keep on appearing as a rigid tableau; and how happy she was when the boy started to move and the artist saw himself compelled to give the sign to lower the curtain again!

If the distressing feeling of not being able to go to greet a good friend had been added during these last moments to Ottilie's other emotions, she now felt an even greater embarrassment. Should she move towards him clad in this strange costume and jewellery? Should she change? She did not hesitate, but took the latter course and tried meanwhile to pull herself together and become calmer, and only succeeded in regaining harmony within when she could at last greet the newcomer dressed in her usual clothes.

CHAPTER VII

In that the architect wished what was most agreeable
to his hostess, it was pleasant for him to know that they
had the company of the estimable assistant now that he
himself finally had to leave: but in that he related their
favour to himself, he felt it somewhat distressing to see
himself replaced so soon, and, as his modesty might
conceive it, so well and so completely. He had still been
hesitating, though now he felt an urge to be away; for he
did not wish to experience in the present what he would
have to endure after he had departed.

He was greatly cheered in his half-melancholy feelings
when the ladies gave him on his departure another present, a waistcoat which for some time he had seen them
both engaged in knitting, with a quiet envy of the
unknown happy man whose property it would eventually be. Such a gift is the pleasantest that an affectionate, admiring man may receive; for when he thinks
of the tireless play of lovely fingers that have gone to
make it, he cannot help flattering himself that the heart
also will surely not have remained wholly indifferent
during such a long continuous piece of work.

The ladies had a new man to look after; they were
favourably inclined towards him, and he was to feel
comfortable as their guest. The female sex cherish a
special, inward and constant loyalty, which nothing
on earth will make them desert; in outer, social relations,
on the other hand, they are glad to let themselves be
easily swayed by the man who happens to be occupying
them at the moment; and so by refusal and amenability,

obstinacy and pliancy, it is they who really are in command, and in civilised society no man dares to withdraw from this régime.

The architect had practised and demonstrated his talents, more or less as it suited his own fancy, for the entertainment and the use of the ladies, and the occupations and amusements of the household had been arranged according to these plans and purposes; but through the presence of the assistant a different way of life soon asserted itself. His great talent was his ability to speak well and treat in his discourse human problems, particularly in relation to the education of the young. And thus a quite perceptible contrast to their previous manner of life developed, the more so since the assistant did not wholly approve of the way they had been spending so much of their time.

He said nothing at all about the *tableau vivant* which greeted him on his arrival. But when the ladies took pleasure in showing him the church and chapel and all that was concerned with it, he could not conceal his own views and opinions about it. 'As far as I am concerned,' he said, 'I'm not at all happy about the closeness, indeed the combination, of what is sacred with what is sensuous, nor that certain special rooms have to be dedicated, consecrated and adorned before a feeling of piety can be aroused and cherished. Even the most everyday environment should not be able to disturb in us the feeling of the divine which can accompany us everywhere and hallow every place into a temple. I like to see a family service held in the room where it is usual to eat, to assemble for social activities or to amuse oneself with games and dancing. The highest, most excellent quality of man is without form, and we should be cautious not to depict it in any other way than as a noble deed.'

Charlotte, who already knew his opinions in general and learnt yet more about them in a short time, directed him at once to activity in his own line by ordering the garden-lads, who had been inspected by the architect before his departure, to march along in the large assembly-room, since they looked very well in their cheerful, neat uniforms, with their disciplined movements and natural and lively dispositions. The assistant examined them in his own way, and through various queries and turns of phrase he soon discovered the temperament and capacity of the children, and, without this being apparent, he had instructed and brought them on in less than an hour in a really significant way.

'But how do you do it?' Charlotte said as the boys filed out. 'I listened very attentively; it was only familiar things that came out, and yet I wouldn't know how to set about making them talk in such a short time, with such a lot of cross-talk and sustained argument too.'

'Perhaps one should make a secret out of the advantageous aspects of one's craft,' the assistant replied. 'But I can't keep from you the very simple maxim which enables us to do this and much more as well. Take some subject, material, or idea, call it what you will; hold on to it really firmly; make it really clear to yourself in all its parts, and then it will be easy for you to find out in conversation with a group of children how far they have already developed, and what still has to be stimulated in them or passed on to them. However disconnected and rambling the answers to your questions may be, so long as your next questions pull mind and sense together again and refuse to move from your point of view, the children will eventually have to think and convince themselves only about what the teacher wants them to, and in the way he wants them to. A teacher's greatest mistake is to let himself be led astray by his pupils, and not to know how to keep to the point that he is making at the moment. You try it soon, and you will find it very interesting.'

'How nice!' Charlotte said; 'good educational method is therefore just the opposite of good practical living.

In society one should never labour a point, whereas in teaching the first commandment would be to fight against all distraction.'

'Variety without distraction would be the finest motto for the class-room and for life, if only this balance could be easily maintained!' the assistant said, and wanted to continue further, when Charlotte called to him to look at the boys once more, as their gay procession was just moving across the courtyard. He indicated his satisfaction that the children were made to wear uniform. 'Men should wear uniform from an early age,' he said, 'because they must get used to acting together, losing themselves amongst people of their own type, obeying orders in the mass and working towards a whole. What is more, every kind of uniform encourages a military cast of mind and more precise and smart behaviour, and in any case all boys are born soldiers; one has only to look at their fighting and quarrelling games, and the way they like to attack and climb.'

'So you won't be blaming me on the other hand for not dressing my girls in uniform,' Ottilie put in. 'When I bring them before you, I am hoping to entertain you by a variegated mixture in their clothing.'

'I very much approve,' he replied. 'Women should be dressed in complete variety, each in her own way so that each one learns to feel what really looks well on her and is appropriate to her. A more important reason is that they are destined to be and to act alone all their lives.'

'That seems very paradoxical to me,' Charlotte said; 'after all we hardly ever live just for ourselves.'

'Oh, yes!' the assistant answered, 'certainly, as far as other women are concerned. If we look at a woman as lover fiancée, wife, housewife, and mother, she is always isolated, she is always alone and likes to be so. Yes, even a vain woman is in the same position. Each female temperament excludes another woman, by its very nature; for each woman is expected to do everything that is required of the whole sex. It is different with men. A man needs another man; if there were no other men, he would have to create one; a woman could live to eternity without ever thinking of creating others of her own type.'

'If something true is expressed in an odd way, what is odd eventually seems to be true as well,' Charlotte said. 'We should like to pick out the best from what you have said, and hold together as women among women, and act together too, in order not to concede too great advantages to the men. Indeed, you won't take it amiss if we can't help feeling all the more keenly a certain malicious pleasure when the gentlemen too fail to get on particularly well together.'

The sensible man now examined with great care the method by which Ottilie managed her little pupils and showed his decided approval on this account. 'You very rightly instruct your charges only as far as immediate practical usefulness demands,' he said. 'Cleanliness makes children take pleasure and pride in themselves, and it is more than half the battle if they are induced to carry out what they have to do with cheerfulness and self-confidence.'

Furthermore he was greatly satisfied to find that nothing had been done for the sake of appearance and in a superficial manner, but that everything had been carried out with sincere motive and with indispensable needs in view. 'How few words are needed to sum up the whole business of education, if anyone had ears to hear!' he cried.

'Wouldn't you like to try to do it with me now?' Ottilie said in a friendly tone.

'Gladly,' he replied; 'only you mustn't give me away. Boys should be educated to be servants, and girls to be mothers, then all will be well.'

'Mothers!' Ottilie added. 'Women might let that pass,

since, if they can't be mothers, they have to resign themselves to being attendants of some kind; but certainly our young men would think themselves far too good for servants, for it is easy to see that every man thinks he is more capable to command.'

'That is why we must conceal it from them,' the assistant said. 'We flatter our way into life, but life doesn't flatter us. How many people are willing to concede voluntarily what they are forced finally to do? But let us drop these observations which don't concern us here!

'I consider you fortunate that you can apply right methods with your pupils. If your tiniest girls carry dolls around and patch a few rags together for them, while the older ones look after their younger sisters and the family serves and helps itself and its members, the further step into adult life is not a great one, and a girl of this type will find with her husband what she left behind with her parents.

'But the task is very complex among educated classes. We have to have consideration for higher, more delicate, and more subtle relationships, ones that involve a wider social sphere too. We others have therefore to educate our pupils in an outward direction; it is necessary, it is indispensable and very proper not to overstep the mark in the process; for when we think we are preparing children for a wider circle, we can easily drive them into immeasurable spheres without keeping before us what are really the requirements of their inner nature. This is the task which, more or less, is being accomplished or miscarried by educationists.

'I am worried about much that we provide our girls with in the school, because experience tells me how little use it will be to them in the future. What is not immediately discarded and consigned to oblivion, as soon as a woman finds herself in the position of wife and mother!

'Still, I can't deny myself the pious wish, now that I

have dedicated myself to this work, that I may succeed one day, together with a faithful companion, in bringing out in my pupils what they need when they take the step of moving over into the sphere of their own activity and independence; I should like to be able to say that their education, in this sense, is finished. Of course another education always links on with the first, and it is brought out almost every year of our lives, if not by ourselves, then nevertheless by circumstances.'

How true Ottilie found this remark! How she herself had been educated during the previous year by an unsuspected passion! What fresh trials did she not see looming ahead, even when she only looked to the immediate future!

The young man had not mentioned a companion, a wife, without deliberate purpose; for in spite of all his modesty he could not forgo hinting at his intentions in an indirect way; he had in fact been impelled by various circumstances and incidents to take a few steps during his visit to bring him nearer his goal.

The headmistress of the boarding-school was already advancing in years; for a long time now she had been looking round among her colleagues for someone who would come into partnership with her and had finally made the offer to the assistant whom she had every reason to trust, that he should continue to direct the school with her, to be active in it as if it were his own establishment and to be her heir and the sole owner of the institution after her death. The main problem here seemed to be for him to find a suitable wife. He had Ottilie in secret before his eyes and in his heart; but there were various doubts that had been raised in his mind, which, however, had been counterbalanced by favourable events. Luciane had left the boarding-school, and Ottilie could return there more freely; it was true that something of the affair with Edward had been rumoured, but this matter, like other similar episodes, could be passed over with indifference, and even this event could contribute to Ottilie's return. However, nothing would have been decided and no steps would have been taken, had not an unexpected visit given a particular impetus here, for the appearance of strong personalities can never remain without consequences in any circle.

The Count and the Baroness, who so often found themselves being asked about the merits of various schools, since almost everyone is in a quandary about the education of his children, had made up their minds to get to know this school in particular, about which they had heard so many good reports, and in their new circumstances they were now in a position to make such an investigation together. The Baroness, however, had something else in mind as well. When she had last stayed with Charlotte, she had had a full discussion with her about everything relating to Edward and Ottilie. She repeatedly insisted that Ottilie must be sent away. She tried to encourage Charlotte to this, for the latter was still afraid of Edward's threats. They discussed the various solutions, and also mentioned the assistant's liking for Ottilie while discussing the school, and the Baroness made up her mind all the more firmly to make the visit she had planned.

She came, met the assistant, inspected the school and talked about Ottilie. The Count himself liked to talk about her, having got to know her more closely during his most recent visit. She had approached him, indeed, had been attracted to him, because she believed that his substantial and thoughtful conversation would cause her to perceive and become acquainted with things that had hitherto remained quite unknown to her. And while being with Edward had made her forget the world, the Count's presence seemed to make the world desirable for the first time. All attraction is mutual. The Count felt a liking for Ottilie, so that he liked to look on her as his daughter. Here Ottilie was in the Baroness' way for a second time, and to a greater degree than the first time. Who knows what the Baroness would have undertaken against Ottilie at a time when she had been more impetuous in her passions! Now it was sufficient for her if she could make Ottilie less harmful to wives by getting her married off.

She therefore cleverly encouraged the assistant in a gentle but effective way to arrange a little visit to the castle so that he could hasten the accomplishment of his plans and desires, of which he made no secret from the lady.

It was therefore with the headmistress' full support that he undertook the journey, cherishing the fondest hopes within him. He knew that Ottilie was not unfavourably disposed towards him; and if there was some inequality of social rank between them, this would easily be overcome, the attitude of the time being what it was. The Baroness had also given him to understand that Ottilie would always remain a poor girl. Being related to a rich family, it was said, could help nobody; for even with the largest fortune one would feel conscience-stricken at depriving those who were more closely related and therefore seemed to have a greater right to a property of any considerable sum. And certainly it is strange that people seldom make use of the great privilege of disposing of their possessions after their death to the advantage of their favourites, but, apparently out of respect for tradition, only leave their wealth to those who would have the property even if no will had been made.

The assistant's mood as he was on the journey made him feel that he and Ottilie were wholly equal. A good reception made him even more hopeful. It is true he found that Ottilie was not so open with him as previously; but at the same time she was more adult, more refined and, if you like, more generally outgoing than when he had known her before. He was entrusted with insight into much that was particularly related to his profession. But whenever he wanted to approach his own purpose, he was held back by a certain inner shyness.

Once, however, Charlotte gave him an opportunity by saying to him in Ottilie's presence: 'Now you've pretty well examined everything that is going on in my circle; what do you think of Ottilie? You may say what you feel while Ottilie is here, I'm sure.'

The assistant then described with a great deal of discernment and in a quiet manner how he found Ottilie greatly changed, and to her advantage, in her freer manner, her easier approach, and her greater understanding of worldly matters which showed itself more in her actions than in her words; but he believed all the same that it might be to her advantage to return to the boarding-school for a time in order to acquire in a proper sequence and a thorough and permanent manner knowledge which the world passes on fragmentarily, thus causing confusion rather than satisfaction, indeed this knowledge often only comes too late. He did not want the matter to be delayed, he said; Ottilie herself would best know how she had previously been torn away from a planned series of lectures.

Ottilie could not deny this; but she could not admit what she felt on hearing these words, because she scarcely knew how to interpret them in relationship to her own circumstances. There seemed to her to be nothing in the world that was without meaning, when she thought of the man she loved, and she did not understand how there could be meaning of any sort without him.

Charlotte replied to this offer with sensible and friendly words. She said that she and Ottilie had for a long time both wanted Ottilie to return to school. The only thing was that the presence of so dear a friend and helper was indispensable at the moment; but later on she would not raise any objections, if it remained Ottilie's wish to go back there again for a certain time to finish what she had begun and to acquire a complete understanding of courses that had been interrupted.

The assistant was very pleased to hear of this offer; Ottilie could not say anything against it, although she shuddered at the thought of it. Charlotte, on the other hand, was playing for time; she hoped that Edward would meanwhile be back again as a happy father, and then, she was convinced, everything would be all right and Ottilie too would be looked after in one way or another.

After an important conversation which has given all the participants something to think about, a certain pause usually follows which looks like general embarrassment. They walked up and down the room, the assistant browsed through some books and eventually came upon the folio volume which had been lying about since Luciane's visit. When he saw that there were only monkeys in it, he at once slammed it to again. For all that, this incident may have given rise to a conversation, the traces of which we find in Ottilie's diary.

From Ottilie's Diary

How can anyone bring himself to make such careful pictures of horrid monkeys! One is lowering oneself to look on them merely as animals; but one becomes really more malicious when one lets oneself be lured into identifying acquaintances in this disguise.

Altogether, there is a certain perversity in willingly spending one's time on caricatures and grotesques. I am grateful to our good assistant that I have not been tormented with natural history; I could never take kindly to the worms and beetles.

This time he admitted to me that he felt the same way about it. 'We ought to know nothing about nature except what is around us and is directly alive. We have a true relationship with the trees that blossom, grow green and bear fruit around us, with every bush we pass by, and with every blade of grass that we walk over; they are our real compatriots. The birds that hop to and fro on our branches and sing in our foliage belong to us; they converse with us from our youth onwards and we learn to understand their language. We should ask whether every strange creature, when torn from its own environment, does not make a certain anxious impression on us which is only blunted by usage. A certain gay and noisy type of life is needed to make monkeys, parrots and coloured people tolerable around us.'

Sometimes, when I have experienced an inquisitive urge for such exotic things, I have been envious of the traveller who can see such wonders in living, everyday contact with other marvels. But he too becomes a different type of person. No one can walk unpunished among palm-trees, and one's opinions must surely change in a country where elephants and tigers are at home.

Only the scientific investigator of nature is worthy of respect, the man who is able to describe and depict what is most strange and exotic in its very own element, its locality and its surroundings. How glad I should be if I could only once hear Humboldt relating his findings!

A natural-history cabinet can seem to us like an Egyptian tomb, where the various animal and plant idols are kept embalmed. It may be proper for a priestly caste to concern itself with such things in secret semi-obscurity; but they should not find a way into general education, all the less so, since nearer and more worthy subjects can easily be pushed to one side as a result.

A teacher who can arouse our feelings by one single good deed or one single good poem, is doing more than one who passes on to us whole sequences of inferior natural creatures by appearance and name; for the whole result of it is something that we can know already, that the human countenance most excellently and uniquely bears the image of divinity.

Let the individual be free to occupy himself with what attracts and pleases him and seems useful to him; but the proper study of mankind is man.

CHAPTER VIII

THERE are few people who are capable of occupying themselves with events that have recently happened. Either the present holds us forcibly, or we are lost in the past and seek to recall and restore what has been wholly lost, whatever it may have been. Even in great and wealthy families, which owe much to their forebears, it is usual to think more of the grandfather than the father.

Our assistant was aroused to such thoughts on one of those beautiful days when parting winter habitually dissembles spring, while he had been walking through the big old castle garden, admiring the tall avenues of lime-trees and the formal gardens that were the work of Edward's father. They had flourished excellently according to the wishes of him who had planted them, and now that they were ready for the first time to be appreciated and enjoyed, nobody spoke of them any more; they were hardly visited, and the household had turned its fancy and its expenditure to another direction, out into the open spaces.

On his return he made this remark to Charlotte, who took it up not unfavourably. 'As life pulls us along, we believe that we are acting of our own volition and that we are choosing our activity and our pleasures,' she said, 'but indeed, when we look at it more closely, they are only the plans and inclinations of the time, which we are compelled to carry out too.'

'Certainly,' the assistant said: 'and who can resist the current of his environment? Time moves on and with it attitudes, opinions, prejudices and fancies. If a son's

youth happens to coincide with the period of transition,
you can be sure that he will have nothing in common
with his father. If the father lived in a period when one
took pleasure in acquiring things, in securing, limiting
and restricting this property and in confirming one's
pleasure in being cut off from the world, you may be
sure that the son will try to widen out, communicate and
expand himself and to reveal what is locked up.'

'Whole periods resemble this father and son whom you
describe,' Charlotte added. 'We can scarcely conceive of
those circumstances where every little town had to have
its walls and moats, where every country-seat was still
being built in the midst of a swamp and the meanest of
castles were only accesssible by means of a drawbridge.
Even fairly large towns are now dismantling their forti-
fications, the moats even of princely castles are being
filled in, towns only form large patches, and when we see
that on our travels, we should believe that world peace
has been established and that the golden age is at hand.
Nobody feels comfortable in a garden unless it looks
like open country; nothing in it should remind us of art
and compulsion; we want to draw breath in full, uncon-
ditional freedom. Can you then understand, my friend,
that one could turn back from this state to another, the
previous state?'

'Why not?' the assistant replied; 'every state has its
difficulties, the restricted as well as the uninhibited one.
The latter takes abundance for granted and leads to
extravagant expenditure. Let us confine ourselves to
your example, which is striking enough. As soon as there
is a shortage, self-restriction is imposed once more.
People who are compelled to make use of their land once
more build walls round their gardens in order to ensure
themselves of their produce. This gradually results in a
new view of things. The utilitarian once more gains the
upper hand, and even the large owner comes finally to
believe that he must make use of everything. Believe

me, it is possible that your son will neglect all the park grounds and retire again behind the serious walls and below the high lime-trees of his grandfather.'

Charlotte was secretly pleased to hear a son prophesied for her, and therefore pardoned the assistant his somewhat unfriendly prophecy about what might happen one day to her dear, lovely park. She therefore added in quite a friendly manner: 'Neither of us is as yet old enough to have experienced such conflicts more than once; but when we think back to our early youth and remember what we heard older people complaining about, taking consideration of countries and towns as well, there's not much to object to in the remark. But oughtn't we to do something to counteract this natural process, so that father and son, parents and children can be brought into agreement? You have been so kind as to predict for me a boy; but will he have to grow up in conflict with his father, and destroy what his parents have built, instead of completing and perfecting it, as he can do if he continues in their spirit?'

'But there is a sensible way of preventing this,' the assistant added, 'though it is one that is seldom used by people. The father should raise his son to the level of joint-ownership, let him be a partner in building and planting operations and allow him, as he allows himself, a certain amount of harmless arbitrariness. One activity can be woven into another, but not stuck on to it like a patch. A young shoot can be easily and gladly joined to an old branch, whereas a grown branch can no longer be joined to it.'

The assistant was pleased that he had chanced to say something pleasant to Charlotte just at the time when he would have to leave and that he had thus assured himself of her goodwill once more. He had been away from home too long already; but he could only make up his mind to return when he had become fully convinced that he would first have to let Charlotte's approaching time of childbirth pass before he could hope for any decision relating to Ottilie. He therefore accepted the circumstances and returned to the headmistress with his prospects and hopes.

Charlotte's confinement drew near. She kept more in her own rooms. The women who had collected around her were her intimate company. Ottilie looked after the household, while scarcely daring to think what she was doing. She had become fully resigned; she wished to continue to be as serviceable as she could to Charlotte, the child and Edward; but she did not see how it could be possible. Nothing could save her from complete confusion except the daily performance of her duty.

A son was happily born, and the women all maintained that he was the image of his father. Only Ottilie could not agree with this in her heart when she congratulated the mother and warmly welcomed the infant. Charlotte had already been highly sensitive to her husband's absence during the arrangements concerning her daughter's coming marriage; now the father was to be missing from his son's birth as well; he was not to decide the name which the child would be known by in future.

The first of all the friends to come with his congratulations was Mittler, who had made special arrangements so that he should at once receive news of this happening. He appeared, and in a cheerful mood too. He scarcely hid his triumph in Ottilie's presence and was quite outspoken about it to Charlotte; he dismissed all worries and waved aside all momentary obstacles. The christening was not to be postponed long. The old priest, with one foot in the grave already, should bind together past and future by his blessing; the child was to be called Otto; he could have no other name but that of father and friend.

It needed Mittler's decided importunity to overcome the hundredfold objections, the arguing, hesitating, faltering, knowing better or knowing differently, vacillating, believing and changing belief, since what usually happens on such occasions is that new misgivings keep on arising again when the old ones have been allayed, and, when one is trying to take everything into consideration, it always happens that some factors are not handled rightly.

Mittler undertook to make all the announcements of the birth and the arrangements for visiting godparents; all the letters were to be prepared at once, for he was particularly concerned about announcing an event which he considered so fortunate and significant for the family to the rest of the world, which included some people of malicious and gossiping intent. And indeed the earlier impassioned episodes had not escaped the public which in any case is convinced that everything that happens only happens so that it shall have something to talk about.

The christening ceremony was to be dignified, but restricted and brief. They came together, and Ottilie and Mittler were to hold the child as godparents. The old priest, supported by the sexton, entered with slow steps. The prayers were spoken, the child was placed in Ottilie's arms, and when she looked affectionately down at the infant she was not a little surprised by his open eyes; for she thought she was looking into her own; such a resemblance would have surprised anyone. Mittler, to whom the child was then handed, was similarly startled, for he saw in his features such a striking resemblance to the Captain as he had never previously experienced.

The weak condition of the good old priest had prevented him from carrying out the baptismal ceremony with more than the bare liturgy. Mittler, however, full of the occasion, remembered his own earlier official functions, and in any case had a way of thinking immediately in any circumstances how he would now speak and express himself. This time he could restrain himself all the less as he was surrounded only by a small company

of none but friends. Towards the conclusion of the proceedings he therefore began to place himself expansively
in the position of the priest, making a cheerful speech
about his duties and hopes as a godparent and dwelling
all the longer on these as he thought that Charlotte's
contented look was expressive of her approval.

The vigorous speaker failed to notice that the good
old man would have been glad to sit down; he was much
less aware that he was about to be the cause of a greater
evil; for after he had described with emphasis the relationship of everyone present to the child and had thereby
put Ottilie's self-control to something of a test, he finally
turned to the old man with these words: 'And you, my
reverent elder, can now say with Simeon: "Lord, now
lettest thou thy servant depart in peace; for mine eyes
have seen the salvation of this house." '

He was now in full swing to complete a final perora-
tion, but he soon noticed that the old man to whom he
held out the child certainly seemed to be bending towards
him, but then suddenly sank back. He was only just
caught as he fell and brought to a seat; and in spite of all
attempts at resuscitation he had to be pronounced dead.
Ottilie alone looked at the dead man, who had still retained his friendly, engaging mien, with a touch of envy.
Her soul's life had been killed; why should her body still
be preserved?

Although the unhappy events of the day led her often
in this way to ponder upon transience, parting and loss,
she was consoled by strange manifestations by night
which reassured her of her loved one's life and
strengthened and animated her own life. When she laid
herself to rest at night and was still hovering in that
sweet sensation between sleeping and waking, it seemed
to her as if she were looking into a very brightly, though
gently illumined room. Here she saw Edward quite
plainly, though not dressed as she had seen him before,
but in military attire, each time in a different position,

though one that was completely natural and not at all fanciful—standing, walking, lying down, riding. The figure, delineated to the smallest detail, moved readily before her without her doing anything herself, without her desiring it or making an effort of the imagination. She sometimes saw him surrounded particularly by something mobile that was darker than the light background; but she could scarcely distinguish these shadowy forms which at times appeared to her as people, horses, trees and mountains. Usually she went to sleep during this phenomenon and when she awoke again in the morning after a peaceful night she was refreshed and consoled; she felt convinced that Edward was still alive and that she was still in the closest harmony with him.

CHAPTER IX

S PRING had come later, but more quickly and more joyfully too, than usual. Ottilie now discovered in the garden the results of her previous work; everything was springing forth, turning green and blossoming at the right time; many things that had been prepared in beds within well-constructed glasshouses now proceeded to develop further through the action of nature from outside, and everything that had to be attended to ceased to be merely hopeful effort, as it had been up to now, and became cheerful pleasure.

But she had to console the gardener for many a gap among the potted plants and for the spoilt symmetry of many a treetop that had been caused by Luciane's wildness. She cheered him by saying that all this damage would soon be restored; but his feelings were too deep and he had too high a conception of his craft for these reasons for consolation to have been of much effect on him. Just as a gardener may not let himself be distracted by other hobbies and interests, there should be no less interruption of the quiet growth which the plant needs for its fruition, whether permanent or transitory. A plant is like wilful people from whom one can obtain anything so long as one treats them in their own fashion. A quiet eye and an unruffled consistency in doing what is needful at all hours and seasons are perhaps required of nobody more than of a gardener.

The good man possessed these qualities in a high degree, which is one reason why Ottilie was so glad to work with him; but for some time now he had no longer been able to practise his real talent with ease. For although he knew very well how to carry out all that was necessary as far as the orchard and kitchen-gardens were concerned and the demands of the older type of ornamental garden as well (as indeed one man will succeed better at one task than another), and although he could have challenged nature herself in the treatment of an orangery, of flower-bulbs, and of carnation and auricula plants, the new ornamental trees and fashionable flowers had remained unfamiliar to him, and he had a kind of fear of the limitless field of botany that was being revealed in the course of time with its strange, buzzing names. What the master and mistress had begun to order the previous year he considered an unnecessary expense and waste of money, all the more so as many rare plants had to be disposed of and as he was not on particularly good terms with the commercial gardeners who in his opinion did not treat him with sufficient honesty.

After various attempts he had made a kind of plan in which Ottilie encouraged him, especially as it actually depended on Edward's return; Edward's absence was felt, in this and many other instances, to be becoming daily more regrettable.

As the plants now became more firm in their roots and thrust forth their branches, Ottilie felt ever more attracted to these gardens. Just a year ago she had come here as a stranger and insignificant person; how much she had learnt during that time!—but, unfortunately, how much also she had lost since then! She had never been so rich and never so poor. At that moment she felt that both conditions were alternating within her, indeed crossing over each other most closely, so that she could think of no way of escape except to take up the most immediate task she could find with good will, or even passion.

It may well be imagined that whatever was particularly dear to Edward also attracted her careful attention most strongly; indeed, why should she not hope that he himself would now soon be coming back and that he would notice with grateful presence of mind the thoughtful solicitude that she had devoted to him in his absence?

But in a very different way too she had been caused to be active on his behalf. She primarily had undertaken to look after the child, whom she was in a position to care for directly, since it had been decided not to give him to a wet-nurse, but to bring him up on milk and water. He was to enjoy the fresh air during the fine season; and she liked best to take him out herself, walking with the sleeping, unconscious infant among flowers and blossoms which might one day greet him in his childhood with their friendly laughter and between young bushes and plants which seemed destined by their own youth to grow up with him. When she looked around her, she did not conceal from herself what conditions of grandeur and wealth the child was born into; for almost everything which the eye could see was to belong to him one day. How desirable it was therefore that he should grow up before the eyes of his father and mother and should be a confirmation of a renewed, happy union!

Ottilie felt all this so purely that she thought to herself that it was really true, and she did not consider herself at all in this situation. It became suddenly clear to her under this clear sky and bright sunlight that her love, to be complete, would have to become completely unselfish; indeed she thought at some moments that she had already attained this level. All she desired was her friend's well-being, and she believed herself capable of renouncing him, even of never seeing him again, if only she knew that he was happy. But she had definitely made up her mind that she would never belong to another man.

The gardening arrangements ensured that the autumn would be as magnificent as the spring. All the so-called

summer flowers, all those things which cannot cease
blooming in autumn and boldly go on growing in order
to face the cold weather, asters in particular, had been
sown most plentifully and, being planted everywhere,
would form a sky of stars over the earth.

From Ottilie's Diary

We copy into our diaries a good thought that we
have read or a striking remark we have heard. But
if at the same time we took the trouble to select
peculiar remarks, original points of view and the
occasional clever phrases that occur in our friends'
letters, we should become very rich. One keeps
letters, never to read them again; eventually one
destroys them for reasons of discretion, and in this
way the most beautiful and most direct breath of life
disappears irrevocably for ourselves and for others.
I am going to resolve to make good this oversight.

Once again then the fairy-tale of the year's development is being repeated. Now we have arrived, thank
goodness, at the prettiest chapter. Violets and lilies
of the valley are, as it were, the chapter-headings or
vignettes. We are always pleasantly impressed when
we come upon them again in the book of life.

We scold the poor, especially the youngsters, when
they loll about the streets begging. Do we not notice
that they are at once active as soon as there is something to do? Nature has scarcely had time to display
her friendly treasures before the children have got
round to making a trade of it; none of them begs any
longer, they all hand you a bunch of flowers; the
child plucked the flowers while you were still asleep,
and as he begs he looks at you in a friendly way, like
his own gift of flowers. Nobody looks pitiable when
he feels to some extent that he is entitled to make a
request.

Why now does the year sometimes seem so short in
one's memory, at other times so long? This is how it
happened to me with last year, and it is nowhere more

striking than in the garden how what is transient and what is permanent are bound closely together. And yet nothing is so fleeting that it does not leave some trace, something of itself behind.

One can put up with winter too. One can fancy oneself expanding more freely when the trees stand before us so ghostly and transparent. They are nothing, but neither do they conceal anything. But once buds and blossoms are here, one becomes impatient for foliage to be fully out, for the countryside to take bodily shape and for the trees to press towards us like human figures.

Everything that is complete in its own way must develop beyond itself and become something else, something incomparable. The nightingale is still a bird in many of the notes it sings; then it transcends its own class and seems to want to indicate to all birds what singing really means.

A life without love and the closeness of the beloved is only a *comédie à tiroir*, a poor routine play. One pulls open one drawer after another and shuts them to again, and hurries off to the next one. Anything that is good or important only hangs together in a haphazard manner. One must everywhere be starting again from the beginning and would be glad to end anywhere.

CHAPTER X

For her part Charlotte felt cheerful and well. She was pleased with the lovely boy whose promising appearance occupied her eyes and mind every hour. Through him she obtained a new approach to the world at large and to the property. Her old activity awakened again; she saw in the past year, wherever she looked, much that had been done, and she was glad about this achievement. Impelled by a curious feeling she climbed up to the arbour with Ottilie and the child; and as she placed the child on the little table as if on a domestic altar and saw two further empty seats, she thought of former times, and new hope for herself and Ottilie rose up.

Young women perhaps look modestly around at this or that young man, quietly considering whether they would like to have him as a husband; but anyone who has to look after a daughter or a female ward will cast glances in a wider circle. This is what was now happening in Charlotte's case; to her mind a marriage between the Captain and Ottilie did not seem impossible, since after all they had once sat side by side in this cottage. She had heard that the particular prospect of an advantageous marriage of the Captain had not materialised.

Charlotte went on climbing, and Ottilie carried the child. The former gave herself over to all kinds of thoughts. A shipwreck may also take place on dry land; it is fine and praiseworthy to recover from this and to put oneself right as quickly as possible. After all life is only calculated in terms of profit and loss! Who does not make some arrangement and find himself disturbed in it! How often we follow one path and are led away from it! How often we are diverted from an aim which is sharply fixed in our mind's eye in order to attain another, higher one! A traveller is highly annoyed if he breaks a wheel of his coach while he is on his way, and gains through this unpleasant accident the most agreeable acquaintances and connections which affect his whole life. Fate grants us our wishes, but in its own way, in order to be able to give us something more than we wish for.

With these and similar thoughts Charlotte climbed to the new building on the top of the hill, and here her reflections were fully confirmed. For the surrounding country was much more beautiful than one could have thought. Everything that was disturbingly trivial had been removed from round about, while all that was good about the landscape, that which nature and time had done to it, received a clear emphasis and attracted the eye, and already the young plants were green; they were intended to fill certain gaps and link up the separate parts in a pleasant manner.

The house itself was almost habitable, and the view, in particular from the upper rooms, most varied. The more one looked round, the more beautiful things were to be discovered. What effects the various times of day, and the moon and the sun, must have! It was most pleasant lingering here, and the desire to build and create was reawakened in Charlotte now that she found that all the heavy work had been done. All she needed now to finish off the building in a short time was a joiner, a paper-hanger and a painter who knew how to cope with stencils and light gilding. The cellar and the kitchen were quickly put to rights; for in view of the distance from the castle it was necessary to have all that was needed about one. Thus the women and the child lived up there, and unexpected walks were open to them from the summer-house which formed a new centre. They took

218

great pleasure in the fresh open air in this higher altitude during most beautiful weather.

Ottilie's favourite walk, either by herself or with the child, was to go down to the plane-trees by a comfortable path which then led to the spot where one of the boats was moored which were usually used for crossing the lake. She frequently enjoyed a trip on the water, but she did not take the child, since Charlotte showed anxiety about this. However, she did not fail to visit the gardener daily in the castle garden and to show a friendly interest in his care for the many young plants which were now all enjoying the fresh air.

The visit of an Englishman during this fine season of the year was very welcome to Charlotte; he had got to know Edward while travelling, had met him a number of times and was now curious to see the beautiful grounds of which he had heard tell so much that was good. He had with him a recommendation from the Count and also introduced a quiet, but very pleasant man as his companion. As he strolled through the neighbourhood, sometimes with Charlotte and Ottilie, sometimes with his companion and occasionally on his own, it could be seen from his observations that he was an enthusiastic connoisseur of such parks and that he must have planned quite a number of them himself. Although no longer young, he was concerned in an agreeable manner for anything that would add attraction and significance to living.

It was in his company that the women really first enjoyed their surroundings. His trained eye appreciated every effect quite freshly, and he enjoyed what had been done all the more since he had not known the district previously and was scarcely able to separate what nature had provided from what had been added by man.

It may indeed be said that the park grew and became enriched by his comments. He could already recognise in advance what the new, growing plantations promised.

He did not fail to notice any spot where some form of beauty could be emphasised or observed. He drew attention to a spring which, if it were purified, promised to shed lustre on a whole group of bushes; or to a cavern, which, if cleared and enlarged, could give a pleasant resting place, as it would only be necessary to fell a few trees in order to have a view of magnificent masses of cliff. He congratulated the owners that there still remained so much to be done and pleaded with them not to hurry matters, but to reserve for future years the pleasures of this creative and organising work.

He was, incidentally, by no means a trouble to them when they were not in company together; for he spent the greater part of the day capturing the picturesque views of the park in a portable camera obscura and then drawing them, and in this way he could acquire for himself and others a fine record of his travels. He had been doing this for a number of years already in all places of interest and had acquired in this way a most pleasant and interesting collection. He showed the ladies a large portfolio that he took about with him and entertained them both by the pictures and by his commentaries. It gave them pleasure to travel through the world so comfortably here in their solitude and to watch moving past them coasts and harbours, mountains, lakes and rivers, towns, citadels and many another spot that has a name in history.

Each of the two women had a special interest; Charlotte's was the more general, an interest in anything historically noteworthy, while Ottilie preferred to dwell on those parts which formerly Edward used to talk a lot about and where he had been glad to linger and whither he had frequently returned; for everyone knows certain details of place, either near or far, which attract him and which appeal to him or excite him in a particular way, according to his character, or because of a first impression, particular circumstances or habit.

She therefore asked the English lord which part he had liked best and where he would now set up his home if he had to choose. Then he could point to more than one lovely district and tell them easily in his curiously accented French what he had experienced there to make that place dear and valued to him.

But when asked where he usually stayed now and to what place he preferred to go back, he explained without awkwardness, though to the surprise of the ladies, as follows:

'I have accustomed myself to being at home wherever I am, and in the end I find nothing more comfortable than that other people should build, plant and make domestic efforts on my behalf. I don't want to go back to my own property, partly for political reasons, but principally because my son, for whose sake I had really done and arranged everything, and whom I was hoping to transfer it to and to enjoy it with a while, has no interest in the estate, but has gone to spend his life in India, where, like so many others, he may devote it to a higher purpose or even sacrifice it altogether.

'It is true, we make much too much preliminary expenditure for life. Instead of starting at once to make ourselves contented in moderate circumstances, we diffuse our energies more and more and are always making things more uncomfortable for ourselves. Who is there now to enjoy my buildings, my park, my gardens? Not myself, nor even my family: strange guests, inquisitive visitors, restless travellers.

'Although we are well off, we are constantly only at home half the time, especially in the country, where we miss much that we are used to in town. The book that we want most is not at hand, and something that we need most urgently has been forgotten. We are always settling in domestically and then leaving once more, and when it is not our own will and fancy that compel us, we

221

are affected by circumstances, passions, chance, necessity and I don't know what else.'

The English lord did not suspect how closely his comments had affected his friends. And how often any of us may come into this danger when he makes a general statement, even in company whose circumstances are on the whole well known to him! A chance wound of this nature, even coming from well meaning and good-natured people, was nothing new to Charlotte; and the world lay in any case so clearly before her eyes, that she felt no special hurt if someone inconsiderately and carelessly compelled her to turn her glance here or there to an unpleasant spot. Ottilie, on the other hand, in her half-awakened youthfulness felt more by intuition than she saw, and could turn aside her glance, indeed was compelled to do so, from what she did not care to and was not meant to see; she was extremely upset by these confidences, for the pleasant veil was violently torn from her, and it seemed to her as if all the labour that had been expended up to now on houses and courtyard, garden, park and all the surroundings was quite peculiarly in vain, because the man to whom it all belonged was not enjoying it and because he too, like this present guest, had been driven to roaming around the world, and since in Edward's case it was through his closest and dearest ones, it was the most dangerous form of restlessness for him. She had accustomed herself to listening in silence, but on this occasion she was in the most distressing position, and one which the visitor's further conversation, now continued with cheerful and idiosyncratic deliberateness, tended to exacerbate rather than to ease.

'I now believe that I am on the right track,' he said, 'since I habitually regard myself as a traveller who gives up much so that he can enjoy much. I am used to change, indeed it has become a necessity for me, just as one always expects fresh décor at the opera, simply because there have been so many changes of scenery

before. I know what to expect from the best as well as
from the worst hotel; however good or bad it may be,
I nowhere find anything I am used to, and in the end it's
all the same whether you are dependent on a habit that
has become a necessity or on the most arbitrary chance.
At least I haven't the irritation now of finding that something has been mislaid or lost, or that my daily living
room is unusable because I've got to have it repaired,
or that my favourite cup has been broken and that for
quite a time I can't enjoy drinking from any other. I
am spared all this, and if the roof begins to burn over
my head, my servants pack up and we make off to the
courtyard and then to the town. And with all these
advantages, when I come to work it out, I haven't spent
any more at the end of the year than it would have cost
me at home.'

In the course of this account Ottilie could see in her
mind's eye only Edward, as he must be moving along on
trackless ways with resignation and difficulty, or lying
in danger and trouble on the battlefield, accustoming
himself in face of so much uncertainty and risk to being
homeless and friendless, and to jettisoning all he had
simply in order not to lose it. Fortunately for her the
company separated for a while. Ottilie found a spot
where she could weep freely in solitude. No dull pain had
seized her more violently than this clear vision which
she strove to make even clearer to herself, just as one
habitually inflicts pain on oneself when one is once likely
to be tormented from outside.

Edward's state seemed to her to be so wretched and
miserable that she decided at all costs to do what she
could to further his reconciliation with Charlotte, to conceal her grief and her love in some quiet spot and to
elude them by some kind of activity.

In the meantime the nobleman's companion, a quiet,
sensible, observant man, had noticed the blunder in the
conversation and revealed the similarity of the situations

to his friend. The latter knew nothing of the family's circumstances; but his companion had made himself acquainted, both in advance and even more so during his stay in the house itself, with all that had happened and was still happening there, for nothing aroused his interest while travelling so much as the strange happenings which are occasioned by natural and unusual relations, or by the conflicts of what is lawful with what is uncontrolled, of commonsense with higher reason, of passion with prejudice.

The nobleman was sorry, but without becoming embarrassed about the matter. We should have to be totally silent in company, if we were not at some time to fall into a trap; for it is not only important comments, but even the most trivial remarks which can clash in an unharmonious manner with the interests of those who are present. 'Let us make good the matter this evening,' the nobleman said, 'and hold back from all general topics. Let the company hear something from the many pleasant and significant anecdotes and stories with which you have filled your brief-case and enriched your memory during our travels!'

But even with the best intentions the visitors did not succeed this time in cheering their friends with harmless entertainment. For after the companion had aroused their attention and excited their interest to a high degree by a number of tales—strange, meaningful, humorous, moving and terrifying—he thought he would close with an incident that was quieter, though certainly unusual, and he did not suspect how closely it was to touch his hearers.

'THE STRANGE YOUNG NEIGHBOURS
Novella

Two young people from neighbouring families of rank, a boy and a girl whose respective ages would allow

224

them one day to become man and wife, were brought up together with this pleasant prospect in view, and the parents of both children looked forward gladly to a future marriage. But it was soon noticed that the intention appeared to be going awry, since a strange antipathy developed between their two fine characters. Perhaps they were too much alike. They were both turned in upon themselves, clear about what they wanted and firm in their intentions; each was loved and respected by his companions; they were always opponents when they were together, always constructive for themselves alone and mutually destructive whenever they met, not competitive in a friendly manner but constantly fighting for an aim in view; very well disposed and affectionate, yet displaying only hatred and malice in their relations to one another.

This strange relationship showed itself already in their childhood games, and continued as they grew older. And just as boys play at war, separating into sides and fighting battles with one another, similarly the obstinately courageous girl put herself on one occasion at the head of an army and fought against the other side with such violence and bitterness that this latter would have been put shamefully to flight if her one opponent had not resisted very stoutly until he finally disarmed and captured her. But here she still resisted in such a violent manner that he had to take off his silk neckerchief and tie her hands together with it in order to defend his eyes from her and at the same time not to harm her.

She never forgave him for this, indeed she made so many secret arrangements and attempts to injure him that their parents, who had noticed these strange passions for a long time now, came to an agreement among themselves and decided to separate the two hostile young people and to give up their aspirations to a loving union.

The boy soon distinguished himself in his new surroundings. Every kind of instruction took effect with him. His own inclination and that of his well-wishers led him to a military career. He was popular and respected wherever he went. His robust nature seemed to have only a beneficent, comforting effect upon others, and he was quite contented in himself, without any clear realisation that he had lost the only opponent whom nature had intended for him.

The girl on the other hand came all at once into different circumstances. Her age, her increasing refinement and even more a certain inner feeling deflected her from the violent games which she had practised up to now in the company of boys. On the whole she seemed to be lacking something; there was nothing around her that would have been worth arousing her hatred.

A young man who was older than her former neighbour and opponent, who possessed rank, wealth and character, and was popular in society and with women, devoted his whole attention to her. It was the first time that a friend, admirer and servant had interested himself in her. The preference that he gave her above many who were older, more educated, more brilliant and more assuming, pleased her very much. His continuing, though not importunate attentions, his loyal support on various awkward occasions, his attitude to her parents, which was open, yet quiet and no more than hopeful, since she was certainly still very young; all these things attracted her to him, and they were helped by usage and outer appearances, which were taken for granted by other people. She had been referred to so often as betrothed that she eventually came to think of herself thus, and neither she nor anyone else thought that any further trial would be necessary when she exchanged rings with him who had been assumed to be her fiancé for so long.

The quiet course which the whole matter had taken had not been hastened by the official engagement either. On both sides it was agreed to let things go on as before;

they enjoyed being together and wished to enjoy the favourable time of year as the springtime before more serious life in the future.

Meanwhile the youth had developed in distant parts in a most satisfactory manner, had risen to a well-deserved stage in his career and came on leave to visit his family. He confronted his beautiful young neighbour once more, in a wholly natural, but still strange manner. Recently she had only known family feelings of a friendly, bridal character, and was in harmony with all that was around her; she believed herself to be happy, and was happy in in a certain way. But now for the first time after a long interval something stood opposed to her: it was not something to be hated; she had become incapable of hatred, in fact the childish hatred, which had really only been an obscure recognition of inner value, now expressed itself in happy surprise, pleasant curiosity, polite concession, and a coming closer that was half willing and half reluctant, though inevitable; and all this was mutual. The long separation provided material for fairly lengthy conversations. Even that episode of childish unreasonableness seemed an amusing memory to them now that they were more enlightened, and it was as if they must at least make good their teasing hostility through friendly, attentive behaviour and as if that violent misjudgement was not to remain, but to become an outspoken appreciation now.

For his part everything stayed within sensible and desirable bounds. His rank and position, his desires and ambitions occupied him so fully that he accepted easily enough the beautiful betrothed woman's friendliness as a gratifying additional gift without regarding it therefore as having any special relationship to himself or without begrudging her to her fiancé, with whom, incidentally, he was on the best of terms.

Matters were different with her, however. She seemed to herself as if she had been awakened from a dream.

The fight with her young neighbour had been her first passion, and this violent struggle was, after all, only a violent, so to speak innate liking concealed under the form of resistance. Furthermore, it seemed to her when she looked back as if she had always loved him. She smiled at the hostile way she had searched with weapons in her hand; she was willing to remember only the pleasantest feelings when he had disarmed her; she imagined that she had felt the greatest bliss when he was tying her up, and everything that she had undertaken to injure and annoy him only seemed to her now to have been an innocent means of directing his attention to herself.

If someone had been able to bring out these feelings which she kept wholly to herself and to develop them and share them with her, he would not have reproved her; for undoubtedly the fiancé could not stand comparison with the neighbour as soon as one saw them together. Whereas one could withhold a certain trust in the one, the other aroused fullest confidence; if one would gladly have the one man's company, one desired the other as close friend; and if one were thinking of a higher kind of sympathy and of unusual circumstances, one might have had some doubts about the one, as against complete certainty with regard to the other. Women have a special, innate feeling for such relationships, and they have reason as well as opportunity to develop it.

The more the beautiful betrothed woman cherished such thoughts to herself in secret, the less anybody was in a position to say what would be favourable to the fiancé and what attitude and obligations were advisable or necessary, indeed, what inevitable necessity seemed to require irrevocably; the more the beautiful young woman's heart favoured its own partiality. On the one hand she was indissolubly tied by society, family, fiancé and her own assent, while on the other the ambitious youth made no secret at all of his opinions, plans and prospects,

but showed himself only as a faithful and not even particularly fond brother towards her; and now there was
even talk of an impending departure. Thus it seemed as
if her old, childish spirit was reawakening with all its
cunning and violence and reluctantly preparing at a
higher stage of life to act in a more significant and destructive manner. She made up her mind to die, in order
to punish the man, who had been once hated and was
now so violently loved, for his indifference, and to be
wedded for ever, since she was not to possess him, at
least to his imagination and regrets. He should not be
rid of the image of her as she lay dead, and he should
not cease to reproach himself for not having recognised,
investigated and esteemed her personality.

This strange madness accompanied her everywhere.
She concealed it in all sorts of forms; and although she
appeared to people to be behaving strangely, nobody
was alert or discerning enough to discover the true, inner
cause.

Meanwhile friends, relations and acquaintances had
exhausted themselves in the arrangements of various
kinds of entertainment. Hardly a day passed without
something new and unexpected being arranged.
There was scarcely a pleasant spot with a view which
had not been decorated and prepared for the reception
of many light-hearted guests. Our young arrival wanted
to play his part too before leaving again, and he invited
the engaged couple together with a fairly close family
circle to take part in a river-trip. They boarded a fine,
large, well appointed ship, one of those yachts which
provide a small lounge and a number of little rooms and
try to transfer the comforts of dry land to life on the
water.

They sailed along the big river to the accompaniment
of music, as it was in the heat of the day; the company
had assembled in the lower rooms, where they passed the
time with games of skill and chance. The young host,

229

who could never remain inactive, had taken the rudder
to relieve the old ship's captain who had fallen asleep at
his side; and the one who was awake now needed all his
wits about him, as he was approaching a spot where
two islands made the river-bed narrow and caused a
dangerous current by stretching out their flat banks of
pebble now on one side, now on the other. The careful and
alert steersman was almost tempted to waken the ship's
captain, but he believed he could manage it and steered
the ship towards the narrow part. At this moment his
beautiful enemy appeared on deck, a wreath of flowers
in her hair. She removed the wreath and threw it to the
steersman. 'Take this as a memento!' she called out.
'Don't disturb me!' he called back to her, catching the
wreath; 'I need all my strength and powers of concen-
tration,'—'I shan't disturb you again,' she cried, 'you
won't see me any more!' After saying this she hastened
to the ship's prow and from there she leaped into the
water. Some voices called: 'Help, help, she's drowning.'
He was in the most terrible dilemma. The old captain
woke up at the noise and attempted to take the rudder
which the younger man wished to relinquish to him, but
there was no time to change over: the ship ran ashore,
and at that very moment, throwing off the most cumber-
some of his clothes, he dived into the water and swam
after the young woman.

Water is a friendly element for those who are familiar
with it and know how to treat it. It carried him, and as
a good swimmer he could control it. Soon he had reached
the beautiful girl who had been torn from him; he seized
hold of her, and managed to lift her up and transport
her; they were both carried along violently by the river
until they had left islands and islets far behind them and
the river began to flow broadly and easily again. Now
for the first time he plucked up heart and recovered from
the first pressing emergency when he had acted without
thinking, in a purely mechanical way; he looked around

with head stretched aloft and swam with all his strength
towards a flat, bushy spot which ran pleasantly and con-
veniently into the river. Here he brought his beautiful
catch on to dry land; but there was no breath of life in
her to be found. He was in despair, when a well used
path running through the undergrowth met his eyes. He
picked up the dear burden once more, and noticed a
solitary cottage which he soon reached. There he found
helpful people, in fact, a young couple. It did not take
long to explain the misfortune and the urgent need.
He thought over what was required, and this they did for
him. A bright fire was soon burning, woollen blankets
were spread over a couch, furs, skins and anything that
was warm were brought along. The desire to save overcame any other type of thought. Nothing was left undone
to restore the beautiful, half-rigid, naked body to life
again. The efforts were successful. She opened her eyes,
saw her friend, and put her heavenly arms round his
neck. She remained like this a long time; a stream of
tears poured from her eyes, and this completed her recovery. 'Do you want to leave me,' she cried, 'since I
have found you again like this?'—'Never, never!' he
cried, not knowing what he was saying or doing. 'But
spare yourself,' he added, 'spare yourself! Think of
yourself for your sake and for mine.'

She now thought of herself and noticed for the first
time what a state she was in. She could not be ashamed
before her lover and rescuer; but she willingly released
him so that he could look after himself; for everything
about him was still dripping wet.

The young couple consulted each other; they offered
the youth and the girl their wedding clothes which were
still hanging in the cottage complete and which had
enough material in them to clothe a couple from head to
foot. Within a short time the two adventurous young
people were not only dressed, but also elegantly decked
out. They looked most charming, gazed at each other

in astonishment when they came together and fell impetuously into each other's arms with unbridled passion, though still half smiling at the fancy dress. The vigour of youth and love restored them to normal health again in a few moments, and all that was missing was music to invite them to dance.

They had found their way from water to dry land, from death to life, from their family circle into a wilderness, from despair to rapture, from indifference to liking and passion, all in one moment; the head was not adequate to grasp this, it would burst or become confused! Here the heart had to do its best if such a startling change were to be borne.

Quite lost in each other, it was some time before they could think of the fears and worries of those who had been left behind, and they themselves could hardly avoid fear and worry in wondering how they were to meet the others again. 'Shall we run away? Shall we hide?' the youth said. 'Let's stay together,' she said clinging to him.

The peasant who had heard their story of the stranded ship hurried to the river-bank without stopping for further questions. The ship was just moving happily along; it had been set in motion again after a great deal of effort. The others were sailing on in an uncertain manner, in the hope of finding again those who had been lost. So when the peasant aroused the attention of the voyagers by his shouting and waving, and ran to a spot where a good landing-place showed itself, continually shouting and waving, the ship turned towards the bank, and what a scene it was when they landed! The parents of the engaged couple pressed to the shore first; the loving fiancé had almost lost his senses. No sooner had they heard that the dear children were safe than these latter stepped from behind the bushes in their strange disguise. They were not recognised until they had come up quite close. 'Who's this?' the mothers cried. 'What do I see?' the fathers exclaimed. The two young people threw themselves down before them. 'We are your children!' they called, 'a loving couple.' 'Forgive us,' the girl cried. 'Give us your blessing!' the youth exclaimed. 'Give us your blessing!' they both called, as everyone around was silent with astonishment. 'Your blessing!' the words were heard a third time, and who could have gainsaid them their request!

CHAPTER XI

The narrator paused, or rather he had already concluded, when he could not help noticing that Charlotte was deeply agitated; in fact she got up and left the room, excusing herself with a silent gesture; for the story was familiar to her. This event had really happened to the Captain and a woman neighbour of his, not precisely as the Englishman had related it, though it was not distorted in its main features, but only rather more developed and decorated as to its details, which is what usually happens to such stories when they are first commonly talked about and are then taken up by the imagination of an intelligent and refined narrator. For the most part everything—and nothing—remains in the end as it was.

Ottilie followed Charlotte, as the two guests requested, and now it was the nobleman's turn to notice that perhaps a mistake had been made yet again, and that the story had been familiar to the family, and had possibly even concerned a relation. ' We must be careful not to do any further harm,' he went on. 'We don't seem to be bringing much happiness to our hostesses in return for the many good and pleasant things we have enjoyed here; let us attempt to take our leave.'

'I must admit that I am kept here by something else and that I should not like to leave the house without having some explanation and closer knowledge of it,' the companion said. 'You were too busy yesterday choosing a really picturesque viewpoint, my lord, when we were going through the park with the portable camera obscura, to notice what was going on otherwise. You

turned off from the main path in order to get to a little
visited spot by the lake which offered you a good view.
Ottilie, who was with us, hesitated to follow and offered
to make her own way to the spot by boat. I sat down in
the boat with her and took pleasure in the skill of the
beautiful oarswoman. I assured her that I had not been
conducted so pleasantly across the waters since I had
been in Switzerland, where most attractive girls also
take the place of the ferryman; but I couldn't refrain
from asking her why she had in fact declined to take that
side path; for really there was a kind of anxious embarrassment in her evasion. "So long as you won't laugh
at me," she replied in a friendly manner, "I can certainly give you some information, although even for me
there's a secret about it. I have never taken that side-
path without being overcome by a quite peculiar feeling
of dread which I don't have anywhere else and which
I can't explain. Consequently I would rather not lay
myself open to such feeling, especially as it is followed
immediately afterwards by a headache on the left side
of my head, which I suffer from fairly frequently on
other occasions." We landed, and Ottilie conversed with
you, while I examined the spot which she had clearly
pointed out to me in the distance. But how surprised I
was when I discovered a very definite trace of coal,
which convinced me that with some excavation one
might well find a rich seam below.

'Excuse me, my lord, I see you smiling and I know
full well that you will condone my passionate interest
in these things, which you have no belief in, only because
you are a wise man and a friend; but it is impossible
for me to leave here without making the pendulum experiment on the dear girl.'

When this matter came up for discussion, the nobleman never failed to repeat yet again his arguments
against it; these his companion took up modestly and
patiently, but still insisted on his own opinion and

desires. He too repeated his belief that the matter should not be given up because such experiments were not always successful, in fact research should be carried on all the more seriously and thoroughly, since there were certainly many connections and kinships which were at present concealed from us between inorganic materials, just as between organic and inorganic or organic and organic.

He had already spread out his apparatus of gold rings, iron and sulphur ore and other metal substances, which he always took with him in a handsome small chest, and now as an experiment lowered metals, suspended by threads, over the other metals which had been laid out. 'I don't begrudge you the pleasure I read on your face that you are anticipating when nothing will move for me here, my lord,' he said while he was making preparations. 'For my operations are only an excuse. When the ladies come back, I want them to be curious about the odd things we are doing here.'

The womenfolk returned, Charlotte at once understood what was happening. 'I've heard a lot about these things,' she said, 'but I've never seen them in action. As you've got everything so well prepared, perhaps you will let me see if maybe it will work with me.'

She took the thread in her hand, and as she was taking the experiment seriously, she held it steadily and without emotion; but there was not the slightest trace of movement to be seen. Then it was Ottilie's turn. She held the pendulum over the metals below even more quietly, unconcernedly and unselfconsciously. But at that moment the suspended object was agitated as if in a definite whirlpool; it turned, as the metals were changed underneath, now to one side, now to the other, at one time in circles, at another in ellipses, or else moved in straight ones; this was as the companion alone expected, indeed it surpassed his expectations.

The nobleman himself started somewhat, but his friend could not restrain his pleasure and eagerness, and kept on requesting a repetition and variation of the experiments. Ottilie was complaisant enough to submit to his requests until she eventually asked him in a friendly way if he would release her since her headache had begun again. Surprised, even delighted at this, he assured her enthusiastically that he would cure her completely of this trouble if she would entrust herself to his treatment. There was a moment's uncertainty; but Charlotte, quickly understanding what the conversation was about, declined this well-intentioned offer because she was unwilling to permit something on her premises which had always aroused in her strong feelings of apprehension.

The visitors left, and although the ladies had been affected by them in a strange way, Charlotte and Ottilie had been left with the desire to meet them again some day. Charlotte now made use of the fine weather to complete her return visits in the neighbourhood, and found that she could hardly get through her visits, since everybody in the district had been punctiliously concerned on her account, some people with genuine sympathy, others simply as a matter of habit. At home she was fortified by the presence of her child; he was certainly deserving of all love and care. They saw him as a kind of wonder-child, even a prodigy, most pleasing in appearance, in size, proportions, strength and health; and the double resemblance, which continued to become more obvious, was even more surprising. In his features and figure the child came to look more like the Captain, while his eyes came to be ever less distinguishable from Ottilie's.

Led on by this strange kinship and perhaps even more by the fine feeling that women have, who can embrace with delicate fondness the child of a man they love, even if the child is not their own, Ottilie became as good as a

237

mother to the growing child, or perhaps another kind of mother. If Charlotte was away, Ottilie stayed on her own with the child and his nurse. For some time now Nanny had obstinately kept away, being jealous of the boy on whom her mistress seemed to lavish all her affection, and had returned to her parents. Ottilie continued to take the child out of doors and got into the habit of going for even longer walks. She took the child's bottle with her so that she could give him milk, if need be. She usually took a book with her, and in this way, with the child on her arm, reading and strolling about, she made a most attractive *penserosa*.

CHAPTER XII

THE main purpose of the campaign had been attained, and Edward, distinguished with decorations, had been honourably discharged. He at once went back to his little farm where he found detailed news of his family waiting for him; without their noticing or knowing about it, he had had them closely watched. As he approached, his quiet dwelling-place had a most friendly appearance; for in the meantime many things had been arranged, improved and encouraged according to his instructions, so that the gardens and surroundings made up for what they lacked in extent and breadth by their inner and immediately appreciable qualities.

Edward, who had become accustomed in his quick-moving way of life to taking firm decisions, now made up his mind to carry out a plan that he had had long enough time to think over. First of all he got in touch with the Major. They were very glad to see each other again. Youthful friendships, like blood relationships, have the considerable advantage that they can never be fundamentally injured by confusions and misunderstandings of any kind and that the old relationship can be restored in time.

While joyfully welcoming him, Edward asked how his friend was and heard how fortune had favoured him completely according to his wishes. With half-joking confidentiality Edward then asked if a close relationship with a fair lady were in the offing. His friend denied this with full seriousness.

'I cannot and may not be secretive,' Edward went on;

'I must reveal my thoughts and intentions right away. You realise my passion for Ottilie and have known for a long time that it is because of her that I plunged into this campaign. I won't deny that I had wanted to be rid of my life, which without her was of no further use to me; but at the same time I must confess to you that I couldn't bring myself to despair utterly. Happiness with her was so lovely and desirable that it was impossible for me to renounce it completely. So many a comforting presentiment, so many good omens had confirmed me in the belief, the illusion perhaps, that Ottilie could be mine. A glass inscribed with our initials was thrown into the air when the foundation stone was laid, and did not shatter; someone caught it, and it is now in my hands again. ''I will put myself in the place of the glass, then, to act as a sign as to whether our marriage is possible or not,'' I said to myself, when I had spent so many anxious hours at this lonely spot. ''I will go off in search of death, not like a madman, but as one who hopes to live. Ottilie is to be the prize for which I am contending; she it is whom I hope to win behind every hostile battle-array, in every entrenchment and in every beleaguered fortress. I will work miracles in my desire to remain unscathed, in the sense, that is, of gaining Ottilie, and not losing her.'' These feelings have led and supported me through every danger; but now I am in the position also of someone who has attained his object and overcome all obstacles, there no longer being anything in his way. Ottilie is mine, and anything that still lies between this thought and its realisation I can only consider as unimportant.'

'You are obliterating with a few strokes everything that could and should be raised as an objection to you,' the Major replied. 'I leave it to you to recall your relationship with your wife in its true value: but you owe it to her and yourself not to let this be obscured in your mind. But how can I think of your having a son without at the same time saying that you and Charlotte belong to each other for ever and owe it to this child to live together and care together for his education and future well-being.'

'It is a mere parent's fancy to imagine that their presence is so necessary for the children,' Edward replied. 'Any living creature can find food and care; and even if a son doesn't have such a comfortable and sheltered childhood after his father's early death, he may for that very reason adapt himself more quickly to the world by recognising at an early age that he has to fit in with other people, which is something which we all have to learn sooner or later, after all. And this isn't the situation here at all: we are rich enough to be able to care for a number of children, and it is by no means an obligation or a good deed to heap so many good things on to one person's head.'

While the Major was thinking of indicating in a few words Charlotte's worth and Edward's long-standing relationship with her, his friend hastily broke in again: 'We have been foolish, as I see only too well. Anyone who thinks he can realise his former youthful wishes and aspirations after he has reached a certain age always deceives himself; for every decade of a man's life has its own happiness, hopes and prospects. He is an unfortunate man who is compelled by circumstances or his own illusions to return to the past or to anticipate the future. We have been foolish; must this folly last a lifetime? Must we renounce something that is not forbidden by the code of our times because of some kind of hesitation we may have? There are so many occasions in life when a man may go back on his intentions or his actions, but yet it shouldn't be possible just where it is a matter of the whole and not the part, of the whole complex of life and not this or that particular condition?'

The Major did not omit to put before Edward the various ties to his wife and family, to his property and to society in a skilful and emphatic way; but he failed to arouse any sympathetic response.

'All these things have come before my mind in the heat of battle, when the ground was trembling with the continuous thunder of cannon, when bullets were hissing and whistling by and my comrades were falling right and left, my horse shot and my hat riddled with bullets; I have borne them in mind when resting by the quiet fire by night under the starry vault of heaven. On such occasions all my obligations have been in my thoughts; I have thought them through and felt them intensively; I have been fully aware of them and I have made my peace with them, repeatedly and now, for ever.

'In such moments (how can I conceal this from you?) you too were in my mind, you too were part of my circle; for have we not belonged together for a long time? If ever I have been in your debt, I am now in a position to pay it back with interest; if you have ever owed me anything, you now see yourself in a position to make it good to me. I know that you love Charlotte, and she is worthy of your love; I know that she cares for you, and indeed why should she not recognise your value? Receive her from my hand, and lead Ottilie to me, and we shall be the happiest men alive!'

'Just because you want to bribe me with such great gifts I must be all the more cautious and self-disciplined,' the Major replied. 'This suggestion, which I respect, instead of making things easier, only makes them more difficult. It becomes a matter that concerns myself as well as you; it affects the destiny, the good name and the honour of two men whose previous spotless reputation is in danger of appearing in a very strange light to the world on account of this strange action, if we are not to call it by any other name.'

'This very fact that we have a spotless reputation entitles us to let ourselves be criticised one in a way,' Edward answered. 'Someone who has proved himself to be a reliable man throughout his life can make an action reliable even if it might seem dubious in the case of other people. As far as I am concerned, I feel myself justified by the recent ordeals that I have imposed upon myself and by the difficult and dangerous deeds that I have performed for other people in doing something now for myself. As far as you and Charlotte are concerned, that can be a matter for the future; but neither you nor anybody else is going to hold me back from carrying out my plans. If others are co-operative, I'm ready to fit in with everything; but if I'm to be left to do everything myself or even to be opposed, a crisis is bound to develop, which may take any course.'

The Major felt it his duty to oppose Edward's intentions as long as possible, and he now used a clever step against his friend by seeming to give way and merely bringing up the formalities and business details by which these separations and new ties were to be effected. This revealed so much that was unpleasant, tiresome and dubious that Edward felt himself being placed into the worse of moods.

'I can see,' he cried finally, 'that if you want to obtain anything, you have to wrest it forcibly from your friends just as much as from your enemies. I shall keep firmly in view what I want and what is indispensable to me; I shall seize hold of it, and what is more, soon and quickly. Such relationships can't be stopped and started, as I know full well, without much falling that has stood upright, and without much giving way that had been expected to hold firm. You can't finish this sort of thing by thinking it over; in the light of reason all rights are alike, and if the scale rises on one side, there is also a counterweight to be put on. So make up your mind, my friend, to act on my behalf and your own, to disentangle, unravel and join up again these circumstances for me as well as for yourself! Don't let yourself be put off by any considerations; we have given the world something

to talk about already in any case; people will talk about
us once again and then they will forget, just as they
forget everything else that ceases to be new, and will
let us go our way as best we can without their bothering
any more about us.'

The Major had no alternative to this and had to admit
in the end that Edward should treat the matter once and
for all as something that was known and taken for
granted, that he should discuss in detail how everything,
was to be arranged and look forward to the future with
gaiety, even joking about it.

Then he became serious and thoughtful again, and
went on: 'It would be criminal self-deception if we were
to give ourselves over to the hope and expectation that
everything would settle itself automatically and that
chance would guide and favour us. It is impossible for us
to save ourselves this way or to restore our mutual peace
of mind: and how shall I be able to console myself since
I am the innocent cause of it all! It was my insistence
that persuaded Charlotte to take you into the house, and
Ottilie too only came to us as a result of this change. We
are no longer master of the consequences of these actions,
but we are capable of making them harmless and turning
the situation to our own good. Even if you are minded to
turn your eyes away from the lovely, friendly prospects
which I am revealing, even if it is your wish to order us
to sad renunciation—as far as you think such is possible,
as far as it is possible—would there not also be much that
is improper, uncomfortable and annoying about setting
out to return to the old conditions, without there being
anything good or pleasing to result from it? Would the
happy position in which you find yourself now give you
any pleasure if you were prevented from visiting me and
living with me? And after what has happened, it would
surely always be painful. Charlotte and I would only
find ourselves in an unhappy position, for all our wealth.
And if you think, like other men of the world, that the

passing of the years and separation will benumb such feelings and erase such sharply engraved lines, remember that we are talking of those years which we wish to spend in joy and comfort, not in grief and separation. And now at last there is still the most important thing to discuss: even if we might be able to wait, according to our inner and outward circumstances, what is to happen to Ottilie, who would have to leave our house, to be without our care in society and would drift about miserably in the notoriously cold world! You describe circumstances in which Ottilie could be happy without me, without us, and then you will have uttered an argument that is stronger than any other, though one which I can't admit and to which I can't yield; however, I should be quite willing to examine it and think it over again.'

This task was not so easy to carry out, at least no adequate answer to it occurred to our friend, and there was nothing for him to do except to emphasise yet again how important, how dubious and in many respects how dangerous the whole undertaking was and that the least one could do was to consider very carefully how it should be tackled, though only on condition that his friend would not leave him until they had become fully agreed about the matter and had taken the first steps.

CHAPTER XIII

PEOPLE who are complete strangers and are indifferent to one another expose their inmost thoughts to each other, and a certain intimacy must develop. It was all the more to be expected that our two friends would have no secrets between them now that they were again living as neighbours and were going about together daily and hourly. They revived memories of their earlier circumstances, and the Major did not conceal that Charlotte had thought of Ottilie as a suitable match for Edward after he had come back from his travels and that she had later thought of marrying him to the beautiful girl. Edward, confused with delight by this revelation, spoke uninhibitedly of the mutual attraction of Charlotte and the Major which he painted with vivid colours, since it happened to be handy and advantageous to his own point of view.

The Major could not entirely disagree nor yet entirely approve; but Edward only became firmer and more definite. He thought of everything not merely as possible, but as having already happened. All parties simply needed to agree to what they wanted; a divorce could surely be procured; a quick wedding was to follow, and Edward wanted to go travelling with Ottilie.

There are perhaps no more attractive factors that the imagination can envisage than when lovers and young couples are hoping to enjoy their fresh, new relationship in fresh, new surroundings and to test and prove the durability of their union against so many changing circumstances. Meanwhile the Major and Charlotte were

246

to have unrestricted authority to order everything relating to the property, wealth and materially desirable
arrangements, and to arrange them rightly and fairly so
that all parties could be contented. But what Edward
seemed to rely on most of all and to promise as most
advantageous to himself was this: since the child would
stay with the mother, the Major would be able to bring
the boy up, guide him according to his own views and
develop his capacities. Not for nothing had the child
been given at baptism their common name of Otto.

That had all become so firmly fixed in Edward's mind
that he did not care to wait a day longer before nearing
the execution of the plan. On their way to the estate they
came to a little town in which Edward owned a house
where he intended to stay and wait for the Major's
return. But he could not bring himself to stay there as
soon as he arrived, and accompanied his friend a little
further through the town. They were both on horseback,
and, immersed in serious conversation, they went on
riding together.

All at once they saw in the distance the new house on
the heights, and it was the first time that they saw its
red tiles gleaming. Edward was seized by an irresistible
longing; everything was to be settled that very evening.
He now wanted to stay hidden in a village that was quite
close by; the Major should put the position to Charlotte
in urgent tones, should surprise her out of her cautious-
ness and press her by his unexpected proposal to a free
disclosure of her own mind. For Edward, imagining that
her wishes were the same as his own, thought that he
was doing no other than to fit in with her own decided
wishes, and he hoped for such quick agreement on her
part because he could not desire anything other than
this.

He saw the happy solution joyfully in his mind's eye,
and to make sure that this solution would be quickly
announced to him as he lurked waiting, some cannon-

247

shots were to be fired and, if it were night-time, some rockets set off.

The Major rode up to the castle. He did not find Charlotte, but learned that she was at present living in the new building on the hill, though just now she was paying a visit in the neighbourhood, and that she would probably be back later that day. He went back to the inn where he had left his horse.

Edward meanwhile, impelled by uncontrollable impatience, crept out of his hiding place along paths known only to huntsmen and fishermen towards his own park, and it was almost evening when he found himself in the bushes near the lake which he saw for the first time as a complete, whole surface.

That afternoon Ottilie had gone for a walk by the lake. She was carrying the child and reading while she walked, as was her custom. In this way she reached the oak trees near the place where the boat was moored. The little boy had gone to sleep; she sat down, placed him down beside her and went on reading. The book was one of those which attract a tender heart and do not let it go again. She forgot the time and did not think that she would still have a long way back by land to the new building; but she sat sunk in her book, curled in upon herself, and so pleasant a sight that the trees and bushes around should have been animated and provided with sight in order to admire her and take pleasure at seeing her. And just at that moment a reddish shaft of light from the setting sun fell behind her and turned her cheek and shoulder to gold.

Edward, who had succeeded in advancing so far without being noticed and found his park deserted and the whole district lonely, pressed on further. Eventually he broke through the bushes by the oak-trees; he saw Ottilie, and she him; he rushed up to her and threw himself down at her feet. After a long, silent pause in which they both tried to pull themselves together, he told her in a few words why and how he had come there. He told her how he had sent the Major to Charlotte, and that their common fate might perhaps be being decided at that very minute. He had never doubted her love, and she surely too had never doubted his. He begged her to consent. She hesitated, he implored her; he tried to re-assert his old rights and to fold her in his arms; she pointed to the child.

Edward looked at him and was astonished. 'Good God!' he cried, 'if I had reasons for doubting my wife and my friend, this child would be terrible evidence against them. Aren't these the Major's features? I've never seen such a likeness.'

'Surely not!' Ottilie put in; 'everybody says he looks like me.' 'Is that possible?' Edward asked, and at that moment the child opened his eyes, two large, black, penetrating eyes, deep and friendly. Already the little boy was looking at the world in such a sensible way; he seemed to know the two who were standing before him. Edward threw himself down by the child and was kneeling a second time before Ottilie. 'It's you!' he cried, 'they're your eyes. Oh, but let me look into yours. Let me cast a veil over that unhappy hour which gave this creature its existence. Am I to terrify your pure soul with the unhappy thought that man and wife may embrace although they are estranged from each other and that legal intercourse may be desecrated by strong passions? Or rather, since we've got that far, since my relationship to Charlotte must be broken off, and since you are mine, why shouldn't I say it? Why shouldn't I utter the hard words: this child was begotten in double adultery! It separates me from my wife, and my wife from me, whereas it should have united us. Let it bear witness against me, let these splendid eyes say to yours that I belonged to you as I lay in the arms of another; may you feel, Ottilie, truly feel that I can atone for that mistake, that crime only in your arms!

'Listen!' he cried, jumping to his feet; he thought
he heard a shot as the sign that the Major was to give.
It was a huntsman who had fired a shot in the nearby
hills. Nothing further followed; Edward was impatient.

It was only now that Ottilie saw that the sun had sunk
behind the mountains. In the end its light was still reflected from the windows of the building on the heights.
'You must go, Edward!' Ottilie cried. 'We have done
without and been patient for so long. Consider what we
both owe Charlotte. She must decide our fate, let us not
anticipate her decision. I am yours, if she consents; if
she does not, I must renounce you. Let us wait, as you
believe the decision to be so near. Go back to the village
where the Major believes you to be. So much can happen
that will need explaining. Is it likely that a fierce burst
of cannon-fire will announce the success of his negotia-
tions? He may be looking for you this very minute. He
hasn't met Charlotte, I know; possibly he has gone to
meet her, because it was known where she had gone to.
How many different things are possible! Leave me! She
must be coming now. She is expecting me up there with
the child.'

Ottilie spoke in haste. She called all possibilities to
mind. She was happy near Edward and felt that she
must tell him to go now. 'I beg you, I beseech you, my
beloved!' she cried, 'go back and wait for the Major!'
'I will obey your commands,' Edward answered, first
looking at her with passionate desire and then pressing
her close in his arms. She embraced him with her arms
and pressed him most tenderly to her breast. Hope soared
away over their heads like a shooting-star. They
imagined and believed that they belonged to one another;
for the first time they exchanged firm, open kisses, and
it was difficult and painful for them to part.

The sun had set, and the lake was already in half-
darkness and the atmosphere was damp. Ottilie stood
confused and agitated: she looked towards the house on

the hill and thought she saw Charlotte's white dress on the balcony. The way round the lakeside was long, she knew that Charlotte would be waiting impatiently for the child. She saw the plane-trees opposite, and was only separated by the sheet of water from the path which led straight to the house. In her thoughts, as with her eyes, she was already there. The danger of venturing on to the water with the child was forgotten in this eagerness. She hurried to the boat, not feeling how her heart was beating, her feet were faltering and how near she was to fainting.

She leaped into the boat, seized the oar and pushed off. She had to use force, she pushed a second time, the boat swayed and glided a little distance into the lake. Bearing the child on her left arm, the book in her left hand and the oar in her right hand, she too swayed and fell into the boat. The oar slipped away from her to one side and, as she was trying to save herself, the child and the book to the other, all three falling into the water. She was able to seize the child's clothes; but her awkward position impeded her herself as she was trying to get up. Her free right hand was not enough to enable her to turn and sit up: at last she managed this and pulled the child from the water, but his eyes were closed and he had stopped breathing.

At that moment her whole mental alertness returned, but her grief was all the greater. The boat drifted almost into the middle of the lake, the oar was floating far off, she could see nobody on the shore, and in any case what help would it have been to her to see anyone! Entirely cut off, she was drifting on the treacherous, imperious element.

She attempted to help herself. She had heard so often of first-aid to the drowning. Even on the evening of her birthday she had had experience of this. She took the child's clothes off and dried him with her muslin dress. She tore at her clothes and for the first time in her life

251

bared her breast to the open air; for the first time in her life she pressed a living creature to her pure, naked breast—alas, it was a living creature no longer. The cold limbs of the unfortunate child sent a chill to her breast and deep into her heart. Endless tears poured from her eyes and gave an appearance of warmth and life to the outer surface of the rigid little body. She did not desist, she covered him with her scarf, and believed that by stroking, pressing and breathing on him and by kisses and tears she could make up for those aids which were not available to her in her isolation.

It was all in vain! The child lay motionless in her arms, the boat was immobile on the water's surface; but even here her fine spirit did not desert her. She turned for help up above. She went down on her knees in the boat and lifted the benumbed child with both arms above her innocent breast which in its whiteness and, unfortunately too, in its coldness resembled marble. She looked up with glistening eyes and called for help from that source where a tender heart hopes to find the greatest riches, when there is dearth everywhere else.

Nor did she turn in vain to the stars, which were already beginning to shine here and there. A gentle wind arose and drove the boat towards the plane-trees.

CHAPTER XIV

S‚HE hurried to the new house, called for the surgeon and handed him the child. This man who was prepared for any emergency treated the tender corpse stage by stage in the usual way. Ottilie assisted him in everything; she was active, fetching and carrying, moving certainly as if in another world, for deepest misfortune, just as greatest happiness, changes the appearance of all objects; and only when the good man, after trying all possible methods, shook his head and answered her hopeful questions, at first with silence and then with a gentle 'no,' did she leave Charlotte's bedroom, where this had all been happening; she had scarcely entered the living-room when she fell exhausted on her face on the carpet without being able to reach the sofa.

Just at that moment Charlotte's carriage could be heard arriving. The surgeon urgently requested the bystanders to remain behind so that he could go to meet her and prepare her; but she was already entering the room. She found Ottilie on the ground, and one of the maids rushed towards her screaming and weeping. The surgeon came in, and she heard everything at once. But how could she be expected to give up all hope at once! The experienced, skilful and sensible man only asked her not to see the child; he retired in order to deceive her by more operations. She sat on her sofa, Ottilie still lay on the ground, though lifted to her friend's knees, upon which her lovely head lay. Their medical friend walked up and down; while appearing to be concerned for the child, he was in fact concerned for the ladies.

Thus midnight arrived, the deathly silence became deeper and deeper. Charlotte no longer deceived herself that the child would ever come to life again; she demanded to see him. He had been neatly wrapped up in warm, woollen clothes, put in a basket which was placed by her side on the sofa; only the little face was left free; he lay there serene and lovely.

The village had soon been aroused by reports of the accident, and the news at once spread to the inn. The Major had gone up by the usual paths; he went round the house and stopped a servant who was hastening to fetch something from the annexe, thus procuring further details, and asked to see the surgeon. The latter came, astonished to see his old patron, and told him about the present situation, undertaking to prepare Charlotte for his arrival. The surgeon went back in, started a casual conversation, leading her imagination from one subject to another until he finally suggested to her the Major's presence, the certainty of his sympathy and his closeness to her in mind and feeling; he then soon made it clear that he was referring to a real presence. It was enough, she learned that her friend was at the door, informed of everything and desirous of being admitted.

The Major stepped in; Charlotte greeted him with a painful smile. He stood before her. She raised the green silk coverlet which concealed the body, and by the dim light of a candle he saw not without secret horror his own likeness, still and rigid. Charlotte pointed to a chair, and thus they sat facing one another in silence the whole night through. Ottilie lay quietly at Charlotte's knees; she breathed gently: she was asleep, or seemed to be sleeping.

Morning came, the light went out, the two friends seemed to awaken from a heavy dream. Charlotte looked at the Major and said calmly: 'Explain to me, my friend, what fate brings you here to take part in this scene of mourning?'

'This is not the time or place to be secretive, to prevaricate and to tread gently,' the Major answered softly, just as she had put her question, as if they did not wish to awaken Ottilie. 'The position in which I find you is so monstrous that the important reason for my coming loses its value in comparison with it.'

He then confessed to her quite quietly and simply the purpose of his mission, in that he had been sent by Edward; the reason for his coming in so far as his own free will and his own interest had been involved. He referred to both these elements in a very delicate, though honest way; Charlotte listened with composure, and seemed to be neither surprised nor annoyed about it.

When the Major had finished, Charlotte answered in quite a soft voice, so that he was compelled to draw his chair up closer: 'I've never been in circumstances like these before, but in comparable ones I have always asked myself: "What will it be like tomorrow?" I feel clearly enough that the fate of several people is now in my hands; and there's no doubt in my heart about what I have to do, and it doesn't take long to say it. I agree to the divorce. I ought to have made up my mind to it earlier; through my hesitation and resistance I have killed the child. There are certain things which fate carries through obstinately. It is in vain that reason, virtue, duty and everything sacred attempt to obstruct fate: something must happen that seems right to fate, though not to us; and so fate finally intervenes, we may behave as we will.

'But what am I saying! Actually, fate wants once more to put into effect my own wish and intention which I myself thoughtlessly acted against. Didn't I myself in those days put Ottilie and Edward together in my thoughts as a most suitable match? Didn't I myself try to bring the two together? Weren't you yourself aware of this plan, my friend? And why couldn't I distinguish a man's wilfulness from true love? Why did I accept his proposal when I could have made him happy with another wife, if I had remained simply a friend? And just look at this unhappy girl asleep here! I tremble to think of the moment when she will awaken from her almost deathly sleep to return to consciousness. How is she to live and console herself if she cannot hope to give back to Edward through her love what she has stolen from him by being a tool of the strangest chance? And she can restore everything to him by means of the affection and passion with which she loves him. If love can tolerate all things, so in even greater measure it can make all things good. At a moment like this there should be no thought of myself.

'Slip away quietly, dear Major. Tell Edward that I agree to the divorce, that I am leaving it to him and to you and Mittler to start the whole business, and that I am not worried about my future position and that I am right in every sense not to be worried. I'll sign any piece of paper put in front of me; only don't let anybody ask me to collaborate, to think or to take counsel.'

The Major stood up. She stretched out her hand to him across Ottilie's slumbering form. He pressed his lips upon this dear hand. 'And what hope is there for me?' he whispered softly.

'Let me leave that question unanswered,' Charlotte replied. 'We haven't deserved to become unhappy, but neither have we done anything to merit being happy together.'

The Major left, feeling deeply grieved in his heart on Charlotte's account, though without being able to feel sorry for the poor dead child. Such a sacrifice seemed to him to be necessary for their general happiness. He pictured Ottilie with a child of her own on her arm as the most complete substitute for that which she had deprived Edward of; he thought of himself with a son on his knees who would be more justified in bearing his likeness than the departed child.

It was with such flattering hopes and images in his mind that he found Edward on the way back to the inn; Edward had spent the whole night waiting for the Major out of doors, as there had been no fireworks or cannon-fire to announce a happy outcome. He already knew about the misfortune, and instead of feeling sorry for the poor creature, he too saw this accident as a sign indicating that all obstacles to his happiness were being removed at once, though he did not wish to admit this wholly to himself. It was not therefore difficult for the Major to persuade him, after informing him of his wife's decision, to go back to that village and then to the little town, where they could consider the next steps and how to set things in motion.

After the Major had left her, Charlotte remained seated and sunk in her thoughts only for a few minutes; for Ottilie soon stretched herself up, looking at Charlotte with wide eyes. She removed herself from Charlotte's lap, stood up and then faced Charlotte.

'For a second time I have experienced the same sort of thing,' the dear child began speaking in tones of irresistible, delightful seriousness. 'You once told me that during people's lives similar things often happen to them in a similar way and always at important moments. I can now see the truth of that remark and feel compelled to make a confession to you. Shortly after my mother's death, when I was a small child, I drew my stool close up to you; you sat on the sofa as you are doing now; my head lay on your knees, I wasn't properly asleep or properly awake; I was dozing. I heard everything that was going on around me very clearly, especially all the talking; and yet I couldn't move or express myself or indicate, even if I had wanted to, that I was conscious. On that occasion you were talking to a friend about me; you pitied my fate to be left in the world as a poor

257

orphan; you described how dependent I was and how awkward it could be for me unless a special lucky-star were to take care of me. I understood well and precisely, perhaps too rigidly, everything that you seemed to be wishing for me and requiring of me. I made rules for myself about the matter according to my own limited lights; I have lived according to these rules for a long time now, and my behaviour was regulated by them at the time when you loved me and cared for me and took me into your house, and also for some time after that.

'But I have stepped outside my own track, I have broken my rules, I have even lost my feeling for them, and after a terrible happening you explain my circumstances to me, which are more wretched than on the first occasion. Resting in your lap, half rigid, I hear again, as if from a strange world, your gentle voice above my ears; I hear how things look as far as I am concerned; I shudder at myself; but just as I did on that previous occasion, I have also marked out my new path this time as I was lying in almost deathly sleep.

'I am determined, as I was then, and you must learn at once what I have made up my mind to. I shall never be Edward's! God has opened my eyes in a terrible manner to show me what a crime I am implicated in. I wish to atone for it; and let nobody think of diverting me from my intention! My dearest and best beloved, make arrangements in accordance with that. Tell the Major to come back; write to him to say that no steps are being taken. How afraid I was, so that I couldn't move or stir when he went. I wanted to jump up and scream out that you shouldn't let him go with such criminal hopes.'

Charlotte saw Ottilie's condition and felt for her; but she hoped to gain some influence over her through putting her point of view and with the passage of time.

But when she uttered a few words hinting at the future with its alleviation of grief and its hopes, Ottilie cried with emotion: 'No! Don't try to persuade me or go behind my back! At the moment when I hear that you have consented to the divorce, I shall atone for my transgression and crime in the self-same lake.'

CHAPTER XV

W HEN people are living together in happiness and peace, relations, friends and members of one household converse more than is necessary or right about what happens or is said to be happening; they repeatedly confide to each other their plans, undertakings and occupations and, without exactly asking each other's advice, treat the whole of life so to speak on a basis of giving and taking counsel. On the other hand at important moments, just when it would seem that a man would need outside support and encouragement most, one finds that people withdraw into themselves, attempting to act each for himself and in his own way; they conceal from each other their individual plans, and only the result, the goal, the achievement may once more be shared with others.

After so many extraordinary and unhappy incidents a certain quiet seriousness had thus also come upon the two women, and it expressed itself in affectionate forbearance. Charlotte had had the child discreetly removed to the chapel. It lay there as the first victim of an ominous destiny.

As far as she could, Charlotte returned to life, and here she found that it was Ottilie who needed her support. She devoted her time primarily to her, though without letting this be seen. She knew how intensely the dear child loved Edward; bit by bit she had pieced together the scene which had preceded the tragedy and learned about every detail in part from Ottilie herself in part from the Major's letters.

Ottilie for her part made Charlotte's daily life more

tolerable. She was open, even talkative, but there was never any mention of the present or the recent past. She had always been observant and well informed; all this now became apparent. She conversed with Charlotte and entertained her; the latter still cherished the secret hope of seeing a couple she esteemed so much joined together.

But for Ottilie matters lay differently. She had revealed to her friend the secret of her life's course; she was relieved of her previous self-limitation and servitude. By her repentance and her decision she felt also that she had been freed from the burden of that transgression and misfortune. She no longer needed to use force over herself; she had pardoned herself in the depths of her heart only on condition of complete renunciation, and this condition was indispensable for all time.

Some time passed in this way, and Charlotte felt very much that each day the house and park, lakes, rocks and trees were only able to arouse sad emotions in her and Ottilie. It was all too obvious that they would have to have a change of place, but it was not so easy to decide how it should happen.

Should the two women remain together? Edward's earlier wish seemed to require it, and his declaration and threats to make it necessary; but how could it not be recognised that, for all the good will, good intentions and reasonableness they had, they were in a painful situation together? Their conversations were evasive. Sometimes they would like to understand something only by half, and often an expression would be misinterpreted, if not intellectually, then at least emotionally. They were afraid of hurting each other's feelings, and it was precisely this fear that was most easily hurt and itself could most easily inflict hurt.

If they decided to go elsewhere and at the same time to separate, at least for the time being, the old question arose again as to where Ottilie was to go. That large wealthy household had made vain attempts to procure sociable and emulous companions for their daughter and heiress. Charlotte had been invited to send Ottilie there when the Baroness had last invited her, and more recently there had been letters on the subject; she now again spoke about it. But Ottilie emphatically refused to go where she would find what people are accustomed to call high society.

'Dear aunt,' she said, 'let me say something that in any other case it would be my duty to keep silent about and to conceal, or else I may seem to be limited and wayward. Someone who has suffered a strange misfortune, even if he were innocent, has been marked out in a terrible way. His presence arouses a kind of terror in all who see him. People think that they can see from his face the monstrous burden that has been placed upon him; everyone is curious and fearful at the same time. Consequently a house or a town where some monstrous deed has happened remains terrible to everyone who enters there. The light of day is less bright in that place, and the stars seem to lose their brilliance.

'But think of the great, though possibly pardonable indiscretion of people, their silly obtrusiveness and their clumsy good-naturedness towards such unhappy figures. Excuse me for talking like this; but I suffered to an unbelievable degree with that poor girl when Luciane brought her out of the hidden rooms of the house, showed herself friendly to her and with the best of intentions wanted to press her to join in games and dancing. When the poor child became more and more anxious until she finally took flight and collapsed, when I took her in my arms and saw that the company was first frightened and excited, and then really curious about the poor girl, I didn't think that a similar fate was awaiting me; but my compassion, so true and quick, is still alive. I can now turn my compassion against myself and be careful that I don't become the occasion of comparable scenes.'

'But, my dear child,' Charlotte replied, 'you will nowhere be able to avoid the sight of people. We haven't any convents, where in former times such feelings could seek refuge.'

'Solitude is no refuge, dear aunt,' Ottilie answered. 'The best sanctuary is to be found where we can be active. No acts of atonement or asceticism are likely to draw us away from an ominous destiny, if it has made up its mind to pursue us. It is only if I am to serve as an idle spectacle to the world, that I find the world repulsive and terrifying. But if I am found working contentedly and doing my duty untiringly, I can face the eyes of anyone, because I have no reason to fear the eyes of God.'

'Would I be very wrong in thinking that your inclination draws you back to the boarding-school?' asked Charlotte.

'I don't deny it,' Ottilie said; 'it strikes me as being a happy lot to be able to bring up others along the normal paths when we ourselves have been educated in the strangest way. And don't we see from history that men who withdrew into the desert because of great moral catastrophies were by no means concealed and hidden, as they had hoped? They were called back to the world so that they themselves might lead the strays back to the right path; and who could do so better than those who had already had experience of the wrong paths of life! They were called to assist the unfortunate; and who could do this better than those whom no further earthly misfortune could move!'

'You are choosing a strange destiny,' Charlotte said. 'I won't resist you; let it be so, even if only, as I hope, for a short time!'

'How much I must thank you for allowing me this trial, this experience,' Ottilie said. 'If I am not flattering myself too much, I hope it will succeed. When I am there I will remember how many trials I endured and how petty and trivial they were compared with those that I was to endure afterwards. With what gaiety I shall regard the embarrassments of the young pupils, and shall smile at their childish troubles and guide them with a gentle hand out of all their little errors. It isn't suitable for a happy person to be in charge of those who are happy; it is only human nature to make more and more demands of oneself and others, the more one has received oneself. Only an unhappy person who has recovered his balance knows how to foster in himself and in others the feeling that even something that is only moderately good should be appreciated with delight.'

'Let me raise just one other objection against your plan, and it's one that seems to me to be the most important,' Charlotte finally said after some hesitation. 'It doesn't concern you, but rather a third person. You know the feelings of the good, sensible and pious assistant; the way you're going, you will be more valuable and more indispensable to him every day. According to his way of feeling, he is already in a state when he would not care to live without you, and so in the future, once he has got used to your being with him, he won't be able to do his work without you. You will start by being of assistance to him, only to estrange him from the work later.'

'Fate has not dealt easily with me,' Ottilie replied, 'and anyone who loves me oughtn't perhaps to expect fate to treat him much better. However good and sympathetic this friend may be to me, I hope that feelings of pure friendship towards me will develop in him; he will see me as a person apart who can only make up for a monstrous evil that has afflicted herself and others by dedicating herself to that holy power which surrounds us invisibly and alone can protect us against those monstrous intruding forces.'

Charlotte considered quietly everything that the dear child had expressed so cordially. She had enquired on various occasions, though only in the gentlest manner, whether an approach of Ottilie to Edward might not be conceivable; but even the gentlest hint, the least hope or the slightest suspicion seemed to affect Ottilie most deeply; indeed she spoke her mind quite clearly about this on one occasion, as she could not avoid the subject.

'If your decision to renounce Edward is so firm and unalterable, just be careful to avoid the danger of seeing him again,' Charlotte countered. 'When we are absent from someone we love, we seem to be all the more in control of our passions, the deeper our affection is, since we turn the whole violence of our feeling in upon ourselves, which formerly found expression outside; but how soon, how quickly we are corrected of this error when what we believed we could renounce all at once appears before our eyes as indispensable. Do now what you consider most suitable to your position; examine yourself, indeed change your present decision rather: but do so of your own accord, from a free, willing heart. Don't let yourself be caught again into the previous relationship by chance or surprise; it is in consequence of this that a mental split is caused which is unbearable. As I was saying, before you take this step and leave me to begin a new life that will take you who knows where, just consider once more if you really can renounce Edward for all time. If you have made up your mind to this, we will make an agreement to the effect that you will have nothing more to do with him, not even in conversation, if he should visit you and force his attentions upon you.' Ottilie did not hesitate a moment; she gave her word to Charlotte, exactly as she had vowed to herself earlier.

But now Charlotte could not forget that threat of Edward's, that he could only renounce Ottilie as long as she did not leave Charlotte. Admittedly circumstances had changed so much since then and so much had happened that those words, wrung from him in the heat of the moment, were to be considered as cancelled by the subsequent events; but she still did not want to venture or undertake anything remotely likely to upset him, and so in this instance Mittler was asked to find out Edward's attitude.

Since the child's death Mittler had often visited Charlotte, though only for brief moments. This accident, which made the reunion of husband and wife seem highly improbable, had a profound effect on him; but continuing to hope and strive according to his character, he was now secretly glad of Ottilie's decision. He put his trust in the alleviating effects of the passing of time, went on hoping that Edward and Charlotte could be kept together and saw these agitations of passion only as trials of marital love and fidelity.

Charlotte had immediately informed the Major in writing of Ottilie's first declaration and had requested him most urgently to persuade Edward not to take any further steps, to keep quiet and to wait and see whether Ottilie's emotional balance would recover. She had also reported to him what was necessary concerning later events and reactions, and now indeed Mittler was charged with the difficult task of preparing Edward for changed circumstances. But Mittler, well knowing that one accepts a *fait accompli* more easily than one consents to something that has yet to happen, persuaded Charlotte that it would be best to send Ottilie at once to the boarding-school.

Consequently preparations were made for the journey as soon as he left. Ottilie packed her things, but Charlotte could not help noticing that she did not attempt to take the pretty little casket nor any of its contents with her. Charlotte said nothing and let the silent girl do as she wished. The day of departure arrived; Charlotte's carriage was to take Ottilie on the first day to a familiar hotel, and on the second day as far as the school; Nanny was to accompany her and to stay with her as her servant. The impetuous child had found her way back to

Ottilie immediately after the infant's death, and now clung to her, as she had done earlier, according to her nature and her fondness for Ottilie; indeed, she seemed to want to make up for what she had up to now neglected by conversational sociability and to devote herself completely to her beloved mistress. But now she was quite beside herself with happiness at the prospect of travelling too and seeing strange districts, for she had not as yet ever been outside the place of her birth; she raced from the castle down to the village to her parents and relatives, in order to announce her happiness and take her leave. Unfortunately while doing this she came into contact with children who were confined to bed with measles, and she immediately felt the consequences of the infection. There was no wish to delay the journey; Ottilie herself insisted upon it; she had already travelled that way once and she knew the people of the hotel where she was to spend the night; the castle coachman drove her; there was nothing to worry about.

Charlotte did not resist; in her thoughts she too was hastening away from these surroundings, only she still wanted to rearrange the rooms which Ottilie had had in the castle so that they would be suitable for Edward, just as they had been before the Captain's arrival. The hope of restoring an old happiness keeps on flaming up again in man's heart, and once more Charlotte was justified in such hopes, indeed impelled to them.

CHAPTER XVI

W HEN Mittler came to talk to Edward about the situation, he found him alone, his head cupped in his right hand and his arm propped up on the table. He seemed to be suffering very much. 'Is your headache troubling you again?' Mittler asked. 'It is troubling me,' Edward replied; 'and yet I can't hate it, because it reminds me of Ottilie. Perhaps she too is suffering just now, I think, leaning against her left arm and no doubt suffering more than myself. And why shouldn't I bear it just like her? These pains are beneficial to me, I can almost say, desirable; for the picture of her patience, together with all her other good qualities, hovers before my imagination all the more powerfully, clearly and vividly; only in the midst of suffering do we feel in a truly complete way all the great qualities which are necessary for us to bear it.'

When Mittler found his friend resigned to this extent, he did not hide the reason for his coming, though he did recount it in historical sequence, following step by step the way the thought had arisen with the women until it had gradually matured into a purpose. Edward made hardly any critical comments. What little he said seemed to indicate that he would leave everything to them; his present grief and pain seemed to have made him indifferent to everything else.

Scarcely was he alone when he got up and paced up and down the room. He no longer felt his pain, he was occupied with something quite outside himself. Already while Mittler was giving his account Edward's loving imagination had indulged itself ardently. He saw Ottilie alone, or as good as alone, on the well-known road and in a hotel in whose rooms he had so often walked; he thought and pondered, or rather he thought without pondering; he only desired and wanted. He had to see her and talk to her. There could be no discussion of what for, why, or what was to come of it. He did not resist, he had to.

The valet was taken into his confidence, and he at once made investigations to find out the day and hour of Ottilie's departure. The morning came; Edward did not hesitate to make his way alone on horseback to where Ottilie was to spend the night. He arrived there all too punctually; the surprised innkeeper's wife received him with joy; she owed him a great family happiness. He had procured a distinction for her son, who had behaved very bravely as a soldier, by emphasising a deed he had done when Edward alone had been a witness, bringing it with eager commendation to the general and overcoming the opposition of a few begrudging personages. She would do anything for him. She quickly cleared up as much as she could in her dressing-room, which at the same time was also a cloakroom and store-room; however, he announced to her the arrival of a lady who was to have this room, and ordered a room off the corridor at the back to be arranged provisionally for him. The landlady found the business intriguing, and she was glad to be able to do something for her patron who was displaying so much interest and activity in the matter. And as for him, with what emotions he filled out the long, long time until the evening! He examined all round the room where he was to see her; it seemed to him a heavenly resting place in its whole domestic unusualness. What thoughts he had, as to whether he should surprise Ottilie or whether he should prepare her! Eventually the latter alternative gained the upper hand: and he sat down and wrote. She was to receive the note.

Edward to Ottilie

While you are reading this letter, my dearest, I am near you. You must not be frightened or startled; you have nothing to fear from me. I shan't force myself upon you. You will not see me any sooner than you yourself decree.

First of all think of your position and mine. How grateful I am to you that you do not intend to take any decisive step; but such a step is significant enough. Don't take it! Here, at a kind of cross-roads, think it over once more: Can you, will you be mine? Oh, you would be conferring on us all a great blessing, on me in particular an infinite one.

Let me see you again, see you with joy again. Let me put the delightful question by word of mouth, and answer me in your own delightful person. Come to my arms, Ottilie, where you have rested more than once and where you belong for ever!

As he wrote he was overcome by the feeling that what he was yearning for was approaching and would be present very soon now. She would come in at this door, she would read this letter, she really would stand before him as in the past, the presence that he had so often longed for. Would she be the same? Would her appearance and her attitude have changed? He still held the pen in his hand, he wanted to write as the thoughts came; but the carriage drove into the courtyard. With hasty strokes of the pen he added: 'I can hear you coming. Goodbye for a moment!'

He folded the letter and addressed it; there was no time to seal it. He hastened into his room, knowing that he could re-enter the corridor afterwards from there, and at once it struck him that he had left his watch and seal on the table. Ottilie should not see these first; he rushed back again and succeeded in taking them away. He could already hear the landlady's voice in the reception room; she was making for the room to show it to the guest. He hurried back to his room door, but it had shut to. As he had rushed past, he had knocked down the key, which lay inside; the lock had snapped shut and he stood there banished outside. He pushed impetuously against the door; it did not yield. Oh, how he would have liked to slip through the cracks like a spirit! In vain! He hid his face against the door-post. Ottilie entered, and the innkeeper's wife withdrew when she saw Edward there. He could not remain concealed from Ottilie either for a moment. He turned towards her, and so the lovers once more confronted each other in the strangest manner. She looked at him quietly and gravely, without advancing or retreating, and when he made a move to approach her, she stepped back a few paces to the table. He too stepped back again. 'Ottilie,' he cried, 'let me break this terrible silence! Are we only shadows facing one another? But above all, do listen; it is by accident that you find me here right away now. A letter is lying near you which was meant to prepare you. Do read it, I beg you! And then make what decision you can.'

She looked down to the letter, took it up after some hesitation, tore it open and read it. She read it without changing expression, and so too she put it gently away; then she pressed her outstretched, uplifted hands together, placed them against her breast, bending forward just a little, and looked at the man who was making these urgent pleas with such a glance that he was compelled to desist from everything that he might require or want. This gesture tore at his heart. He could not bear Ottilie's look and gesture. It looked completely as if she would sink down at the knees, if he persisted. He hurried desperately out of the room and sent the innkeeper's wife to keep her company.

He paced up and down in the reception room. Night had fallen, and it was quiet in the room. Eventually the landlady appeared and took out the key. The good woman was moved and embarrassed, and did not know what she should do. In the end, as she was moving off, she offered the key to Edward, who refused it. She left the light burning and retired.

In deepest distress he threw himself down on Ottilie's threshold, letting his tears fall. Hardly ever can a pair of lovers have spent the night so close to one another and yet so miserably.

Day broke; the coachman wanted to make a start, the innkeeper's wife unlocked the door and entered the room. She found Ottilie dressed and asleep; she went back and beckoned to Edward with a sympathetic smile. They both stepped in front of the sleeping girl; but Edward could not even bear this sight. The landlady did not dare to wake the slumbering child, but sat down facing her. At last Ottilie opened her lovely eyes and got up on her feet. She would not have breakfast, and now Edward came before her. He asked her urgently to say only a word to explain what her intention was. All he wanted was to do her will, he swore; but she kept silent. Once he asked her lovingly and insistently, if she would be his. Delightfully and with downcast eyes she gently shook her head. He asked if she wanted to go to the boarding-school. She said no, though indifferently. But when he asked if he might escort her back to Charlotte, she replied affirmatively by a hopeful nodding of the head. He hurried to the window to give orders to the coachman; but from behind him she rushed out of the room like lightning down the stairs and into the carriage. The coachman took the way back to the castle; Edward followed on horseback at some distance.

CHAPTER XVII

CHARLOTTE was most surprised to see Ottilie drive up in the carriage and Edward ride on horseback into the courtyard at the same time. She hurried to the entrance. Ottilie got out and came up with Edward. She seized with eagerness and force the hands of the married couple, pressed them together and hurried to her room. Edward embraced Charlotte and burst into tears; he could make no explanation and asked her to have patience with him and to support and help Ottilie. The latter hurried to Ottilie's room, and shuddered when she went in; it had already been completely cleared, only the empty walls were there. It seemed so large and cheerless. Everything had been removed except for the casket, which had been left in the middle of the room, as the servants had been uncertain where to put it. Ottilie lay on the floor, arm and head stretched over the casket. Charlotte concerned herself with her, asked what had happened and received no answer.

She left her maid, who had brought refreshments, with Ottilie and hurried to Edward. She found him in the drawing-room; he told her nothing. He prostrated himself before her, bathed her hands in tears, fled to his room, and when she made to follow him there she was met by the valet who explained things to her as far as he was able. She pieced the rest together for herself, and then at once decided what was needed for the moment. Ottilie's room was refurnished as quickly as possible. Edward found his own rooms just as he had left them, down to the last of his papers.

273

The three appeared to get back to their old ways together again; but Ottilie continued to be silent, and all Edward could do was to ask his wife to show the patience that seemed to be lacking in himself. Charlotte sent messengers to Mittler and the Major. The former could not be found, but the latter came. Edward poured out his heart to the Major, confessing to him each detailed circumstance, and it was thus that Charlotte learned what had happened, what had changed the situation so strangely, and what had so agitated their minds.

She spoke most lovingly to her husband. She would make no other request than that the girl should not be besieged with questions for the time being. Edward felt the value, the love and the good sense of his wife; but his feelings towards Ottilie dominated him exclusively. Charlotte gave him hope by promising to agree to a divorce. He had no confidence in this; he was so sick at heart that hope and faith alternately deserted him; he urged Charlotte to give her hand to the Major; a kind of mad discontent had seized hold of him. Charlotte did as he wished in order to soothe and sustain him. She would accept the Major's suit if Ottilie would agree to marry Edward, but only on the express conditon that the two men would go away together on a journey forthwith. The Major had some distant business to perform for the court to which he was attached, and Edward promised to accompany him. Plans were made, and a certain calm was achieved since at last something was being done.

In the meantime it could be observed that Ottilie was hardly eating or drinking anything and continued to refuse to speak. They spoke to her, but she showed fear; they gave up the attempt. For have we not mostly the weakness that we are reluctant to torment anyone, even for his own good? Charlotte thought over all ways and means, and at last hit upon the idea of summoning the assistant from the school who had considerable authority over Ottilie; he had expressed himself in very friendly terms on hearing of her unexpected failure to arrive, but had not yet received a reply.

They talked about this plan in Ottilie's presence in order not to surprise her. She did not seem to be in agreement with it; she thought it over; eventually a decision seemed to be crystallising within her mind, she hurried to her room and already before the evening sent down the following note to the others.

Ottilie to her Friends

Why should I put into words, my dear friends, what is taken for granted? I have stepped out of my path, and I am not to come back into it. A hostile force that has obtained power over me seems to be obstructing me from outside, even if I had found unity with myself again.

My intention to renounce Edward and to go away from him was wholly sincere. I hoped I should not meet him again. Things have turned out differently; he stood in my presence against his own will. Perhaps I have taken my promise to have no conversation with him too literally. In accordance with my feelings and my conscience at the time I kept silent in my friend's presence, and now I have nothing more to say. By chance, urged on by emotion, I have taken upon myself a strict vow which would perhaps arouse uneasy fears in someone who submits to it after due consideration. Let me adhere to it as long as my heart commands me to it. Do not call in any third person! Do not urge me to talk or to take more food and drink than I strictly need. Help me through this period by your forbearance and patience. I am young, and youth recovers unexpectedly. Tolerate me in your company, bring me happiness with your love, instruct me through your discussions; but leave my inner life to me alone!

The men's departure had been long prepared, but was put off because the particular business of the Major was delayed. How desirable this was to Edward! Aroused again by Ottilie's message and encouraged by her comforting, hopeful words and feeling justified by them to patient waiting, he declared all at once that he would not go away. 'How foolish it would be prematurely to discard what is most indispensable and necessary. What might perhaps still be retained at a time when loss threatens us! And what does that mean? Surely only that man seems to be able to will something, to choose. How often, when possessed by such a foolish illusion, have I torn myself away from my friends hours, even days, too soon, only so that I may not be decisively compelled by the last, unavoidable, agreed time. But this time I want to stay. Why should I leave? Has she not already left me? I have no idea of seizing her hand and pressing her to my heart; I may not even think of it, I shudder so much at it. She has not retreated from me, she has lifted herself up above me.'

And so he stayed, as he wished, as he had to. But there was nothing comparable to the well being he felt when he was in her presence. And she too had the same feeling; she too could not deprive herself of this blessed need. Now as much as ever before they exerted an indescribable, almost supernatural attraction upon each other. They lived under the same roof; but even when they were not consciously thinking of each other, being occupied with other things and pulled this way and that by other people, they drew closer together. If they happened to be in the same room, it was not long before they were standing or sitting near one another. Only close proximity could quieten them, really cause them to be relaxed, and this proximity was enough; it did not need a glance, a word, a gesture or a touch, but only simply being together. Then they were not two people, but only one person in unconscious, complete easiness of spirit, contented within and with the world. Indeed, if one of them had been held fast at the furthest end of the house, the other would have gradually and unintentionally moved in the same direction. Life was an enigma to them, the solution to which they could only find with each other.

Ottilie was quite serene and calm, so that one could be fully reassured about her. She did not avoid society, though she had insisted on eating alone. Nobody else but Nanny attended her.

Whatever usually happens to an individual, happens more repeatedly than we think, because his temperament gives the first indication of this. Character, personality, inclination, direction, milieu, surroundings and habit together form a whole in which everyone swims as if in an element, an atmosphere where alone he is comfortable and at ease. And thus to our astonishment we find people, about whose changeability so many complaints have been made, unchanged after many years and after countless outward and inner stimuli—unchanged.

In this way too everything in the daily life of our friends seemed to be almost back in the old groove. Ottilie still showed her obliging disposition through various kind services, though she remained silent, and the others behaved similarly, each in his own way. In this manner the domestic circle showed itself as an apparent replica of their earlier way of life, and the illusory feeling that everything was as before was pardonable.

The autumn days, comparable in length to those spring days, called the company at much the same time back from the open air into the house. The rich supply of fruit and flowers, which is peculiar to this season, made one think that it was the autumn after that first spring; the time in between had been forgotten. For now flowers were blooming of the type that had been sown during those first days also; now fruit was ripening on the trees which had been seen in blossom at that earlier time.

The Major came and went; Mittler too often put in an appearance. Evenings were for the most part regularly spent together. Edward usually read aloud, livelier and with more feeling, better, even more gaily, if you like, than before. It was as if he wanted to give new life through gaiety as well as through feeling to Ottilie's benumbed condition and to dispel her silence once more. As before, he sat so that she could look over his shoulder into the book, in fact, he became restless and distracted if she did not look over and if he was not certain that she was following his words with her eyes.

All unpleasant, uncomfortable feelings from the middle period had disappeared. No one any longer had hard feelings against anyone else; all bitterness had gone. The Major and Charlotte played the violin and piano, just as Edward's flute playing coincided, as in earlier days, with Ottilie's treatment of the instrument. In this way they spent the time as Edward's birthday drew nearer, the celebration of which had not taken place the previous year. This time it was to be celebrated without festivity in quiet, friendly comfort. Half tacitly and half expressly then, they had come to agreement about it. But as the date drew near, there was an increase in the solemn quality in Ottilie's character, which up to then had been sensed rather than consciously noticed. In the garden she often seemed to be surveying the flowers; she had suggested to the gardener that he should be sparing with summer plants of every kind, and she had lingered in particular among the asters which just this year were flowering in great profusion.

CHAPTER XVIII

T HE most significant thing, however, which the friends observed with quiet attention was that Ottilie had unpacked the casket for the first time and had selected and cut up various pieces of the material from it, sufficient for one single, though complete outfit. When she wanted to pack the rest away again with Nanny's help, she could scarcely manage it; the space was over-full, although a part had already been taken out. The young girl Nanny stared covetously at the things, particularly as she found that all the smaller parts of the outfit had been provided. There still remained shoes, stockings, embroidered garters, gloves and various other things. She begged Ottilie just to make her a present of part of the things. Ottilie refused, but at once opened the drawer of a wardrobe and let the child have her choice; Nanny grasped something with hasty and clumsy hands and at once ran off with the booty to announce and show her good fortune to the rest of the household.

Eventually Ottilie succeeded in arranging everything carefully again; after this she opened a secret drawer that had been fitted into the lid. She had hidden there little notes and letters from Edward, some pressed flowers, souvenirs of walks they had had together at earlier times, a lock of her loved one's hair and various other things. She added one more object—it was the portrait of her father—and closed it all up, after which she hung the tiny key on the little golden chain round her neck once more.

Various hopes had meanwhile stirred in our friends'

hearts. Charlotte was convinced that Ottilie would begin
to talk once more when that day came; for up to now she
had shown a secret activity, a kind of gay contentment,
a smile like that on the face of one who is concealing
something good and agreeable from his beloved. Nobody
knew that Ottilie spent many an hour in great physical
weakness, from which she raised herself up through will-
power only for the periods when she appeared in public.

Mittler had shown himself frequently during this time
and had stayed longer than had been his custom. The
obstinate man knew only too well that there is one certain moment only when the iron may be forged. He
explained away Ottilie's silence and abstinence to suit
himself. Up to now no steps had been taken towards the
divorce; he was hoping to determine the good girl's fate
in some other favourable way; he listened, he yielded,
he gave his opinion and behaved sensibly enough according to his own lights.

But he was always carried away when he found a pretext for expressing himself on subjects to which he
attached a great importance. He lived much on his own,
and when he was with other people he usually had contact with them only through action. But once he began to
talk to friends, his words flowed on, as we have already
seen, without consideration for others, wounding or
healing, helping or harming, just as things might work
out.

On the evening before Edward's birthday Charlotte
and the Major sat together waiting for Edward, who had
gone out riding; Mittler was walking up and down the
room; Ottilie had stayed in her room, laying out the
finery for the morrow and indicating various things to
her maid Nanny who understood her perfectly and
skilfully obeyed the silent orders.

Mittler had just taken up one of his favourite topics.
He was fond of maintaining that nothing was clumsier
and more barbaric, either in the education of children or

the government of peoples, than prohibitions, restrictive laws and regulations. 'Man is active by nature,' he said; 'and if you know how to give him orders, he will get right on with it, and will act and carry out what he is asked to do. I for my part prefer to tolerate mistakes and shortcomings in my own circle until I can prescribe the cure to be put into effect, rather than to get rid of the mistake without having anything positive to put in its place. Man is glad to do what is good and purposeful, if only he can hit upon it; he does it in order to have something to do, and thinks no more about it than he does about the silly tricks that he gets up to through sheer idleness and boredom.

'How annoyed I often become when I have to listen to the way the ten commandments are repeated in confirmation classes. The fifth commandment is quite a pleasant, sensible and positive one. "Honour thy father and thy mother." If the children imprint that properly on to their minds, they can be putting it into practice the whole day through. But as for the sixth, what are we to say to that? "Thou shalt not kill." As if anyone ever had the slightest wish to kill another! You may hate someone, become angry and over-hasty, and as a result of this and all sorts of other things it may well happen that a murder is occasionally committed. But is it not a barbaric idea to forbid children to murder and kill? If it said: "Care for my neighbour's life, remove anything that can be harmful to him, save him even at danger to thyself": these are commandments which are valid among civilised, reasonable people, and yet they are only dragged into the catechism reluctantly as an explanatory footnote.

'And as for the seventh, I find it quite revolting! What? Are we to stimulate the anticipatory curiosity of children about dangerous mysteries, to excite their imaginations to strange images and fantasies which will precipitate with violence just what we want to keep from them? It would be far better for such things to be arbitrarily punished by a secret tribunal than to allow them to be blabbed about in front of church and congregation!'

At that moment Ottilie came in. ' "Thou shalt not commit adultery," ' Mittler went on. 'How crude, how indecent! How different it would sound if it said: "Thou shalt have reverence for the bond of marriage; where thou seest man and wife who love each other, rejoice about it and be glad as at the happiness of a bright day. Should anything in their relationship be troubled, seek to clarify it; thou shalt seek to calm and pacify them, to make clear to them their mutual advantages, thou shalt further the well-being of others with a fine selflessness by making them feel what happiness arises from every duty, and especially from that obligation which binds man and wife indissolubly." '

Charlotte was on tenterhooks, and the situation was all the more distressing to her as she was convinced that Mittler did not know what he was saying or where he was saying it, and before she could interrupt him she already saw Ottilie leave the room, her whole being transformed.

'Perhaps you will spare us the eighth commandment,' Charlotte said with a forced smile. 'All the rest,' Mittler replied, 'so long as I can preserve the foundation which supports the others.'

Nanny rushed in, calling out with a terrible cry: 'She is dying! The young lady is dying! Do come, do come!'

When Ottilie had returned stumblingly to her room, the finery for the next day lay fully spread out on a number of chairs, and Nanny, who had been circling around it with curiosity and admiration, cried out exultantly: 'Just look, miss, these are bridal adornments that are really worthy of you!'

Ottilie heard these words and sank down on to the sofa. Nanny saw her mistress turn pale and become rigid; she hurried to Charlotte, and people came up. The household doctor hurried along; he said it only seemed to be a form of exhaustion. He asked for some broth to be brought; Ottilie refused it with an expression of disgust, indeed she was almost seized by convulsions when the spoon was brought near to her mouth. He asked seriously and hastily, as the circumstances warranted, what food Ottilie had had that day. Nanny hesitated; he repeated his question; the girl confessed that Ottilie had not had anything.

He thought that Nanny seemed more anxious than was reasonable. He took her into another room, Charlotte followed, Nanny threw herself down on her knees and confessed that for a long time now Ottilie had had virtually no food at all. Ottilie had pressed her to eat the meals instead of her; she had kept quiet about it because of the imploring and threatening gestures of her mistress and also, she added innocently, because the food had tasted so good.

The Major and Mittler came in; they found Charlotte busied together with the doctor. The pale, ethereal child sat on the corner of the sofa, apparently conscious. They asked her to lie down; she refused, but indicated that the casket should be brought to her. She placed her feet on it and found this half-lying position comfortable. She seemed to be wishing to take leave, her gestures expressed the most tender attachment to all who were standing around—love, gratitude, apology, and the most heartfelt leave-taking.

Edward heard about the circumstances on dismounting from his horse; he rushed into the room, threw himself down at her side, clasped her hand and bathed it with silent tears. He remained a long time in this position. Eventually he cried out: 'Shall I never hear your voice again? Won't you come back to life with a message for me? Very well, then, I'll follow you across; there we shall speak with other tongues!'

She pressed his hand firmly, looked at him with an

expression full of life and love, and after taking a deep breath and making a divine, mute movement with her lips, she cried with lovely, tender effort; 'Promise me you will live!' but at once she sank back. 'I promise!' he said to her, but he was saying it after her; for she had already passed away.

After a night of weeping, Charlotte was beset by the responsibility of burying the dear remains. The Major and Mittler stood by her. Edward's condition was pitiable. As soon as he could rise out of his despair and think at all coherently, he insisted that Ottilie should not be removed from the castle, she should be waited on, nursed and treated as if she were alive; for she wasn't dead, she couldn't be dead. They did as he wished, at least in that they desisted from doing what he had forbidden. He did not ask to see her.

Yet another shock, yet another worry befell our friends. Nanny had disappeared, after being seriously reprimanded by the doctor; she had been driven to confession through threats, and after making her confession she had been heaped with reproaches. She was found again after a long search, and seemed to be distracted. Her parents took charge of her. Good treatment did not seem to work with her, and it was necessary to lock her in as she was again threatening to flee.

They gradually succeeded in lifting Edward from the most violent despair, but only to his own misfortune; for he now became fully certain that he had lost his life's happiness for ever. They ventured to suggest to him that when she was buried in the chapel Ottilie would still be among the living and would not be without a friendly and peaceful dwelling-place. It was difficult to obtain his consent, and he only finally agreed and appeared to be resigned to everything, on condition that she should be carried out in an open coffin and should lie in the vaults covered only by a glass lid, and that an ever-burning lamp should be set up there.

They dressed the lovely body in the finery which she had prepared herself; a wreath of asters was placed on her head, and they gleamed mysteriously like sad stars. All the gardens were plundered in order to decorate the bier, the church and chapel. They lay devastated, as if winter had already removed all joyful colour from the flower-beds. Early in the morning Ottilie was carried out of the castle in the open coffin, and the rising sun once more brought a glow of red to her heavenly features. The mourners pressed closely to the bearers, nobody wanted to go on ahead, nobody wanted to follow, and everybody surrounded her as if to enjoy her presence again for the last time. Boys, men and women were all moved. The girls were inconsolable, for they felt their loss most directly.

Nanny was missing. They had kept her back, or rather, they had concealed from her the day and the hour of the funeral. They watched her at her parents' where she was in a room looking towards the garden. But when she heard the bells ringing, she realised all too soon what was on foot, and as her nurse left her, being curious to see the procession, Nanny could slip out at the window on to a corridor and from there, finding all the doors shut, she went to the attic.

The cortege was just winding along the clean, leaf-strewn road through the village. Nanny clearly saw her mistress below her, more clearly, more completely and more beautifully than all who were following the procession. Supernaturally, as if supported by clouds or waves, Ottilie seemed to be waving to her servant, and Nanny, confused, hesitating, staggering, fell down.

The crowd scattered in all directions, with a terrible cry. The bearers were compelled by the pressure and the confusion to put down the bier. The child lay quite near to it, and looked as if all her limbs were broken. They lifted her up; and, either by chance or by special dispensation of Providence, she was leaned against the corpse, in fact she seemed to be trying with her last remaining scrap of life to come close to her beloved mistress. But no sooner had her trembling limbs touched Ottilie's dress, no sooner had her powerless fingers touched Ottilie's folded hands, than Nanny jumped up, first raising her arms and eyes towards heaven and then sinking down on her knees in front of the coffin, and stared marvelling, worshipping and enraptured at her mistress.

At last she sprang up as if inspired and cried with holy joy: 'Yes, she has forgiven me! What no man could forgive me, what I could not forgive myself, God forgives me through her glance, gestures and mouth. Now she is again resting so quietly and gently; but you have seen how she sat up and blessed me with unfolded hands, glancing upon me with friendly eyes! You have all heard and can witness that she said to me: "You are forgiven!" Now I am no longer a murderess among you, she has forgiven me, God has forgiven me, and no one can hold anything against me any longer.'

The crowd stood pressing around; they were astonished, they listened and looked about them, and hardly anyone knew what he ought to do. 'Carry her to rest!' the girl said; 'she has played her part and had her share of suffering, and can remain among us no more.' The bier moved on, Nanny followed it first, and they came to the church and the chapel.

Thus Ottilie's coffin now lay enclosed in a strong oak container, with the infant's coffin at her head and her little casket at her feet. They had engaged a woman to keep watch during this first period over the body which lay looking very beautiful under its glass lid. But Nanny would not let anyone else perform this office; she wanted to stay alone with a companion and conscientiously tend the lamp now lit for the first time. She asked so eagerly and persistently that they yielded to her in order to prevent a greater mental illness which, it was feared, might befall her.

But she was not alone for long; for as night fell and the hovering light exercised its full right to spread a brighter glow, the door opened and the architect stepped into the chapel, whose piously decorated walls pressed towards him in the mild light in a manner that was more old-world and mysterious than he would ever have believed.

Nanny sat at the one side of the coffin. She recognised him at once; but with a silent gesture she pointed to her dead mistress. And there he stood on the other side, in youthful strength and charm, but thrust back on to himself, rigid, inward-looking, with drooping arms and folded, piteously wrung hands, his head and eyes turned towards the inanimate body.

Once before he had stood like this, in front of Belisarius. Without thinking he now took up the same position; and how natural the position was this time! Here too something immeasurably fine had fallen from its heights. In the case of Belisarius heroism, cleverness, power, rank and wealth were being mourned as irrecoverably lost; qualities which are indispensable to the nation and its prince in moments of crisis, had not been valued, in fact they had been rejected and pushed aside. As far as Ottilie was concerned, many other quiet virtues that had only recently been drawn out of their rich depths by nature's hand had been quickly destroyed again by that same indifferent hand—strange, beautiful, loveable virtues, the peaceful effect of which the starved world appreciates at all times with blissful satisfaction and marks their absence by longing sadness.

The young man was silent, and the girl too for a time; but when she saw the tears flow copiously from his eyes and he seemed to be dissolving wholly into grief, she spoke to him with such truth and strength, such good will and certainty, that he was astonished at the flow of

287

her words and was able to pull himself together and to imagine his beautiful friend as alive and active in a higher world. His tears dried and his pain became less; he knelt down to take leave from Ottilie and then shook hands with Nanny; that same night he rode away without having seen anyone else.

Without the girl's knowledge the surgeon had spent the night in the church, and when he visited her in the morning he found her cheerful and in good spirits. He was prepared for various forms of abnormality; he thought she might talk to him about nocturnal interviews with Ottilie and other such phenomena, but she behaved naturally, quietly and with full self-possession. She remembered all the circumstances of what had passed with complete exactness, and there was nothing in her conversation that departed from the normal course of truth and reality except the episode during the funeral which she often gladly repeated: how Ottilie had sat up, blessed her, pardoned her and thereby given her peace of mind for all time.

Ottilie's continuously beautiful appearance, resembling sleep more than death, attracted a number of people to the chapel. Those who lived nearby wanted to see her again, and everyone was glad to hear Nanny's account of the unbelievable happening; some scoffed, more were quietly sceptical, and a few had faith.

Any need that cannot find a satisfactory explanation in reality compels one to belief. Nanny, whose bones had been broken before the eyes of the whole world, had been restored to health through contact with that hallowed body; why should not a similar good fortune be available here to others? Loving mothers brought, in secret at first, their children who had been stricken with some distress, and they believed that they perceived a sudden improvement. Faith increased, and eventually there was nobody, however old and weak, who did not come here seeking refreshment and comfort of spirit.

The influx of visitors increased, and it was thought necessary to close the chapel and the church too, apart from the times of divine service.

Edward did not venture to approach the departed one again. He just lived driftingly on and seemed to have no more tears and to be incapable of further grief. His interest in society and his enjoyment of food and drink declined daily. He only seemed to derive some solace from the wine-glass which certainly had been no true prophet to him. He still liked to look at the entwined initials, and his serenely earnest glance seemed to indicate that even now he was still hoping for a reunion with Ottilie. And whereas a happy man seems to be favoured and uplifted by every accessory circumstance and chance, even the slightest episodes appear to be conniving to hurt and destroy him who is in distress. For one day, as Edward was raising the beloved glass to his lips, he put it down again with horror; it was the same and yet different; he missed some small distinguishing mark. Pressure was brought to bear upon the valet, who had to admit that the genuine glass had been broken not long ago and that a similar one, dating from Edward's youth, had been substituted. Edward could not be angry; his fate had already been made explicit by events; why should he be moved by a symbolic happening? But it nevertheless did impress him profoundly. It seemed to make all drinking repugnant to him; he appeared to be deliberately abstaining from food and conversation.

But from time to time he was overcome by restlessness. He again asked for food, and once more became talkative. 'Oh, how unhappy I have been,' he once said to the Major, who was seldom far from his side, 'that my whole efforts have always remained a mere imitation, a false striving! What was bliss to her, has become painful to me; and yet, for the sake of this blessedness I am compelled to take over this distress. I must follow her, this way; but my temperament and my promise restrain me. It is a terrible task, to imitate what is inimitable. I feel now, my friend, that genius is necessary for everything, even for martyrdom.'

In face of this hopeless condition, why should we dwell on the efforts which Edward's near ones—wife, friend, and medical attendant—continued to make for a time? One day he was found dead. It was Mittler who first made this sad discovery. He called the doctor and, in his usual manner, gave an exact account of the circumstances in which the dead man had been found. Charlotte rushed in; a suspicion of suicide stirred in her mind; she thought of accusing herself and the others of some unpardonable carelessness. It was, however, quite clear that Edward had not been expecting his end. He had been spreading out during a quiet moment his remembrances of Ottilie which he kept in a casket and a lettercase, an action that up to now he had carefully hidden from the others; there up were flowers plucked in a happy hour, a lock of hair, and all the notes she had written to him, from the first one on, which his wife had handed to him by a foreboding chance. He could not have wanted to expose all these things to chance discovery. And so this soul lay in indestructible peace, after having been aroused only a little while before to boundless excitement; and as he had gone to rest with thoughts fixed on the hallowed Ottilie, he could indeed be called blessed himself. Charlotte decreed that he should be buried next to Ottilie and that there were to be no further burials in this vault. With this condition she made considerable bequests to the church and the school, and to the priest and the schoolmaster.

The lovers therefore rest side by side. Peace hovers over their graves, happy angelic figures, their kindred too, look down upon them from the vaulted ceiling, and what a happy moment it will be when they reawaken together one day.